Saltwater Fish
Cookbook

SALTWATER FISH COOKBOOK

A. D. Livingston

STACKPOLE
BOOKS

Published by
STACKPOLE BOOKS
5067 Ritter Road
Mechanicsburg, PA 17055

Printed in the United States of America

Illustrations by Marsha McHenry
Cover design by Caroline M. Stover

First Edition

10 9 8 7 6 5 4 3 2 1

Library of Congress Cataloging-in-Publication Data

Livingston, A. D., 1932–
    Saltwater fish cookbook / A. D. Livingston
      p.   cm.
    ISBN 0-8117-2924-9
    1. Cookery (Fish)   2. Marine fishes. I. Title.
TX747.L57   1997
641.6'92—dc21   96-47102
                                                  CIP

ACKNOWLEDGMENTS

The author would like to acknowledge a recipe "Alaskan Hooligan Fry" quoted with permission from *Alaska Magazine's Cabin Cookbook*. Other acknowledgments are made in the text as appropriate. Also, a few of the recipes were used, in slightly altered form, in the author's cooking column for *Gray's Sporting Journal*.

CONTENTS

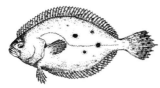

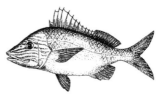

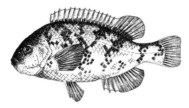

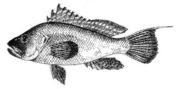

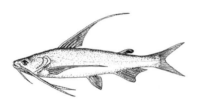

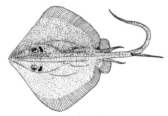

INTRODUCTION

New Zealanders are smart. They naturalized (and nationalized) the Chinese gooseberry, changed the name to kiwifruit, flooded American supermarkets, and counted the money. In an even greater stroke of marketing genius, they took a local fish, the Pacific slimehead, changed the name to orange roughy, jacked up the price, and sold it to American markets. While sniffing around in supermarkets over the past few years, I have asked several fish market clerks what exactly is an orange roughy. They were usually either puzzled, as if they didn't understand my question, or on the defensive, as if I were accusing them of pulling a fast one.

This sort of thing has been going on for a long time at home as well as abroad. And, you'll have to admit, an orange roughy simply tastes better than a Pacific slimehead.

But things do change, albeit very slowly, and American sportsmen are just beginning to realize what culinary treasures we can catch along our Atlantic, Pacific, and Gulf coasts. Still, tons and tons of wonderful fish are thrown back each year because of ignorance, fear, or local custom, or simply because the catch is deemed too ugly to eat. Some of these good fish are thrown out on the beach to rot because they are considered trash, as if unfit to inhabit our waters! Tons of good fish are also killed and wasted by commercial fishermen as unmarketable by-catch. This is a sin.

In any case, I believe that many modern anglers are having problems with knowing what's edible and what's not. The truth is that almost all fish are edible if they are properly handled. I can only hope that this book will help overcome some of the old cultural and regional prejudices. On the other hand, I want to caution the reader not to throw all caution to the wind, and not to accept everything that is written in books and magazines these days. A recent magazine article, for example, said that the roe of any edible fish is also edible. This is simply not the case. Also, some fish can become contaminated with mercury or other toxins in certain areas, because of natural water conditions or pollution. Often the danger here is not in eating a fish or two, but in eating lots of the contaminated fish over a long period. Usually instances of such poisoning are blown all out of proportion to the real danger to most sport fishermen. On the other hand, some large, predatory tropical fish can contain deadly ciguatera poisoning. I have grappled with this problem to the best of my ability in appendix B, and I advise anyone fishing in Florida or the Gulf of Mexico to read this information carefully.

Before using this book, the reader should glance over the table of contents, looking for familiar and unfamiliar fish. Note that some of the chapter titles may be misleading or puzzling to some anglers, but not necessarily to others. "Rockfish," for example, will be understood by many West Coast anglers simply because these bigmouth fish make up a large part of the sportsmen's catch; the angler from the mid-Atlantic seaboard, however, might be puzzled with the text because in that area the popular striped bass is commonly called rockfish.

Since there is so much confusion about what's what, I have tried to include both the scientific and local names for each species. The scientific name is really the best guide to exact identification, but even this is not entirely without pitfalls. Scientists have been known to disagree on what's what, and the names are sometimes changed, creating discrepancies between old writings and new.

Perhaps the best way to find something in this book, if the table of contents doesn't help, is to look in the index, which lists the popular, scientific, and local names for the various species.

The book is organized by edible species, making, I think, for a useful and much needed text on saltwater fish commonly taken by sportsmen, but it doesn't have chapters organized by frying, baking, broiling, and so on. Instead, the emphasis is on what's edible and how it should be handled, followed by a few recipes I consider especially good for that kind of fish. In short, the text emphasizes the edibility of the various species of saltwater fish instead of cooking techniques. For this reason, I am including an appendix on how to cook fish by the various methods.

Finally, I have added an appendix called Ten Steps to Better Saltwater Fish. The emphasis here is on proper handling of the fish after the catch. This is very, very important with saltwater fish, perhaps even more so than with freshwater fish. I might add here that many of our culinary notions about saltwater fish have been formed by old books and old ways of doing things, but the modern ice machine and plastic or Styrofoam ice chest have greatly altered our notions of what's edible and what's not. In short, don't knock it until you try it.

Tight lines—and good eating.

—A. D. Livingston

ONE

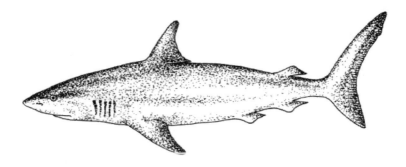

Sharks

Those people who wouldn't dream of eating a shark might be in for a surprise. If properly handled, the meat is mild, white, and succulent. In the recent past, various sharks have been marketed as swordfish, whitefish, or some other such name, and the lowly spiny dogfish shark (which one modern authority, Frank Davis, author of *The Frank Davis Seafood Notebook*, by and large an excellent work, has called oily, coarse, and usually only good for making fish meal, fertilizer, and cat food) is actually the preferred meat in England's popular fish 'n' chips.

Clearly, there are disagreements. Moreover, there are even specific contradictions in the same book. My copy of *McClane's*

The typical shark has larger, flipperlike pectoral fins, a large, high-riding tail, and a pointed head with underslung jaws.

New Standard Fishing Encyclopedia and International Angling Guide, page 158, says of the blue shark, "Although a voracious species, it puts up a poor fight on hook and line, and its flesh is poor and strong in ammonia." Yet on page 867, in a section on sharks as food, the same encyclopedia says, "On the East Coast both mako and blue shark are highly prized. . . ." I'll resist my instinct as a southern good ol' boy to conclude that Yankees relish fish that have poor flesh and smell highly of ammonia; instead, I'll simply say that some of our beliefs about fish in general and sharks in particular are carried over from many years of cultural practices and prejudices.

In theory, I accept the premise that all sharks are edible, but I'll have to add that proper handling is usually more important than species. I also hold the opinion that smaller sharks are better than large ones, but this isn't necessarily true, provided that a big one is dispatched and iced quickly.

The big problem is that most, if not all, sharks contain uric acid, which can give the flesh a bad taste and a strong smell of ammonia. Proper handling can usually prevent this, yielding a mild, white flesh that can be cooked by any method. Remember the following steps:

1. As soon as a shark is landed, it should be gutted and bled. Don't worry about skinning the shark at this time.

2. As soon as it is gutted, the shark should be placed on ice or in slush (see appendix B). This must be done right away, or uric acid will make the flesh smell of ammonia. Smaller sharks can be iced whole. Larger ones should be filleted and cut into chunks. Some experts recommend that the reddish flesh, usually along the lateral line, be cut out. This is not always necessary, and some of this flesh tastes exactly like the rest of the fish.

I have read that steps 1 and 2 should be accomplished within 20 minutes of landing the fish, but this is not always practical with a large fish, which takes a long time to die. In short, be very careful when gutting or otherwise handling a shark. Having several sharp knives will speed up the process.

3. If the meat smells of ammonia after icing, all may not be lost. The smell and taste can sometimes be eliminated by soak-

ing the meat in a solution of 1 cup of salt to 1 gallon of water, or perhaps in seawater. Use ice water or keep the solution and fish in the refrigerator for several hours. Note that slushing the shark fillets or steaks will accomplish both steps 2 and 3.

4. After the initial icing, the flesh should be kept very cold until it is cooked. It can be kept in good condition for several days in the refrigerator, then cooked by a wide variety of recipes.

In support of my stand on eating sharks in general, perhaps I should add a quote from one more or less authoritative publication, *Recipes with a New Catch,* a booklet published with the aid of federal money by the University of North Carolina Sea Grant program: "All species of shark are edible, but most prefer the lemon, mako, and black-tipped shark." Since there are more than 250 species of shark, however, I would like to hedge just a little. One species, **Greenland shark,** *Somniosus microcephalus,* is said to be toxic to man if eaten fresh. It can be made fit for human consumption, I understand, by air-drying the meat or by burying it until it decays, yielding the Icelandic *hakarl* or the Eskimo *tipnuk,* both of which are eaten like cheese. The Greenland shark is caught only on arctic or subarctic waters on both sides of the Atlantic, ranging south to the Gulf of Maine. If you fish those waters, be warned. I have also read that the livers from sharks (as well as polar bears and some marine mammals) taken in northern waters can contain toxic overdoses of vitamin A.

Anyhow, here's my breakdown of some commonly eaten sharks taken from American waters:

Leopard shark, *Triakis semiasciata.* This shark, with a distinctive leopard-spot pattern, roams the Pacific coast from Oregon to Baja. It grows up to 5 feet long, makes good eating, and is commonly caught by sport fishermen.

Lemon shark, *Negaprion brevirostris.* Growing up to 11 feet, this common shark of the Caribbean and the Gulf of Mexico ranges to North Carolina and sometimes strays as far north as New Jersey. It frequents shallow water, where it is sometimes caught by man, and vice versa. The lemon, recognized by its yellow-brown color, makes good eating.

Mako shark, *Isurus oxyrhynchus.* This large shark, growing up to 12 feet long, usually stays near the surface in deep water in the tropical and temperate Atlantic. The mako makes excellent eating and is sometimes classed as gourmet fare similar to the swordfish. It is sometimes steaked and is low in oil content.

Blacktip shark, *Carcharhinus limbatus.* One of the few sharks that hit artificial lures, the blacktip makes excellent eating and is a popular commercial fish. Growing up to 5½ feet, it can be caught in Pacific waters from Southern California to Peru, and in the Caribbean and Gulf of Mexico, ranging up the Atlantic to Cape Cod. In the Gulf, it can be taken on the flats with the fly rod.

Nurse shark, *Ginglymostoma cirratum.* This shallow-water shark, frequently taken by anglers, grows in the Caribbean and Gulf, and in the Atlantic as far north as Rhode Island. It is excellent eating and is often steaked and broiled like swordfish. The fins also have a reputation as gourmet fare.

Bonito shark, *Isurus glaucus.* This Pacific species, which grows to 12 feet, can be caught from Southern California south to Chile and west to Hawaii. It makes good eating.

Spiny dogfish, *Squalus acanthias.* This small shark of the North Atlantic and North Pacific is considered trash in some parts of the United States—although it is the preferred species for the famous British fish 'n' chips and is popular in Scandinavia. This species ranges south to North Carolina. Similar species of dogfish grow in southern waters.

Spinner shark, *Carcharhinus maculipinnis.* This unusual shark of south Florida can be taken on the flats with artificial baits and streamer flies. It often leaps out of the water and spins; hence, its name. It grows up to 8 feet long.

Soupfin shark, *Galeorhinus zyopterus.* This species is taken from British Columbia to Baja California. It grows to more than 100 pounds. It has been fished extensively for its fins and liver (which is high in vitamin A), as well as for its edible flesh. The authentic Chinese soup, by the way, is made with the dried fins, which are sold in oriental markets. Fins from some other species can also be used.

Porbeagle, *Lamna nasus.* Sometimes called mackerel shark, this species can be caught near the shore from the Gulf of St. Lawrence to the Carolinas. The flesh resembles that of swordfish and has been marketed as such. It is best smoked or grilled over charcoal.

Here are a few recipes that will work with most sharks.

Fish 'n' Chips

The meat for this recipe should be white and mild. Cut it into pieces about 3 inches long, 2 inches wide, and ¾ inch thick, or some such size that is easily eaten out of hand. The fish 'n' chips are served in a newspaper rolled into a cone, which is ideal for holding the fish while you eat on the go. Some writers say to line the newspaper with waxed paper, but I don't recommend this because one purpose of the newspaper is to soak up some of the grease. Suit yourself. This recipe has been adapted from *Recipes with a New Catch,* published by the UNC Sea Grant College Program. It calls for a rather elaborate batter. If you want to simplify the recipe, merely dust the shark in fine white stone-ground cornmeal or flour.

> 2 pounds shark fillets, cut into finger-food size
> 2 pounds potatoes, cut into french fry size
> oil for deep frying
> 1 cup flour
> 1 chicken egg, separated
> 5 tablespoons milk
> 5 tablespoons cold water
> 4 tablespoons beer
> ¼ teaspoon salt
> malt vinegar
> more salt

Mix the batter first, starting by pouring the flour into a large bowl. Make a hole in the center and add the egg yolk, beer, and ¼ teaspoon salt, stirring until mixed. Mix the milk and water, then divide into equal parts. Stir half into the batter, stirring as you go until smooth. Then add the rest of the milk mixture 1 tablespoon at a time until the texture is about right for batter. Beat the egg white until stiff, then fold into the batter.

Rig for deep frying, heating the oil to at least 375 degrees. Fry the potatoes a few at a time and drain on absorbent paper, sprinkling with salt. Keep warm. Dip the shark pieces into the batter and fry for 4 or 5 minutes, until nicely browned. Drain on absorbent paper and sprinkle lightly with salt and malt vinegar. Serve both fish and potatoes in a newspaper rolled into a cone.

Blacktip Shark with Yogurt Sauce

Here's a dish with a yogurt mix that can be used as both a baste and a sauce for the fish.

> 2 pounds shark fillets
> 1 cup low-fat yogurt
> 1 tablespoon honey
> 10 drops Tabasco sauce
> salt to taste
> whole milk
> oil

Place the shark fillets in a bowl, cover with milk, and marinate in the refrigerator for 6 hours or longer. Rig for grilling. Mix the yogurt, honey, and Tabasco sauce. Wash the shark fillets and pat them dry with a paper towel. Grease the grill and the shark fillets with oil. Grill the shark for 5 minutes on one side, about 4 inches above a hot fire. Turn and baste with the yogurt sauce. Grill for another 5 minutes, turn, and baste. Grill for another minute or so on each side, or until the shark is done, sprinkling each side lightly with salt. Before serving, I usually cut into a piece to check it for doneness; it should be opaque throughout, but still moist. Serve with the yogurt sauce, vegetables, and perhaps a nice rice pilaf.

Broiled Shark for Two

Most shark fillets can be broiled quite successfully. If the meat has no strong smell of ammonia, it will not need a marinade.

>1 pound shark fillets, 1 inch thick
>1 cup butter
>juice of 2 lemons
>2 tablespoons minced fresh parsley
>salt and pepper to taste
>paprika
>lemon wedges (for garnish)

In a saucepan, heat the butter, lemon juice, and parsley, along with a little salt and pepper; keep the sauce hot. Preheat the broiler. Grease the rack and place it about 4 inches under the heat. Baste the shark fillet on both sides, then place the pieces on the rack. Broil for 5 minutes. Turn, baste, and broil for another 4 or 5 minutes, or until done. Do not overcook. Divide the fillets equally onto 2 plates, spoon the remaining basting sauce over them, and sprinkle the top side with paprika. Garnish with lemon wedges.

Louisiana Shark

Here's a good recipe for fried shark, which I have adapted from *The Official Louisiana Seafood and Wild Game Cookbook.* It calls for Tabasco, but any good Louisiana hot sauce will do.

>2 pounds skinned shark fillets
>1 cup buttermilk
>1 tablespoon Tabasco sauce
>1 cup biscuit mix
>1 teaspoon salt
>peanut oil

Mix the Tabasco sauce into the buttermilk. Put the shark fillets into a nonmetallic container, pour the buttermilk mix over them, and marinate for 30 minutes, turning once or twice. When you are ready to cook, rig for deep frying, heating the oil to at least 375 degrees. Mix the salt in with the biscuit mix. Take the fillets out of the buttermilk and roll in the biscuit mix. Deep-fry a few at a time until the fillets are brown and flake easily when tested with a fork. Serve with Lemon Relish (chapter 27).

Note: The original recipe calls for 2 ounces of Tabasco, which is an entire small bottle. This is too hot for me, but suit yourself and your guests.

Shark Hobo, Greek Style

Here's a recipe to cook by a wood campfire or on a charcoal grill when you are surf fishing. Some fishing piers also allow charcoal grills. I like to cook the dish with shark steaks or fillets, allowing a ½-pound steak or fillet for each person. It's best to cook these in separate packets.

> shark steaks or fillets, about ½ pound
> thinly sliced onion (lots)
> thinly sliced green bell pepper
> thinly sliced red bell pepper
> fresh oregano leaves, chopped
> lemons for juice
> olive oil
> salt and coarsely ground black pepper
> mild paprika

Build a good hot fire and let it burn down to coals. For each fillet or steak, tear off two sheets of heavy-duty aluminum foil. Grease the center of these sheets. Place one sheet on a flat surface and put down a layer of onion rings. Use more than you think you need, because some of these may burn on the bottom; if only lightly burned, however, they have a delightful flavor. Place a steak or fillet atop the onion bed. Sprinkle it with salt, pepper, and paprika. Add a thin layer of onions, red peppers, and green peppers. Sprinkle lightly with oregano. Drizzle about

1 tablespoon of olive oil over the fish and squeeze on the juice of ½ lemon. Place the second sheet of aluminum foil on top and square it up with the bottom sheet. Make a fold of 1 inch all around, then make a ½-inch fold in the first fold. The idea is to seal the packet to hold in the steam. Punch a small hole in the top with a fork tine or knife point to keep the package from bursting open. Put the packet directly onto the hot coals for 20 minutes. Do not turn. Open and enjoy. A loaf of French bread and a bottle of red wine round out the perfect beach lunch.

Note: Steaks or fillets thicker than 1½ inches may require longer cooking times. Remove these from the coals and let them coast a while before opening.

Shark Fin Soup

There are many variations of this recipe, most calling for dried fins from the soupfin shark. Don't hesitate to cook it with the fins of any shark that has been properly salted and air-dried. The key is plenty of salt, which will help draw the moisture out of the fins and aid the preservation process. If you want to dry a few pounds, cut the fins into strips like jerky, lay out on a board, and salt heavily on both sides. Tilt the board in an airy place so that the water will drain off, and resalt from time to time. This process will eventually dry the shark fin. You can speed things up with one of the new forced-air electrical drying units designed for home use.

> ½ pound dried shark fin
> ½ pound lean fresh pork
> 1 pound pork bones
> 1 small chicken (about 2 pounds, dressed)
> 6 cups water
> cornstarch paste (2 tablespoons each water
>   and cornstarch)
> salt

Rinse the shark fin and soak in water for several hours or overnight, changing the water from time to time. Place the shark fin in a stove-top Dutch oven or other suitable pot, add 6 cups of water, and bring to a boil. Reduce the heat, cover tightly, and simmer for 1 hour. Add the pork, pork bones, and chicken. Cover tightly and simmer for 1 hour or so, or until the pork and chicken are tender. Remove and bone the chicken, chop the meat, and return it to the pot. Remove and chop the pork and shark fin. Discard the pork bones, being sure to add any meat back to the pot. Add enough water to make a soup, bring to a boil, stir in some salt, and thicken with cornstarch paste. Serve hot in bowls.

Shark Jerky

The Mexicans love salt-cured and dried shark, and an old processing site in the Gulf of California is called Shark Island. The meat also makes good jerky, and on some sharks the belly meat is just the right thickness, like bacon. Try your favorite jerky recipe, or use the one below, adapted from information distributed by the California Sea Grant, the University of California, and the United States Department of Agriculture cooperating. Any good shark can be used, but Sea Grant folks recommended using blue shark.

1. Start with about 3 pounds shark fillets. Cut the fillets into strips of convenient length, ½ to ¾ inch thick and 2 inches wide. You can cut with or against the grain; cutting with the grain will produce a more chewy jerky. Note that partly frozen shark is much easier to slice.

2. Prepare a sauce with ⅛ cup teriyaki sauce, ⅛ cup liquid smoke, and 6 drops of Tabasco sauce.

3. Place the shark strips on racks. Sprinkle moderately with onion salt, garlic salt, and table salt. Turn the strips and sprinkle the other side.

4. Mix the shark strips and the sauce thoroughly in a large plastic bag. Expel the air from the bag and seal.

5. Marinate for 12 hours in the refrigerator.

6. Remove the shark strips. Place them on oven racks.

7. Turn the oven to 140 degrees. Leave the door ajar. Start checking the jerky after 2 or 3 hours, but leave in the oven until firm, dry, and tough, but not crumbly. It should be rubbery. The curing time will vary and may take as long as 12 hours. A good deal depends on the thickness of the meat, individual ovens (and thermostatic controls), and sometimes on the species of shark.

8. Store the strips in airtight jars in a cool place. Enjoy.

TWO

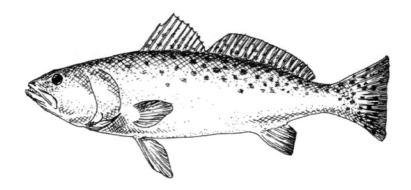

Weakfish and Speckled Trout

Although these fish are perhaps the most popular among sports-men in the Gulf and up the Atlantic seaboard, there is much confusion and some dissension over the names. First, weakfish are not weak. That unfortunate tag probably came about because of their tender mouths, making it necessary for the angler to pull them in gently. Also, thousands of people who catch and eat them don't know them by the name weakfish. The California angler, for example, might be skeptical about calling the white sea bass a weakfish, and the people of Louisiana would probably take offense if their beloved speckled trout was called a weakfish.

The spotted seatrout, shown above, and the weakfish are similar. Both have one or two prominent canine teeth at the tip of the upper jaw.

To add to the confusion, all of the weakfish are members of the large croaker and drum family. Local names include sea trout, spotted sea trout, trout, speckled trout, and squeteague.

There are several kinds of weakfish, and all make very good eating if they are properly handled. All tend to have soft flesh, making it important to dress and ice them as soon as possible. In fact, some become soft so quickly that they are often considered to be trash fish. All of these fish can be taken with cut bait, live bait, or artificial lures, including jigs, plugs, spoons, soft plastics, and flies. Thousands of anglers make the larger species their primary target, and night fishing for weakfish is popular in some areas. Most of the weakfish can be taken in the surf, in shallow bays, in brackish water at one time or another, fishing from small boats, in the surf, on piers or jetties, up saltwater creeks, or even by wading to deeper holes in shallow bays. The various species are as follows:

Weakfish, *Cynoscion regalis.* Sometimes called the common weakfish, gray weakfish, squeteague, or yellowfin, this fish is very popular in the Northeast, ranging from New England down to Florida. Hot spots are between Long Island and North Carolina. Although a few individuals attain weights of 18 or 20 pounds, these fish average from 1 to 5 pounds.

Spotted sea trout, *Cynoscion nebulosus.* Also called speckled trout, speck, or simply trout, this species ranges from New York south to Florida, and throughout the Gulf of Mexico. It is very popular in Florida and along the Gulf Coast. These fish can grow to 12 pounds, but mature fish average 4 pounds and the average catch is probably between 1 and 2 pounds. They are excellent eating, popular as a market and restaurant fish, especially in New Orleans, where they are called simply trout, as in trout amandine, or speckled trout.

Silver sea trout, *Cynoscion nothus.* Also called silver trout, this is a small species that grows to about 10 inches. They are very good panfish, but they should be iced as soon as they are caught. They don't freeze well. Try these (dressed in the round) sautéed and served with a sauce, deep fried, or skillet fried. The silver trout is usually caught in the ocean, except during the cooler months, when it tends to go into bays. It ranges from Chesapeake Bay south to Florida, and throughout the Gulf of Mexico.

Sand sea trout, *Cynoscion arenarius.* The sand sea trout, also called sand trout or white trout, ranges from the Gulf coast of Florida west to Texas and Mexico. This is a small species, with the average size being about 1 pound, that is almost always caught in bays. They are delicious eating, but they don't keep well and the flesh tends to soften. It's best to put them on ice immediately after they are caught, then cook them within a few hours. If properly handled, they are gourmet fare when fried.

White sea bass, *Cynoscion nobilis.* Also called California white sea bass, this species is really a weakfish. By whatever name, it is one of the most popular saltwater species on the West Coast. Although it ranges from Alaska to South America, most of the hot spots occur south of San Francisco. Found near kelp beds, these fish are popular party boat quarry, and the average weight is about 10 pounds. They can grow to 80 pounds. In Mexico, these weakfish are called white corvina. Actually, the white sea bass is a single member of a larger clan, the corvinas, covered below.

Corvinas, *Cynoscion* spp. Not to be confused with the corbina (a whiting), the corvina clan of the Pacific coast includes such weakfish cousins as the white sea bass, above, and the totuava, below, both of which are popular with sport fishermen. Most of the rest of the corvinas are of more interest to commercial anglers, partly because they prefer the deeper waters. Besides, most of the other corvinas are found below the Mexican border. One exception is the orangemouth corvina, which was successfully stocked in the Salton Sea, where it proliferated. All make good eating, and Frank Davis, a New Orleans culinary sport, allows that they can be substituted for speckled trout.

Totuava, *Cynoscion macdonaldi.* The largest of the weakfish, the totuava grows up to 225 pounds and is found only in the middle and upper Gulf of California. It's called totoaba in Mexico. A popular sport fish within its range, the totuava is also very good eating. The larger specimens can be steaked or filleted and cut into fingers, which are delicious when deep-fried. According to A. J. McClane, the air bladder was in great demand by orientals for use in soup during the early part of this century, causing extensive commercial fishing and a drastic depletion in the totuava population.

Here are some recipes that work nicely with the various kinds of weakfish. Most of the recipes are interchangeable, since all of these fish have mild white flesh with a similar texture. Some of these dishes are traditional in some areas.

Weakfish Peconic

Long Island's Peconic Bay was once a weakfish hot spot, and J. George Frederick's *Long Island Seafood Cook Book* lists several recipes for the fish, including the following adaptation. The recipe works best for fish in the 1- to 2-pound range. Allow one fish per person, unless you've got light eaters. I prefer to leave the heads on the fish, if my pan is long enough to accommodate the whole fish. Also, it's best to cook the fish one or two at a time, depending on the size of the boiler. The idea is to cook the fish without lowering the temperature of the water when they are put into the pan.

> 3 or 4 weakfish
> fresh seawater or salted water
> juice of 1 lemon
> salt and pepper
> Egg Sauce (chapter 27)
> parsley and lemon quarters (garnish)
> new potatoes (cooked separately)

Rig for poaching, making sure that your fish will fit into your boiler. Rub the dressed fish inside and out with lemon juice, then wrap each one in cheesecloth and twist the ends for use as a handle. (The ends can be secured with string, pipe cleaners, or twist-ties.) As soon as the water comes to a rolling boil, lower a fish into it and simmer for 15 minutes or so, figuring 10 minutes per inch of thickness at the widest part. Serve a whole fish on each plate, garnished with a lemon quarter and sprigs of fresh parsley, along with new potatoes and egg sauce.

Baked Weakfish

Weakfish can be delicious when baked. They tend to dry out, however, and should not be overcooked. Basting with sauce will help, as in this recipe.

> 3- to 4-pound weakfish
> 8 ounces sliced fresh mushrooms
> 1 medium onion, chopped
> 1 cup dry white wine
> juice of 1 lemon
> 2 tablespoons chopped fresh parsley or cilantro
> butter
> salt and pepper to taste

Preheat the oven to 350 degrees. In a skillet, sauté the mushrooms and onion in 1 tablespoon of butter for 4 or 5 minutes. Add the wine, parsley, salt, and pepper; stir about and keep warm. Place the fish in a well-greased baking pan of suitable size, then pour the mushroom mixture over it. Bake in the center of the oven for 40 minutes, or until the fish flakes easily, basting several times with pan juices. Place the fish on a heated serving platter. Pour the pan juices and mushrooms back into the skillet; add the lemon juice and 1 tablespoon butter. Bring to a light boil, then simmer for a few minutes, stirring as you go. Pour the mushroom sauce over the fish. Serve hot with French bread and vegetables. Feeds 3 to 4.

Easy Trout Amandine

There must be a thousand recipes for this dish, which can be made in a skillet. Or a sauce or topping can be used over broiled, sautéed, or fried fish. Or use this easy recipe.

> 4 small whole speckled trout or fillets
> ½ cup butter
> flour
> salt and pepper
> cayenne (optional)
> Amandine Topping (chapter 27)
> parsley (garnish)

Sprinkle the trout with salt, black pepper, and perhaps a tiny pinch of cayenne; dust lightly with flour. Sauté in melted butter over medium heat until done on both sides, cooking in two or more batches and using more butter if needed. When the fish are done, carefully place them on a heated serving platter or individual plates, spread generously with amandine topping, and garnish with parsley sprigs. Serve with rice and steamed vegetables.

For a more elaborate preparation, see Catfish Amandine, chapter 21.

Trout Meunière

As I pointed out in my *Trout Cookbook*, where a version of this recipe was published, fish meunière, a French formula, is popular in New Orleans, where it is made with what the locals call speckled trout. The French prepare a special meunière sauce and apply it to broiled fish. Americans tend to pan-fry the trout in butter, then stir up a sauce in the pan drippings. For this recipe, I prefer to work with fillets from fish of about 2 pounds each.

4 speckled trout fillets
¾ cup butter
½ cup chopped parsley
juice of 1 lemon
cream
flour
salt and pepper

Melt the butter in a skillet and bring to heat—but not to the smoking point—and warm a serving platter. Sprinkle the fillets with salt and pepper, roll them in heavy cream, and then sprinkle them with flour. Sauté the fillets on both sides until the meat flakes easily when tested with a fork. Remove the fillets from the skillet and place them on a heated serving platter. The butter left in the skillet should be lightly browned. If it isn't, cook it a little longer. Stir in the lemon juice and chopped parsley. Cook and stir for a minute or two, shaking the skillet as you go, then pour the sauce over the fillets on the serving platter. Eat hot. Feeds 2 to 4.

Trout en Papillote

Here's a tasty dish that I like to use for cooking any sort of small or medium-size weakfish or sea trout. If the fillets are thicker than 1 inch, increase the cooking times by 5 or 10 minutes. Although this dish can be cooked in aluminum foil, I find it easy to use brown grocery bags or plastic baking bags of suitable size. If you are courting or feeding Frenchmen, use parchment paper. Also see Pompano en Papillote, chapter 11.

2 pounds sea trout fillets
½ red bell pepper, sliced into rings
½ green bell pepper, sliced into rings
1 large onion, sliced into rings
½ cup melted butter (divided)
juice of 1 lemon or lime
1 teaspoon Hungarian paprika
salt and pepper

Preheat the oven to 375 degrees. Brush the fillets with about half the melted butter, then sprinkle them inside and out with salt and pepper. Place the baking bag on its side in an ovenproof pan. Pour the rest of the butter into the bag, then make a bed with the pepper and onion rings. Add the lemon juice. Sprinkle the fillets with paprika, then place them, skin side down, onto the bed of onions and peppers. Close the bag (following the directions on the package) and puncture the top with the tine of a fork. Bake for 25 minutes. Remove the pan, then slit the bag. Serve the fillets directly on plates, spooning some onions and peppers onto each serving, along with some of the sauce from the bag. Feeds 4.

Sea Trout Turbans Florentine

I devoted a whole chapter of my *Complete Fish & Game Cookbook* to cooking stuffed fillets, rolled into a turban shape. All of those recipes will work with any mild white-fleshed saltwater fish, such as sea trout or cod, but I don't want to repeat myself here. So here's a Texas recipe to try. Ideally, the fillets should be about 8 inches long from a long-shaped fish of about 1½ pounds. The fillets should be boned and skinned.

> 4 fillets, about 8 inches long
> 1 package frozen spinach (10-ounce size)
> 2 cups seasoned bread croutons
> ¼ cup melted butter
> 1 beaten chicken egg
> ½ teaspoon chopped fresh thyme
> salt and pepper
> Shrimp Sauce (see chapter 27)
> pimento (garnish)

Thaw, drain, and chop the spinach. Place the fillets skin side up on a flat surface, then brush them with melted butter and sprinkle with salt and pepper. Preheat the oven to 350 degrees. In a bowl, mix the croutons, remaining melted butter, spinach, egg, and thyme. Divide the spinach mixture into 4 equal portions, then place one on each fillet. Starting with the tail end, roll each fillet around the stuffing. Pin shut with round toothpicks. Carefully place the rolls flat side down on a greased baking dish. Bake for 25 to 30 minutes, or until the thickest part of the fillets is opaque. Serve hot, topped with hot shrimp sauce and garnished with strips of pimento.

A. D.'s Fried Sand Trout

The sand trout is one of the world's best fish for frying my way, provided that it is iced down and cooked right away. This makes it ideal for cooking on shore or even in a boat. Since the fish tend to be small, they can be cooked whole. The larger ones, however, should be filleted or cut in half lengthwise. I've touted this basic recipe before, so I'll keep it short here. The purist or the doubting Thomas should read the section on frying in appendix A. Of course, the sand trout can be cooked successfully with any good frying recipe. Here's my way:

> small sand trout, whole
> peanut oil
> fine stone-ground cornmeal
> salt and pepper

Pan-dress or fillet the trout. Salt and pepper the fish, then shake them in a bag with cornmeal. Heat about an inch of peanut oil in a cast-iron skillet to at least 375 degrees, just below the smoking point. Fry the fish for a few minutes on each side, until nicely browned. If you aren't on a low-oil diet, serve with hush puppies, french fries, and coleslaw, along with plenty of iced tea.

Silver Trout with Soy Sauce

This skillet dish can be used with any mild white fillets of about ¼ pound each, and the usual catch of silver trout is ideal.

> 4 silver trout fillets
> 1 medium onion, chopped
> ½ green bell pepper, chopped
> ½ red bell pepper, chopped
> 2 tablespoons soy sauce
> 2 tablespoons rice wine or sherry
> 1 tablespoon peanut oil
> ½ tablespoon brown sugar

Mix and warm the soy sauce, rice wine, and brown sugar. Heat the oil almost to smoking in a skillet, then sauté the fillets for 3 or 4 minutes, turning once. Remove the skillet from the heat and carefully remove the fillets, putting them on a heated platter or plate. On medium heat in the remaining oil (add a little more if necessary), sauté the onion and peppers for 4 or 5 minutes. Carefully place the fillets in the skillet, cover, and simmer for about 10 minutes. Serve with rice and steamed vegetables.

Corbina with Sauce

In Latin America, the corbina is popular on both the Atlantic and the Pacific coasts. This delicious recipe depends on a sauce made from the pan drippings—often the best kind. Although fillets are specified in the ingredients, small fish can also be used whole.

> 1½ to 2 pounds corbina fillets
> ½ cup olive oil
> onion slices
> 2 chicken egg yolks
> juice of 1 lemon or lime
> salt and pepper

Preheat the oven to 350 degrees. Salt and pepper the fillets on both sides, then place them, skin side down, in a well-greased baking dish or pan. Top each fillet with a slice of onion, then sprinkle with lemon juice and olive oil. Bake in the center of the oven for 20 to 30 minutes, or until the fish flakes easily when tested with a fork. Carefully remove the fillets (still topped with onion) to a heated serving platter, using a spatula. Then pour the liquid from the baking dish into a saucepan. Add the egg yolks, heat, and stir until the sauce bubbles and thickens. Pour the sauce over the fish. Serve hot. Allow from ⅓ to ½ pound per person.

Seviche

Mexicans are fond of an uncooked fish appetizer called seviche, usually served with chopped tomatoes, onions, and peppers. The corbina is a popular fish for seviche, although some Latin Americans prefer a fatty fish such as mackerel. There are thousands of recipes, including some from the South Pacific, where this dish might have originated. The distinguishing ingredients, however, are raw fish and fresh lime or lemon juice.

Always use fresh juice rather than canned or bottled. Fresh tomatoes are also recommended. I sometimes skin these, but I usually leave the seeds in, although some Mexican cookbooks say to remove them. I do, however, get the seeds and pith out of the peppers, lest the seviche be too hot.

>   1 pound corbina fillets, skinless
>   1 cup freshly squeezed lime juice
>   2 large tomatoes, skinned and chopped
>   1 medium white onion, sliced into rings
>   ½ yellow or green bell pepper, chopped
>   2 or more pickled serrano or jalapeño peppers, seeded
>   1 tablespoon fresh cilantro or parsley, minced
>   2 tablespoons olive oil
>   salt and pepper

Cut the fillets into ½-inch cubes, put them into a nonmetallic bowl, and pour the lime juice over them. Refrigerate for 12 hours or overnight, stirring a time or two with a wooden spoon. Shortly before serving, drain the fish and put it into a nonmetallic bowl. Add the onions, hot peppers, bell pepper, cilantro, tomatoes, olive oil, salt, and pepper.

Eat your seviche cold as a salad, appetizer, or light lunch. The last batch I made was scooped up with boats made from large, mild Vidalia onions and saltine crackers. Good stuff.

Note: Use lemons if you don't have a ready supply of limes. Also try minced fresh chili peppers if you've got them.

THREE

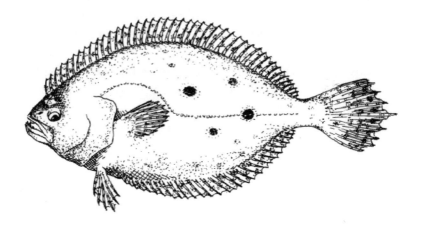

Flounders and Other Flatfish

The flatfish range in size from the hand-size dabs to the large Pacific and Atlantic halibuts. Regardless of size, they all share the familiar flounder shape and all have two eyes on one side of the head. Actually, they start life as normal little fry, with an eye on either side. But as they grow older, and apparently become more and more bottom oriented, they swim on one side or the other and their eyes migrate to one side of the head or the other, depending on whether they are right-eyed or left-eyed flatfish species.

The flounders and soles vary greatly in size and markings, but the shape is always the same. All are flat bottom species, with both eyes on the top.

Although they are generally considered to be bottom fish, and many tend to bury themselves in the sand with only their eyes sticking up, some species will come up to take live or cut bait or artificials. In some areas, they are taken at night with spears in shallow waters.

Most of the flounders have very small scales, and the smaller ones don't have to be scaled. They also have a small body cavity, making it very easy to remove the innards. When dressed whole, preferably with the head on, they can be broiled, baked, or grilled. Larger flatfish can be filleted, and the very large ones (halibuts and sometimes large flukes) can be filleted and cut into steaks or fingers. Flounders of about a pound are often stuffed and served on individual plates or platters. Since the stuffing is exposed in the middle of the fish, such recipes as Flounder Stuffed with Crab, given later in this chapter, make an attractive as well as tasty dish.

Note that some of the soles have a rather tough skin and should be skinned. Other than that, all of the flounders make very good eating, and (for all practical considerations) size is the important factor. In other words, a 10-inch summer flounder from the Atlantic can be cooked exactly like a 10-inch sand dab from California. Further, either fish taken from local waters makes better eating than a 10-inch Dover sole shipped from foreign waters. Actually, much of what is served in American restaurants as "soles" is actually flounder.

The flatfish family, comprising more than 200 species in the Atlantic and Pacific, includes the halibuts, soles, flukes, plaices, dabs, and turbots. Since all are good eating and easily recognized as being in the flatfish family, I don't see much point in making a long list here. If you catch a fish that looks like a flounder, eat it. I was recently amused by a passage in a modern book for fishermen in which the author said of the hogchoker (*Trinectes maculatus*): "The flesh is reported to be flavorful. However, it would be a very hungry or adventurous soul indeed, who would sit down to eat a plate of Hogchokers." Well, I say, when skinned, beheaded, and cooked, a hogchoker is just as pretty as any other flatfish.

All of these fish have mild flesh and, for this reason, they are popular in France for use in recipes that feature one or another of their hundreds of sauces. It seems to me that in French cookery the sauce becomes more important than the fish, and if I were to attempt to do justice to the French method, or fully expose the injustice of it, the length of this book would double. Even if I set forth detailed recipes, with references within references, some Frenchmen and even some Americans would claim that a flounder simply can't compete with a sole. My 1941 edition of the American translation of *The Escoffier Cook Book,* for example, carries the following American editorial note: "The real Dover sole (Limande) is rare here and a fine fillet of flounder might do to replace it although of course it can never replace the fine quality and firmness of the real sole." Crap.

In any case, the sole and other flatfish are very popular in many parts of the world and have given us some fine international recipes. A few of these are set forth here.

Istanbul Flatfish

Here's a dish that was named, in Turkish, for a sultan's pleasure palace in Istanbul. I have adapted the recipe from *A Turkish Cookbook,* by Arto der Haroutunian. After trying it a couple of times, I decided that the Turks are right up there with the French when it comes to the pleasures of sauced sole—and they have recognized the great culinary advantage of the American tomato. If you don't have sole, any small flatfish will do.

> **The Fish**
> 6 small flatfish, drawn
> 2 ounces butter
> juice of 1 large lemon
> 1 teaspoon salt
> flour
> lemon wedges (garnish)
> fresh tarragon leaves (garnish)

The Sauce
12 anchovies, minced
6 fresh tomatoes, chopped
1 medium onion, minced
1 clove garlic, minced
2 tablespoons butter
1 tablespoon chopped fresh thyme
1 teaspoon lemon zest
½ teaspoon salt

Make the sauce first. Heat the butter in a skillet. Sauté the onion for 5 minutes, then stir in the tomatoes, garlic, lemon zest, and salt. Cook for 2 or 3 minutes. Stir in the anchovies and thyme. Simmer for 5 to 10 minutes, or until the liquid has cooked off. Set the skillet aside, but keep it warm.

Rub the fish with lemon juice, then sprinkle with salt. Melt the butter in a large skillet. Shake the sole in a bag with some flour, then fry them one at a time for 5 to 10 minutes, depending on size, or until nicely browned on each side, turning once. Place the fish on a heated serving platter and pour the sauce over it. Serve hot, garnished with lemon wedges and fresh tarragon leaves. Enjoy.

Flounder Stuffed with Crab

Stuffed flatfish make a very attractive and tasty dish, especially when stuffed with crabmeat. I highly recommend this dish for summer flounder, sand dabs, and other small flatfish of ¾ to 1 pound each. In other words, serve a whole stuffed fish for each plate. The measures below feed 6 people but can be adjusted. It's best to make the stuffing first, preferably with fresh crabmeat. Frozen or even canned crab can also be used. The commercial crabmeat imitations will also work, but not quite as nicely as the real thing.

Crab Stuffing

1 pound crabmeat
2 cups soft bread cubes
2 chicken eggs, whisked
⅓ cup butter
1 medium onion, finely chopped
3 cloves garlic, finely chopped
½ rib celery, finely chopped, with green tops
¼ green bell pepper, finely chopped
¼ red bell pepper, finely chopped
1 tablespoon finely chopped fresh parsley
salt and pepper to taste

In a skillet over medium heat, sauté the onion, garlic, bell peppers, celery, and parsley in butter for 3 or 4 minutes. Stir in the crabmeat, bread cubes, chicken eggs, salt, and pepper; turn off the heat but leave the skillet on the burner while you prepare the flounder and preheat the oven to 350 degrees.

The Fish

6 fresh small flounder, ¾ to 1 pound each
¾ cup butter
juice of 3 lemons
2 teaspoons salt
Hungarian paprika

When you dress the fish, leave the heads on unless you think your guests might object. (Remember that flatfish will have both eyes looking up.) Lay the fish on the flatter side; then, with a small, sharp blade of a pocketknife, make a cut dead center from head to tail. Next, carefully work the knife blade along backbone and rib bones on either side of the cut. This will form a nice pocket for the stuffing. Note that the stuffing will be exposed on top, from one end of the fish to the other, making a very attractive and easy-to-eat dish.

Stuff each fish liberally. Quickly melt the butter, mixing in the lemon juice and salt. Brush the stuffed fish with the butter

28

mix. Place each fish on a large sheet of heavy-duty, lightly greased aluminum foil. Fold the foil up and over the fish, bringing the ends together. Make a 1-inch fold along the edge of the foil, then make another fold in the first fold. The idea is to seal in the steam to help cook the fish. Place the packages on a large baking sheet (or on 2 baking sheets) and cook them in the preheated oven for 20 minutes. Then switch the oven to broil, open the packages, baste again with the lemon butter, sprinkle the stuffing with paprika, and broil until the stuffing starts to brown. Serve hot.

Note: You can also cook this dish on a grill or in the coals of a fire. Merely put the sealed package on the grill over a hot fire for 25 minutes or directly onto hot coals for 20 minutes.

Broiled Summer Flounder

Here's a recipe that I like for cooking a whole flounder of 1½ to 2 pounds.

> 1 whole flounder
> ½ cup dark soy sauce
> ¼ cup sake, vermouth, or sherry
> ¼ cup butter
> 2 teaspoons honey
> 1 teaspoon freshly grated ginger root
> 1 tablespoon sesame oil
> ½ teaspoon pepper

Dress the fish whole, with or without the head. Marinate for 2 hours in a mixture of soy sauce, sake, honey, and grated ginger root. Make a long cut down the middle of the fish, lengthwise. When you are ready to cook, preheat the broiler and warm a greased broiling pan. Remove the fish and drain, saving the marinade. In a saucepan, heat the marinade along with the sesame oil, melted butter, and pepper to make a basting sauce. Grease a broiling pan and heat it. Put the flounder, cut side up, in the pan, and place it about 4 inches under the heating element. Brush the flounder all over, getting a liberal amount of sauce into

29

the cut. Broil for about 10 minutes, or until the fish flakes easily when tested with a fork, basting twice. Serve hot.

Thai Flatfish

Here's a good recipe that works nicely for flounder. I have adapted it from *The Taste of Thailand,* by Vatcharin Bhumichitr, who said that fish from northern waters, such as lemon sole, are especially suited for the recipe. I tried it with a flounder taken from the Gulf of Mexico. Ideally, each person is served a whole fish. Of course, the fish must be small enough to fit into your skillet.

> 1 skillet-size flounder, dressed
> 4 long red fresh chili peppers, seeded and chopped
> 4 tablespoons stock or water
> 2 cloves garlic, chopped
> 2 tablespoons Thai Fish Sauce (chapter 27)
> 2 tablespoons sugar
> 2 tablespoons flour
> juice from 2 lemons
> peanut oil
> fresh cilantro leaves (garnish)

Heat about ½ inch of oil in the skillet and fry the fish until done, browning on both sides. Set aside but keep hot. Drain the oil from the skillet, retaining about 2 tablespoons. Sauté the garlic until golden. Add the chili peppers and stir-fry for a few seconds. Stir in the fish sauce, then the lemon juice, sugar, and stock. Mix the flour with a little water and add a little at a time to the skillet, stirring as you go, until the sauce thickens. Pour the sauce over the fish. Serve with rice and steamed vegetables. Garnish with cilantro leaves.

Beer Batter Halibut

Here's a recipe by John Sadusky, adapted from *Alaska Magazine's Cabin Cookbook.* Sadusky says that light-colored beer is best, as the flavor of dark-colored beer is too strong.

> 2 pounds halibut fillets, cut into 1-inch chunks
> oil for deep frying
> 1 bottle beer (12-ounce size)
> 1 cup flour
> 1 tablespoon paprika
> 1½ teaspoons salt

Rig for deep frying, heating the oil to at least 375 degrees. Mix the beer, flour, paprika, and salt. Dip a few pieces of fish in this batter and drop them into the hot oil. Do not overload the fryer, which would cause the temperature to drop too low. Fry for only a few minutes. The fish is done when it floats in the oil, although I usually allow it to brown for a few more seconds. But do not overcook halibut unless you want it dry and chewy. Drain on paper towels or a brown bag. Serve hot.

Halibut for the General

Here's a dish reported in *A General's Diary of Treasured Recipes,* by Brigadier General Frank Dorn. He got it, he said, from the bachelor mess at Fort McKinley, a few miles from Manila. Although he listed halibut in the list of ingredients, he said that having a variety of excellent seafood, including shark and barracuda, was one of the pleasures of living in the Philippines before World War II. Anyhow, it's a simple dish that I highly recommend. The general specifies Bermuda onions, but Vidalias or other large, mild onions will work. The halibut steaks should be about ¾ inch thick and should be cut into pieces about 3 inches across.

1 pound halibut steaks
large onion slices, ½ inch thick
bacon
1 cup white wine
¼ pound butter
salt and pepper to taste
tartar sauce

Preheat the oven to 400 degrees. Melt the butter in a roasting pan just large enough to hold all the fish pieces without overlapping. Add the white wine, then bring to a boil. (This can be done by placing the roasting pan across two stove burners.) Place the fish steaks in the pan, topping each piece with a slice of onion. Cross two strips of bacon, cut to the size of the fish pieces, on each piece of fish and onion. Sprinkle with salt and pepper. Bake uncovered in the center of the oven for 10 minutes. Cover the pan, reduce the heat to 350 degrees, and cook for 20 minutes. Serve hot with pan juices and tartar sauce.

Sand Dab Armenian

This Armenian dish is usually made with fillets from small sole, but any small flatfish will do. Thin fillets are necessary. The rolled fillets can be pan-fried in clarified butter, but it's easier to deep-fry them in olive oil, which is excellent for frying and isn't too expensive if purchased by the gallon.

8 small sand dab fillets (¼ pound each or less)
8 green onions minced with half of green tops
1 cup fine bread crumbs
2 chicken eggs, beaten
olive oil
¼ cup minced fresh parsley
¼ cup minced fresh dill weed
salt and pepper
lemon wedges (garnish)

Heat 1 tablespoon of olive oil in a small pan or skillet. Sauté the onions for 3 or 4 minutes, then mix in the parsley and dill. Remove from the heat and divide into 8 parts (1 part for each fillet). Brush each fillet with olive oil, sprinkle with salt and pepper, spread equally with the onion mix, roll up, and fasten with round toothpicks. Dip in beaten egg, coat with bread crumbs, and deep-fry until golden brown and cooked through. Remove the toothpicks. Garnish with lemon wedges. Serve with fried potatoes and pickled peaches. Feeds 4.

FOUR

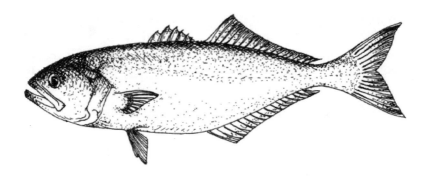

Bluefish

A New York editor, who wanted me to poop up the bluefish in a book I was doing for him, was speechless when I told him that the blue-fish is considered trash along parts of the Gulf of Mexico. Long considered excellent table fare in the Northeast if cooked and eaten while quite fresh, the bluefish is typical of what an unbiased cook runs into when he starts researching saltwater fish. This great culinary gap between North and South is sometimes explained by saying that the bluefish is either wonderful or awful, depending on where it is caught and how long it is kept. I accepted this for many years, but I saw the light when I went to work with Lew Childre, the great fishing tackle maker, during the 1970s.

The bluefish, sometimes called marine piranha, has a mouthful of teeth and knows how to use them.

Lew told me flatly that saltwater fish were better eating than freshwater, then served up some bluefish freshly caught from the Gulf of Mexico. To my surprise, they were outstanding. Moreover, Lew's bluefish were fried, which isn't the preferred method of cooking bluefish, except perhaps for the small ones. Being oily and tending to be strong, bluefish are usually grilled, broiled, or baked. The flesh tends to be dark, but it lightens up when it is cooked.

Although bluefish are better on the day they are caught, the real key is to ice the catch immediately. (Some people bleed them first by cutting them just above the tail.) Even so, bluefish should not be kept long under refrigeration and do not freeze too well.

While I worked with Lew, he entertained a French hook manufacturer, who grew wildly excited when a bluefish bit one of his hooks in two. About this fish's voracity there is no doubt. Bluefish will hit anything that moves in the water. They will also bite when out of the water, and apparently can see quite well. So when handling these fish, watch your fingers; they can take one off. Bluefish (*Pomatomus saltatris)* are also called choppers and marine piranha, and the small ones (up to about 10 inches) are called snappers.

In any case, here are some recipes for freshly caught bluefish, north or south.

Baked Bluefish with New Potatoes

For this recipe you'll need a bluefish of about 3 pounds, or 2 or more smaller fish. Fillet and skin the bluefish. Retain the head, fins, and bony parts.

3 pounds bluefish
8 ounces fresh mushrooms, sliced
2 cups water
½ cup Chablis
½ cup bread crumbs
¼ cup melted butter
1 medium onion, chopped
1 tablespoon fresh parsley
1 teaspoon flour
salt and white pepper
new potatoes (cooked separately)

Put the fish head, bony pieces, and fins into a pan. Add the water, onions, parsley, and flour. Bring to a boil, cover, reduce heat, and simmer for 20 minutes. Strain the stock. Pull the meat off the backbone and head, flaking it.

Preheat the oven to 350 degrees. Place the fillets into a baking pan of suitable size. Pour the stock over the fish but do not quite cover. Top the fillets with the mushrooms, bread crumbs, flaked fish, melted butter, salt, white pepper, and wine. Cover the dish with aluminum foil. Bake for 20 minutes. Remove the foil and bake until brown. Serve hot with new potatoes and green peas.

Pan-Fried Snappers

Young bluefish, from 7 to 9 inches long, are delicious when pan-fried (sautéed) like brook trout. I prefer to scale the snappers, gut them, and cook them whole. Allow at least a snapper per person—and I'll take 2, if available, thank you.

4 snappers
8 slices bacon
flour
salt
lemon (garnish)

Fry the bacon in a skillet until crisp. Drain. Sprinkle the pan-dressed snappers with salt, dust with flour, and sauté in the bacon drippings until nicely browned, turning once. Serve hot along with the bacon, green salad, and bread. If you've got a lemon, quarter it and place on the table for those who want a little juice on their fish.

Flaked Bluefish Casserole

Here's a tasty dish that can be made easily from leftover bluefish, or from freshly poached fish.

> 1 pound dressed bluefish
> 1 can cream of celery soup (10¾-ounce size)
> 2 hard-boiled chicken eggs, sliced
> ¼ cup milk
> 1 cup crushed potato chips
> 1 teaspoon salt
> ½ teaspoon pepper
> 1 can small green peas (8½-ounce size)

Preheat oven to 350 degrees. If you are starting with uncooked fish fillet, poach it for about 10 minutes, until it flakes when tested with a fork; then drain and flake it. Mix the soup and milk in a casserole dish. Stir in the eggs, fish flakes, salt, pepper, and drained peas. Bake for 25 minutes. Sprinkle the top with crushed potato chips and bake for another 5 minutes. Feeds 2 to 4.

Creole Sauce Bluefish

I love a good creole sauce over any baked fish, and this recipe is one of my favorites for fresh bluefish.

> bluefish, 4 to 5 pounds, dressed whole
> 3 large tomatoes, chopped
> 2 medium onions, finely chopped
> 8 ounces fresh mushrooms, finely chopped
> ½ red bell pepper, finely chopped
> ½ green bell pepper, finely chopped
> 3 cloves garlic, minced
> 1 can tomato sauce (8-ounce size)
> 1 cup white wine
> 2 tablespoons olive oil
> 1 tablespoon chopped fresh parsley
> 2 bay leaves
> salt and cayenne pepper
> fresh parsley for garnish

Preheat the oven to 350 degrees. Heat the oil in a skillet. Sauté the onions, peppers, mushrooms, and garlic for 5 minutes. Add the tomatoes, tomato sauce, chopped parsley, and bay leaves. Simmer on very low heat for 30 minutes, then discard the bay leaves. Keep the sauce warm.

Grease a baking pan or ovenproof dish large enough to hold the bluefish. Mix some salt and a little cayenne pepper, then sprinkle the fish inside and out. Pour the wine into the baking pan and place the fish in it. Spread the sauce over the fish and bake in the center of the oven for 30 minutes, or until the fish flakes easily with a fork. Garnish with fresh parsley and serve hot. Feeds 4 or 5.

Buzzards Bay Bluefish

Here's an old recipe that I have adapted from Suzanne Cary Gruver's *The Cape Cod Cook Book*. The result is purely excellent, provided that the salt pork does not put you off for reasons of health. To dress the bluefish for baking, gut and draw it, leaving the head on. If you don't want to serve the fish with the head, leave it on during the cooking, then cut it off before serving. For accurate cooking time, weigh the fish after drawing it.

> 4- to 5-pound bluefish
> 2 cups bread crumbs
> 6 slices salt pork about 4 inches long
> 2 tablespoons melted butter
> 2 tablespoons minced onion
> ¾ teaspoon sage
> salt and pepper
> flour
> water

Preheat the oven and a baking pan to 350 degrees. Mix a little salt and pepper, then rub it onto the fish inside and out. To make a stuffing, mix the bread crumbs, melted butter, onion, and sage. Add just enough water to make the stuffing moist but not really wet. Stuff the fish and sew it up or close it with skewers. Place the salt pork in the bottom of the baking pan, spaced out. Place the stuffed bluefish on the salt pork. Sprinkle with salt, pepper, and flour. Bake in the center of the oven for 15 minutes per pound of fish. Baste several times with pan drippings.

Broiled Bluefish with Oyster Sauce

Broiling is an ideal way to cook bluefish, and thousands of recipes can be used. Here's one of my favorites. When filleting the fish, leave the skin on. Fillets from 3-pound fish are ideal. I usually like to allow ½ pound of fillet per person, but the oyster sauce is quite rich, so a ¼-pound serving will do, especially if you have plenty of vegetables and perhaps rice or french-fried potatoes.

> 2 pounds bluefish fillets
> ½ cup melted butter
> juice of 1 lemon
> oyster sauce (see note below)

Mix the butter and lemon juice, brush the fillets, and broil about 4 inches from the heat for about 15 minutes, or until the meat is opaque throughout, basting from time to time. Carefully transfer the fillets to a heated serving platter or plates, then top with oyster sauce.

Note: For convenience, I usually use bottled Chinese oyster sauce for this recipe, available in the oriental section of most supermarkets, but I also make such a sauce from time to time (see chapter 27).

Beach Bluefish

Gather some dry driftwood and build a good fire. When it burns down to coals, rig a large, flat-hinged grilling basket about 4 inches from the coals. Draw and butterfly the bluefish. Grill for 5 or 6 minutes on each side, or until the meat flakes easily when tested with a fork. While grilling, baste two or three times with seawater. Enjoy.

Baked Bluefish

Although the bluefish isn't as highly touted in the South, here's a recipe that I have adapted from *The Official Louisiana Seafood & Wild Game Cookbook*. In addition to lots of basil and cayenne, the measures call for a 4-pound bluefish. This is the weight of the fish before it is filleted. In my opinion, the French bread crumbs are made by crumbling some French bread, although a New York editor once told me that bread crumbs are not made from bread. The Louisiana book listed 1 tablespoon of cayenne. I reduced this to 1 teaspoon. If you feel frisky and have guests who like hot stuff, increase the measure at will.

4-pound bluefish, filleted
2 or 3 cups of French bread crumbs
2 cups chopped fresh parsley
2 cups chopped fresh sweet basil
½ cup grated Parmesan
½ cup olive oil
5 tablespoons minced fresh garlic
1 teaspoon cayenne pepper
1 teaspoon salt
lemon slices (garnish)

Preheat the oven to 350 degrees. Grease a baking dish large enough to hold the two fillets side by side. Mix the salt and cayenne, then sprinkle evenly over the fish. Baste the fish with olive oil and place them on the greased baking dish. Mix the remaining olive oil with the rest of the ingredients and spread on top of the fish. Bake in the center of the oven for 20 minutes. Serve with lemon slices, rice, steamed vegetables, and French bread. Feeds 4 to 6.

FIVE

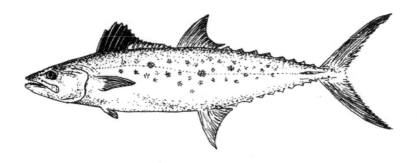

Mackerels

All of the mackerels make good eating and can be cooked by any method. The flesh is rather oily, however, making it ideal for grilling, broiling, or smoking. These fish are often filleted and cooked with the skin left on, and the meat is pulled off the skin at the table with a fork. For frying, they should be skinned. As with many other saltwater species, mackerels should be dressed and iced as soon as they are caught and should be eaten within a few days.

King mackerel, *Scomberomorus cavalla.* Growing up to 100 pounds, the king mackerel, also called king, kingfish, and cavalla, is the largest of all the mackerels. It ranges the western

---

The Spanish mackerel has pronounced bronze or yellow spots. Other mackerels are of similar shape.

Atlantic from Brazil to North Carolina and sometimes ventures as far north as Cape Cod. It is often cut into steaks for broiling or grilling.

Cero, *Scomberomorus regalis.* Weighing up to 15 pounds, this species ranges from Brazil to Cape Cod, being abundant in south Florida. The larger fish are often steaked; smaller ones, filleted. They make excellent eating.

Sierra, *Scomberomorus sierra.* This Pacific mackerel ranges from Southern California to Peru. It is a popular sport fish in western Mexico. Good eating, it weighs up to 12 pounds.

Spanish mackerel, *Scomberomorus maculatus.* These popular fish can weigh up to 20 pounds, but they are usually much smaller. The Spanish mackerel is excellent when smoked or grilled, although some experts don't rate it so highly. This is an Atlantic species, ranging from Brazil to the Chesapeake Bay. A similar species, **Monterey Spanish mackerel** *(Scomberomorus concolor),* grows in the Pacific to the Gulf of California; once it was common in Monterey Bay, where it was considered to be a delicacy, but it no longer frequents these waters.

Atlantic mackerel, *Scomber scombrus.* This small mackerel, usually between 1 and 2 feet in length, occurs from the Gulf of St. Lawrence to North Carolina. A similar species, **Pacific mackerel** *(Scomber japonicus),* ranges from the Gulf of California to the Gulf of Alaska. Both are important commercial species.

Since all of the mackerels make good eating, size is usually of more importance than exact identification when selecting a recipe. In any case, here are some favorites to try.

Broiled Kingfish Steaks

King mackerel are ideal for broiling and grilling. Either fillets or steaks will work. For best results, the steaks should be about ¾ inch thick.

The Fish
4 to 6 kingfish steaks
½ cup melted butter
juice of 2 lemons
¼ cup chopped fresh parsley

The Marinade
¼ cup olive oil
juice of 2 lemons
½ teaspoon crushed fennel seed
½ teaspoon dried basil
½ teaspoon pepper
½ teaspoon salt

Mix the marinade ingredients. Put the steaks into a non-metallic container, pour in the marinade, mix, cover, and refrigerate for 2 hours or longer. When you are ready to cook, preheat the broiler. Mix a sauce with the butter, lemon juice, and parsley in a small pan, bring to a simmer, stir, remove from the heat, and keep warm. Grease a broiling pan. Drain the kingfish steaks, discarding the marinade. Put the steaks into the broiling pan, brush with the warm basting sauce, and broil close to the heat (about 4 inches) for 4 or 5 minutes. Turn the steaks, baste, and broil for another 4 or 5 minutes, or until the fish is done. Heat the basting sauce again, then serve it along with the broiled fish and boiled new potatoes. Serve with lots of green salad and hot French bread.

Variation: Omit the parsley and lemon from the basting sauce, substituting 3 minced or crushed cloves of garlic.

Kingfish Steaks with Mango Salsa

This recipe works with steaks about ¾ inch thick, and with fillets of about the same thickness.

The Fish
2 pounds king mackerel steaks or fillets
olive oil
salt and pepper

The Salsa
¾ cup chopped fresh tomato
¾ cup mango cubes (½-inch dice)
¾ cup finely chopped onion
¼ cup chopped red bell pepper
¼ cup chopped green bell pepper
¼ cup chopped fresh cilantro
2 cloves garlic, minced
1 fresh jalapeño, seeded and minced
1 tablespoon olive oil
1 teaspoon fresh lemon juice
½ teaspoon salt

Heat the oil in a skillet, then sauté the onion, peppers, garlic, and cilantro for 5 or 6 minutes. Stir in the rest of the salsa ingredients, then simmer for a few minutes. Keep hot. Preheat the broiler. Select a broiling pan large enough to hold the steaks without overlapping, brush the broiling pan with olive oil, and preheat it. Arrange the steaks in the heated broiling pan, baste with olive oil, and sprinkle with salt. Broil about 4 inches from the heat for 5 or 6 minutes. Turn each steak carefully with a thin spatula, baste with olive oil, sprinkle with salt and pepper, and broil for another 5 minutes, or until the fish flakes easily when tested with a fork. Do not overcook. Top each steak with salsa, then broil for 1 minute. Serve immediately.

Variation: For a quicker and less expensive version, use a prepared salsa heated in a saucepan.

Easy Mackerel Fillets

Here's an easy recipe for baked fillets from small mackerel, a pound or so. It can also be used to advantage with small bluefish or pompano fillets. Be sure to try this one. The cooking times given are for fillets from small mackerel; thicker fillets may require more cooking time, and very thick fillets may burn on the outside before the inside gets done, because of the high oven temperature.

> 2 pounds small mackerel fillets
> Italian salad dressing
> 1 ½ cups crushed cheese crackers, such as Ritz
> 2 tablespoons olive oil
> salt and pepper to taste
> paprika

Preheat the oven to 500 degrees. Put some salad dressing in a plate or platter and the crushed crackers in another. Sprinkle the fillets with salt and pepper, roll them first in the salad dressing and then in the cracker crumbs. Arrange the fillets skin side down on a well-greased baking sheet or shallow pan. Brush the fillets with olive oil, then sprinkle them with paprika. Bake them in the center of the oven for 12 minutes, or until the fish flakes easily when tested with a fork. Feeds 4 to 6.

Fried Mackerel

Because the mackerels are on the oily side, most authorities recommend that they not be fried. I agree, because I think there are better ways to prepare them, such as smoking or grilling. I confess, however, that I do from time to time fry the smaller mackerels and find them to be delicious.

Fillet the fish, leaving the skin on. Cut the fillet into 3 segments, and cut each segment in half lengthwise. The reason for the latter cut is to keep fish from curling. (I save and fry the backbone left from the filleting process; this piece makes the best eating, I think, and can be eaten like corn on the cob.)

After sprinkling the pieces with salt and pepper, shake them in a bag of fine stone-ground cornmeal and fry them in hot oil until browned on both sides. Serve hot.

Note that coarsely ground, gritty cornmeal won't stick to the slick skin side of the fish too well.

Grilled Spanish Mackerel

Spanish mackerel of about 1 pound or less are easy to fillet and grill. The mild flavor and high oil content make marinades and basting sauces unnecessary. Also, the fillets tend to lie flat instead of curling lengthwise. I always leave the skin on Spanish mackerel fillets. In this recipe, the fillets are served skin side down. Anyone who doesn't want the skin can pull the meat off with a fork.

>
> Spanish mackerel
> sour cream
> Tabasco sauce
> salt

Fillet the mackerel and grill over medium-high heat for 5 minutes skin side down. Turn the fillets and grill them for another 5 minutes, or until done. Do not overcook. The timing will vary a little either way, depending on your cooking rig and source of heat. When the fillets are done, place them skin side down on individual serving plates or platters. Sprinkle lightly with salt, then spread lightly with a mixture of sour cream and Tabasco sauce. Since the sauce goes on after the fillets are grilled, it's easy to vary it to taste. Start with a mild sauce for those who want it, then stir in a little more Tabasco for those who want something hotter. Other commercial or homemade sauces can also be used. Try a good mayonnaise.

A single fillet will make a serving—but I'll want another one. If you are feeding people who really like fish, allow a ¾- or 1-pound mackerel (undressed weight) per person.

Hot-Smoked Mackerel

Mackerel are very good when hot-smoked. I normally use Spanish mackerel because they are readily available to me, but other species can also be used. Fish of about 1 pound can be gutted and smoked whole, with or without the heads. Larger fish should be filleted, butterflied, or merely cut in half lengthwise. Any sort of smoker-cooker can be used, but I prefer the two-rack silo-shaped models fueled with charcoal. Electric models are nice for the patio, but the charcoal models can be used anywhere. For wood chips, I prefer fresh green wood. (Any readily available hardwood, such as oak, hickory, or apple, will do.) Dried chips or chunks can also be used after soaking them in water. Here's all you'll need:

> small mackerel or fillets
> salt
> water
> Tabasco
> melted butter or bacon drippings
> wood chips or chunks

For each pound of fish, mix a cup of salt in a gallon of water. Soak the fish in a nonmetallic container for at least 30 minutes, then let the fish dry in the open air.

Build a charcoal fire (or heat the electric unit) in your smoker. When the coals are hot, add some wood chips and pour some water into the pan. Grease the racks and put the fish down. Cover and smoke for several hours, or until the fish flakes easily when tested with a fork. (Also, see the instructions that came with your cooker.) Add more charcoal and wood chips—and keep water in the pan. (One purpose of the water is to hold the temperature down, since converting water to steam uses up the heat; it's called latent heat of vaporization.) Baste a few times with a mixture of melted butter or bacon drippings and Tabasco to taste.

Variation: You can use the same recipe with outdoor grills that are large enough to use the indirect method. Some of these units will cook the fish more quickly. Again, experience with your cooker is the best guide.

Jamaican Mackerel

Here's a dish that is popular in Jamaica, calling for salt mackerel. I sometimes cook it with salt mackerel purchased in the supermarket, but it's easy enough to salt your own. Simply mix 2 cups of salt in a gallon of water and soak a few mackerel fillets in it for a week or longer in the refrigerator. Be sure to weight the fish down with a bowl or some nonmetallic object so that they stay completely submerged. Turn the fish every few days if you feel the need to do so. Small fillets work best. Of course, if you are into preserving fish by the salting process, have at it.

This recipe also calls for coconut milk, a standard ingredient in island cookery (see chapter 27), and for green bananas. The latter can sometimes be purchased in supermarkets—especially when a new shipment comes in. If you don't have saltwater Jamaicans to feed, you can get by with semiripe bananas. The recipe calls for a fresh Scotch bonnet pepper. If you can't find one, use any hot green chili—just don't loose the seeds or inner pith into the dish unless you want hot stuff. Also, beware of those tiny island peppers.

>
> 1 pound salt mackerel fillets
> 3 cups Coconut Milk (chapter 27)
> 3 medium tomatoes, peeled and chopped
> 2 green onions with tops, chopped
> 1 medium onion, chopped
> 1 clove garlic, minced
> 1 green banana, peeled and sliced into 2-inch pieces
> 1 Scotch bonnet pepper
> 1 teaspoon chopped fresh thyme
> freshly ground pepper to taste

The night before cooking, place the salt mackerel in fresh water and put it in the refrigerator overnight, changing the water several times if convenient. Drain it and cut the fillets into bite-size chunks. Put the coconut milk into a large skillet. Bring it to a boil, then add the tomatoes, onions, green onions, garlic, and thyme. Prick the pepper with a fork, but don't let the seeds out, and add it to the skillet. Simmer until the mixture thickens. Add the mackerel chunks and cook for 5 minutes. Add the sliced green bananas and simmer for another 5 minutes, or until the fish is done. Serve hot, sprinkling some freshly ground pepper over each serving to taste, with rice and hot bread.

SIX

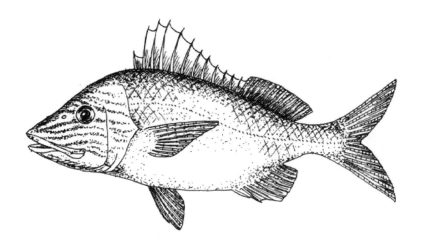

Pigfish and Other Grunts

The grunt family of fish comprises some 175 species worldwide. Fortunately for the angler who isn't a stickler for exact identification, all the grunts that are caught from North American coastal waters are not only edible but also delicious. Here are a few of the more commonly caught grunts.

Pigfish, *Orthopristis chrysopterus.* Also called hogfish, this species is caught in coastal waters and salty bays from the Gulf of Mexico, around Florida, and up the Atlantic coast to Massachusetts. Sometimes quite plentiful, they can be taken on cut

---

The grunt has a large mouth for its size—and mean, spiny dorsal fins. It makes a grunting noise by grinding its teeth, amplifying the sound with an air bladder.

bait, jigs, or other artificials fished near the bottom. In the northern part of their range, they are caught mostly during the warmer months; in the Caribbean and Gulf of Mexico, all year. Although pigfish grow up to 3 pounds, the average catch is about ½ pound and hand-sized. Their meat is grayish white, resembling that of the snappers and groupers. The larger fish can be baked or cooked by any method, or filleted, but the smaller ones are best pan-fried or deep-fried. It's best to ice the fish soon after they are caught, but they keep well and do not require immediate dressing. They also freeze well.

Tomtate, *Haemulon aurolineatum.* This fish is more tolerant of colder waters and ranges as far north as Cape Cod. Because of their small size (8 inches maximum length, but usually only 3 or 4 inches), tomtates are often thrown back, but even the smaller ones are very, very good eating if you learn how to deal with the bones (see chapter 23).

Blue-striped grunt, *Haemulon sciurus.* Excellent eating, this beautiful grunt is easy to catch on cut bait, flies, jigs, or even small plugs. It is popular as a food fish in the West Indies and south Florida, where it is sometimes quite plentiful. The average size is about 10 inches.

White grunt, *Haemulon plumieri.* This common grunt, which averages about 10 inches in length, ranges from Brazil to the Chesapeake Bay. It is excellent eating and is an important commercial fish in the West Indies.

In addition to those discussed above, several tasty grunts live in Florida waters, south to Brazil. These include the cottonwick; the tasty but small French grunt; the Caesar grunt, a market fish in the West Indies; the beautiful and tasty pork fish; the small but delicious smallmouth grunt, a reef fish that also frequents shallow water along the shore; the Spanish grunt, another market fish in the West Indies; and the white margate, a larger species that grows up to 2 feet in length and is often filleted.

Although exact identification can be a full-time job, a grunt is a grunt. Most of them are pretty fish, and some of them are spectacular. As the late Byron Dalrymple once wrote, "The grunts as a group are gaily and beautifully colored, with canary yellow and bright aqua and blue stripes and streaks, spots and spangles their stock in trade."

On the whole, the size is more important than the exact species when you are dealing with grunts. They can be cooked by any method that suits the size of your catch. Here are a few recommendations.

Island Fried Pigfish

In the Caribbean, pigfish and other small grunts are often fried with their heads on. Any good frying recipe will work, but I prefer a cast-iron skillet, peanut oil, and a cornmeal coating, provided that fine stone-ground meal is available.

> pigfish or other small grunts
> peanut oil
> white stone-ground cornmeal
> salt
> hot pepper sauce (such as Tabasco)

Scale and gut the fish, leaving the heads and tails on. Sprinkle sparsely with hot pepper sauce, then let sit for an hour or so. When you are ready to cook, heat about ¾ inch of oil in a skillet. Sprinkle some salt on the fish and inside the body cavity. Shake the fish 2 or 3 at a time in a bag with a little meal, then fry them in hot oil (at least 375 degrees) for 3 to 5 minutes on each side, depending on size. Do not overcrowd the skillet. Serve hot with hush puppies and french fries or fried plantain chips.

Grunt Soup

Here's an old Irish recipe for small, hand-sized grunts.

>10 grunts
>1 quart water
>¼ cup butter
>1 medium onion
>1 tablespoon chopped fresh parsley
>1 tablespoon chopped fresh chives
>1 tablespoon flour
>½ teaspoon salt
>¼ teaspoon pepper

Scale and draw the fish, leaving the heads on. Put the fish into a pot of suitable size and pour in 1 quart of water. Add the salt. Bring to a boil, reduce the heat, and simmer for about 10 minutes, until the fish flakes easily from the bone. While the fish are simmering, melt the butter in a skillet and chop the onion. Sauté the onion for about 3 or 4 minutes, then stir in the flour slowly. Leave the skillet on very low heat. Meanwhile, remove the fish from the pot and flake the meat from the bones. Strain the liquid, put it back into the pot, and bring to a gentle boil. Go back to the skillet, stir the onions and flour, and cook for another 10 minutes, or until the onions are browned. Add to the liquid in the pot, along with the chives, parsley, and pepper. Mix in the flaked fish, then simmer for about 5 minutes. Serve as an appetizer, or as a meal, along with boiled potatoes, bread, a green vegetable, and perhaps salad.

Grilled Grunts

Although grilling is one of the best ways to cook hand-sized fish, the method is not used as often as frying, simply because it is difficult to turn the fish without breaking them up. An adjustable, hinged grilling basket is highly recommended.

    10 small grunts
    ½ cup melted butter
    ¼ cup fresh lemon juice
    ¼ cup cider vinegar
    ¼ cup Worcestershire sauce
    ¼ cup dark brown sugar
    Tabasco sauce
    salt

Scale, draw, and wash the grunts. Sprinkle the batch with a little Tabasco sauce, turning and stirring them about to coat all sides. Set the grunts aside for an hour or longer. When you are ready to proceed, build a wood or charcoal fire and let it burn down to coals. While waiting, heat the lemon juice, butter, vinegar, Worcestershire sauce, salt, and brown sugar in a saucepan or basting pot. Keep warm. When the coals are ready, baste both sides of the fish, then place them on a rack 4 or 5 inches above the coals. Cook for 6 minutes, turn, baste, and grill for 4 or 5 minutes, until the fish are done. Baste again, turn, baste, and serve hot.

Tanzanian Grunts

This fried fish dish doesn't have a meal or flour coating, and it is eaten merely fried or served with a tomato sauce. I have adapted the recipe from *Good Tastes in Africa,* to which it was submitted by Emily Bauv of Tanzania. Although the kind of fish wasn't specified in the list of ingredients, the instructions indicated that they should be sliced on a slant at the sides, leading me to believe that they were fried whole and were therefore on the small size. I think ½-pound grunts work just right. Also, the original recipe specified ½ cup of vegetable oil, but I prefer more—about ½ to ¾ inch in my skillet. Suit yourself.

The Fish
2 pounds whole grunts
salt
cooking oil

The Sauce
2 large tomatoes, sliced
1 small to medium onion, chopped
2 fresh chili peppers (jalapeño will do)
2 tablespoons fresh lemon or lime juice
½ teaspoon curry powder
salt and pepper

Dress the grunts whole, then cut three diagonal slices on either side. Sprinkle salt on the fish, inside and out. Heat about ½ inch of oil in a skillet, then fry the fish on medium-high heat until browned on both sides, turning once.

Remove the fish to a heated platter. Quickly pour off most of the oil from the skillet. Then sauté the onion for about 6 minutes. Remove the seeds and cores from the peppers, then chop them finely and add them to the onion, along with the tomatoes and curry powder. Cook for about 10 minutes. Stir in the lemon juice, salt, and pepper. Pour this sauce over the fish. Serve hot.

SEVEN

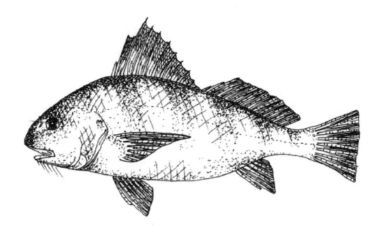

Spots, Croakers, and Other Drums

In all of the drums, the male has a specialized muscle that can cause the swim bladder to make repeated contractions, thereby producing a sound that can be heard for some distance. In some cases, the female can also make this sound. These fish, all in the drum family, are closely related to the weakfish and sea trout (chapter 2); they are also related to the whitings (chapter 23). The drums usually have one or more barbels on the lower jaw and a lateral line that extends only to the caudal fin. Exact identification isn't too important, simply because most of these fish

The family of croakers and drums comprises 260 species. Most of these fish produce a drumming sound with their air bladders. The black drum, shown above, grows well over 100 pounds and has a beard.

can be good eating if properly handled. Here are a few of the more commonly caught species:

Atlantic croaker, *Micropogon undulatus*. This croaker grows to about 4 pounds, but 1 pound is the average. It is common from Texas to the Chesapeake Bay, and can be caught as far north as Cape Cod. The smaller ones are very good when pan-fried. Sometimes called hardhead, this croaker is available in some markets.

Black drum, *Pogonias cromis*. The largest of the family, these drums grow to 100 pounds or better. The smaller ones are delicious when properly handled. Specimens up to 10 pounds can be baked or poached, but larger ones tend to be quite coarse, suitable mostly for soups or chowders. The black drum can be caught in coastal waters from Cape Cod to South America.

Redfish or red drum, *Sciaenops ocellata*. Sometimes called channel bass, this member of the drum family was made world famous by chef Paul Prudhomme's blackened redfish. It is easily identified by a spot on its tail and the absence of chin barbels. Ranging from Cape Cod to Texas, this fish is very, very popular in the Gulf of Mexico, and a "slot limit" is in effect in some areas; that is, small fish and large fish, over and under specified lengths, must be released. Check the current local laws. The smaller ones, often called puppy drum along the Carolina coast, are good when prepared by any method. Try cutting fillets into fingers and deep-frying them. Larger ones, over 10 pounds, are quite coarse and are best when used in stews.

Spotfin croaker, *Roncador stearnsi*. Distinguished by a large black spot at the base of the pectoral fins, this popular surf fish of the Pacific coast grows up to 9 pounds. Sometimes called golden croaker, it is edible but not highly regarded as table fare. The smaller ones are good when fried, but the larger ones should perhaps be poached, flaked, and used in recipes that call for fish flakes.

Spot, *Leiostomus xanthurus*. Similar to the Atlantic croaker, the spot grows up to about 2 pounds, but the average catch is about ½ pound. They are plentiful from New Jersey to Mexico, but they do range a little farther north. The spot is very good if eaten when fresh. Because the flesh tends to turn soft quickly, it should be iced immediately after catching. The flesh is sometimes wormy, but this condition causes no problem to humans (except perhaps psychological) if the fish are cooked properly.

In any case, here are some of my favorite recipes for the various species of drums and croakers.

Texas Black Drum

This is an excellent recipe for baking fillets from black drum. The flavors of bacon and onion combine nicely with fish.

> 2 pounds black drum fillets
> 8 thin slices bacon
> 1 medium to large onion, thinly sliced
> ½ cup soft bread crumbs
> ¼ cup finely chopped fresh parsley
> 1 tablespoon fresh lemon juice
> salt and pepper

Preheat the oven to 350 degrees. Place the fillets in a well-greased baking dish, then sprinkle them with the lemon juice, salt, and pepper. In a skillet, fry the bacon until crisp. Drain the bacon, crumble it, and mix it with the bread crumbs and parsley. Cook the onion slices in the bacon drippings until tender. Arrange the onion slices over the fillets, then sprinkle the top with the bacon and bread crumb mixture. Drizzle a little—but not much—of the bacon drippings over all. Bake for 25 minutes, or until the fish flakes easily when tested with a fork. Feeds 4 to 6.

Carolina Spot and Sweet Potatoes

Although the spot has a good flavor, the flesh tends to be on the soft side. It can, however, be firmed up by salting it for a few days. At one time, salting was a common method of preserving fish both commercially and on a small scale for home consumption. Since the advent of mechanical refrigeration, the practice has become less important, but salt fish are still popular in some areas because of the unique flavor. In any case, the following recipe is from the Outer Banks of North Carolina.

> 4 spot
> 2 pounds salt
> 4 sweet potatoes
> butter
> water
> white vinegar

Scale and fillet the fish, discarding the backbones or using them for fish stock or fish flakes. Pour a little salt in the bottom of a nonmetallic container. Sprinkle both sides of the fish heavily with salt and place them skin side down into the container. Pour the rest of the salt on top, spreading it evenly. Place the container in the refrigerator or a cool place for 4 days.

Remove the fish from the container and wash off the salt. Soak in cool, fresh water for 4 hours, changing the water from time to time. While soaking the fish, place the sweet potatoes in a 350-degree oven and bake until soft and the skin starts to shrink.

Put the fish into a large pan and cover them with water. Bring to a quick boil, reduce heat, cover, and simmer for 10 minutes or until the fish flakes easily when tested with a fork. Carefully place a fish and a sweet potato on each plate. Peel the sweet potato, slit it lengthwise, and put some real butter in the slit. Sprinkle the fish lightly with vinegar. This is soul food. Enjoy.

Frank's Best Croaker

For this recipe I am indebted to *The Frank Davis Seafood Notebook*, by Frank Davis, who allowed that any lean or medium oily fish could be used. He specified croaker, he said, because he believed this to be the best recipe there is for that fish.

> 2 pounds croaker fillets
> 1 cup crushed cracker crumbs
> ½ cup Parmesan cheese
> ½ cup oil
> juice of 1 large lemon
> 2 cloves garlic, minced
> 1 teaspoon tarragon vinegar
> 1 teaspoon onion powder
> ½ teaspoon garlic powder

Mix the cracker crumbs, cheese, onion powder, and garlic powder; set aside. Next, mix the oil, vinegar, lemon juice, and fresh garlic. Put the fillets into a nonmetallic container, pour the marinade over them, and place in the refrigerator for about an hour, turning every 15 minutes.

When you are ready to cook, preheat the oven to 500 degrees. Remove each fillet from the marinade, roll it in cracker crumbs, and place it on a greased baking pan or pizza pan, making sure the fillets do not touch each other. Put the platter into the center of the oven for 12 to 15 minutes, or until the fish flakes easily when tested with a fork. Feeds 4. Serve with potato salad and green peas.

Croaker Italian

Here's a good dish to feed people who are not overly fond of croaker or other fish. It can be made with leftovers, but it's really best to poach fresh fish. The recipe calls for 1 pound of flaked meat, which will require about 2 pounds of undressed croaker. Exact measurements aren't necessary.

1 pound cooked croaker, flaked
1 package frozen spinach (10-ounce size)
1 pound chopped fresh tomatoes
1 medium to large onion, chopped
4 ounces sliced mushrooms
1 cup chicken broth or Fish Stock (chapter 27)
2 tablespoons olive oil
1½ tablespoons flour
4 cloves garlic, minced
salt and pepper
freshly grated Parmesan cheese
linguine or spaghetti, cooked separately

Thaw the spinach. Heat the oil in a large skillet. Sauté the mushrooms, onion, and garlic for a few minutes. Add the flour, stirring well with a wooden spoon. Add the chicken broth, tomatoes, salt, and pepper. Bring to a boil, reduce the heat, cover, and simmer for 10 minutes. Stir in the croaker flakes and spinach. Serve hot over linguine, topping with Parmesan to taste. Hot buttered Italian bread and *vino* go nicely with this dish.

Croaker in Hot Tomato Sauce

Here's a dish that I like to cook with any mild fish that isn't too flaky after being poached; the fish will be cut into bite-size cubes, and these shouldn't come apart too easily. Try the recipe with croaker, sheepshead, or redfish. Purists will want to seed the tomatoes, but I don't bother.

> 1 pound skinless croaker fillets
> 4 medium tomatoes, peeled and chopped
> 1 large onion, finely chopped
> 4 cloves garlic, finely chopped
> 1 bell pepper, seeded and chopped
> 2 or 3 green jalapeño peppers, seeded and chopped
> 3 tablespoons tomato puree
> 1 tablespoon lemon juice
> ½ cup sherry
> ¼ cup olive oil
> ½ teaspoon sugar
> salt and pepper to taste
> chopped parsley
> rice (cooked separately)

Poach the fish fillets for about 10 minutes, then cut them into 1-inch chunks. Drain. Heat the olive oil in a large skillet. Sauté the onion, garlic, bell pepper, and jalapeño for 5 minutes. Add the tomatoes, tomato puree, sugar, salt, and pepper; simmer and stir for 15 minutes. Then stir in the lemon juice and sherry. Next, add the fish chunks, being careful not to break them apart. Simmer for 5 minutes. Sprinkle the dish with chopped parsley. Serve with rice and steamed or stir-fried vegetables.

Dahi Machi

Here's a dish from India, combining fish and yogurt, that works nicely with croaker. Use fillets rather than whole or pan-dressed fish.

> 1½ to 2 pounds croaker fillets, cut into chunks
> ¾ pint yogurt
> 2 medium onions (used separately)
> 4 green chili peppers (see note below)
> 2 tablespoons peanut oil
> 2 tablespoons butter
> juice of 1 lemon
> 1 tablespoon grated fresh ginger root
> 2 teaspoons dry turmeric powder
> salt

Finely chop one of the onions, then mix it into the yogurt, along with the grated ginger, turmeric, chopped chili peppers, and salt. Put the fish chunks into a nonmetallic bowl and pour the yogurt mixture over them, tossing to coat all sides. Marinate for at least 1 hour in the refrigerator. Heat the oil and the butter in a skillet. Slice the second onion and sauté for 5 minutes. Add the fish and the marinade, cover the skillet, and simmer for 15 minutes, or until the fish flakes easily when tested with a fork. At the last minute, sprinkle the fish with the lemon juice and toss lightly. Serve hot with lots of fluffy white rice.

Note: Be warned that this dish can be exceedingly hot if you chop the green chili peppers without first removing the seeds and inner pith. Although the dish is served very hot in India, you may want to moderate it somewhat.

Lucille's Old Drum Stew

I found this stew recipe in a book called *Coastal Carolina Cooking*, which attributed it to Lucille Truitt of Oriental. The recipe calls for cornmeal dumplings, as do several similar fish stew recipes in the book. I have added a recipe for these, along with my recipe for crackling bread. According to Lucille, there are three kinds of drums, according to size. A puppy drum is from 10 to 12 inches long. A yearling is from 18 to 20 inches. (I don't know what happened to those between 12 and 18 inches.) And an old drum is from 28 to 30 inches. These, she says, can be nailed to a board at the tail and then scaled with a hoe.

In any case, be sure to try this stew with an old drum or any good fish with flaky flesh, such as large grouper.

The Stew
2 pounds old drum boneless fillets, cut into chunks
4 medium potatoes, quartered
1 medium onion, diced
¼ pound salt pork
cornmeal dumplings (below)
water

Put the potatoes into a large pan or stove-top Dutch oven. Cover with water, bring to a boil, reduce heat, and simmer for 20 minutes. While the potatoes simmer, mince the salt pork and fry out the fat in a skillet. Fry it until the bits of pork are quite crispy. Layer the onions over the potatoes, and layer the chunked fish over the onions. Remove the salt pork bits (cracklings) from the skillet, drain them on a brown bag, reserving them for the crackling bread, and pour the drippings into the stew. Shake the pan to settle the ingredients. Add a little more water if needed. Bring to a simmer, then reduce the heat, cover, and simmer for 20 minutes, or until the broth thickens. Add the cornmeal dumplings and simmer for another 5 to 10 minutes. Serve hot in bowls.

Note that this recipe doesn't list salt and pepper. The salt pork grease may provide enough salt to suit your taste, but you may want to add some pepper. Many of the Outer Banks recipes call for flaked red pepper, which I highly recommend, especially in conjunction with cornmeal dumplings, in modest amounts.

The Cornmeal Dumplings
1 cup fine stone-ground white cornmeal
¼ cup boiling hot water
¼ cup broth from the fish stew
salt

Mix the cornmeal, hot water, and broth from the stew. (The broth will help hold the dumplings together, or keep them from cooking apart.) Stir in some salt. Form the dough into small patties and carefully put them into the stew. Cook for 5 to 10 minutes, as directed above. Since we have cornmeal and some crispy bits of salt pork on hand, I can't resist adding crackling bread to the menu, and I trust that Lucille Truitt won't object, although she might argue with the fine details.

The Crackling Bread
2 cups fine stone-ground white cornmeal
water
cracklings from above
salt
cooking oil

Mix the cornmeal with enough hot water to make a soft dough. Stir in the cracklings and salt. Heat the cooking oil in a skillet. Add a little more water to the dough, if needed. The dough should drop easily from a tablespoon and should flatten slightly when it comes in contact with the bottom of the skillet. Fry on medium-high heat until nicely browned on both sides, turning once. Serve with the stew. If you're in the mood for real soul food, crumble the leftover crackling bread into a glass, cover it with thick, cold buttermilk, and eat with a spoon.

Slot Limit Redfish

A fellow by the name of Woods King, Jr., down on the Florida side of the Gulf of Mexico, once took me to task about a hot sauce that I called piripiri, saying in his letter that it was called Peri-Peri in

South Africa. I wrote back that it may be called Peri-Peri in South Africa, but that in Mozambique it is called piripiri and in Togo it is called Pili Pili. I went on to add that I was hot at work on this book, and I asked whether he had a good saltwater fish recipe to share. He replied that the first time he ate Peri-Peri sauce it was in Lourenço Marques, Mozambique, back in 1949. "At the time, I was staying in a very fancy hotel, and the sauce was served along with an octopus-based soup. Very delectable combination, I might add."

He didn't offer the recipe for octopus-based soup, but he did say that his wife had a wonderful way of cooking redfish of intermediate size. "We have a slot limit on redfish here, so I'm generally talking about 5- to 8-pound fish that have been cleaned, skinned, and filleted.

"For the two of us she mixes a cupful of Hellman's mayonnaise with about a capful of dry vermouth. She spreads this mixture with any implement that's handy on the upper side of the fillets. If she thinks about it, she sprinkles on some paprika for color and some freshly ground pepper. Then she broils it until there's some brown in the mayonnaise and it starts to bubble (approximately 10 minutes).

"She frequently serves this with a twice-baked potato, green beans amandine, and a dry chardonnay, or Chablis.

"Certainly Gulf of Mexico fish of a number of species have spoiled much of my yearning for fish available in Ohio, including walleye, which is pretty much the local favorite there. Even fresh Dover sole poached at a well known London fish house fails to surpass the above described redfish. I suggested to my wife that she direct the recipe toward another favorite of ours—blacktip shark. No, she says. Larger and smaller fillets require other styles. She does, however, cook snook and trout (spotted weakfish) of the size indicated in the same fashion."

I might add that another saltwater sport from the Gulf of Mexico recommends using mayonnaise on broiled king mackerel, but he uses Kraft mayonnaise instead of Hellman's—and he doesn't recommend dry vermouth for anything.

Grilled Redfish

Here's a recipe that works on an open grill, such as those usually found in state and national parks beside the sea. Of course, it can also be cooked on the patio. For best results, use coals from a hardwood fire. Charcoal, gas, or electric heat can also be used. The oyster sauce used in the recipe is a tasty Chinese condiment made from dried oysters. It can be purchased in the oriental section of most large supermarkets, or you can make your own if you've got fresh oysters (chapter 27).

> redfish fillets
> ½ cup oyster sauce
> ½ cup melted butter
> juice of ½ lemon
> ¼ teaspoon Tabasco sauce (or to taste)
> aluminum foil

To fillet the fish, merely cut along the backbone from the tail to the head, leaving both the skin and scales on the fillet. Build a hot fire. Mix the butter, oyster sauce, lemon juice, and Tabasco; keep warm for basting. (If you are grilling outdoors, the sauce can be mixed ahead of time.) When the coals are hot, grease the rack and place the fillets on it skin side down. Baste the tops of the fillets with the warm sauce. Cover each fillet loosely with aluminum foil. Grill for about 15 minutes without turning, or until the fish flakes easily when tested with a fork. (If the scales and skin burn a little, don't worry about it.) Lightly baste the tops of the fillets again and serve, placing a fillet onto each plate or serving platter skin side down. The cooked meat is pulled off the skin with a fork, or perhaps with the fingers. Serve with hot baked beans, sliced Vidalia onions, and hot bread.

Blackened Redfish

I covered this phenomenon at some length in my book *Cast Iron Cooking,* on which the following recipe is based. Apparently, the original recipe for blackened redfish was created by professional chef Paul Prudhomme in Louisiana. My guess is that the dish was born of necessity when a cook accidentally burned somebody's order of pan-fried fish, which happened to be the last fillet in Prudhomme's place! In any case, the popularity of the dish put an inordinate demand on the Gulf Coast commercial and sport fishery, in that it required redfish of a certain size. In order to blacken properly, a fish fillet has to be from ½ to ¾ inch thick. Ideally, fillets of this size must be taken from a relatively small redfish. This requirement for thin fillets, in turn, created a demand for these smaller fish; this in turn placed a great demand on the commercial and sport fishery and helped spread the notion that larger redfish are not fit to eat. Though it is true that large redfish, which grow up to 80 pounds, are coarse and taste none too good, smaller fish, 15 pounds and under, are quite toothsome when cut into fingers and fried.

Many other kinds of fish are quite suitable for making "blackened redfish." Even some rough fish can be blackened. A recent issue of *Outdoor Life* magazine, for example, set forth an article about a Texas couple who bagged gar by bow fishing—and blackened the fillets.

Although much emphasis has been put on prepared Cajun "blackening" spice mixes, I think the real secret is of technique and specification. First, the cookware must be extremely hot, and cast iron is the only common cookware material that will withstand such temperatures. Second, the thickness of the fillet must be such that it will brown and form a crust on the outside while staying moist and succulent on the inside. Third, spices provide both flavor and crust, almost like a batter provides a crust in frying.

Be warned that true blackening produces clouds of smoke, and this rules out the kitchen stove. Even a stove with a powerful overhead vent may cause problems. Although I have blackened fish and meat successfully in a kitchen fireplace, I believe that it's best to do your blackening outside. But it is difficult to heat cast iron hot enough for true blackening, and ordinary charcoal on a grill simply will not get hot enough to do the job. Wood chips will help. But by far the best bet for obtaining the required heat is from a gas-fired burner, such as those used for heating large fish fryers. Just any gas burner won't do. Some camp stoves, for example, won't put out enough heat. Also, a good deal depends on your cast-iron skillet or griddle. In any case, cast-iron pieces will start turning white on the cooking surface when they are hot enough. Don't worry. It's hard to get cast iron too hot for proper blackening.

Having said that technique and exactness are the keys to this recipe, I'll have to add that the spice mix can be varied quite a bit. I prefer to use the spices set forth by *Chef Paul Prudhomme's Louisiana Kitchen,* although I change the proportions from one batch to the next. Hotness aside, I feel that lots of paprika is needed to give the spice mix body. It is very important that a thick coat of spices cover the fish flesh, and I use lots of paprika as a sort of filler. I also cut back on the cayenne. There are other mixes. Frank Davis, for example, adds 12 crushed bay leaves and some basil, although he calls the recipe Paul Prudhomme's Blackened Redfish. *The Official Louisiana Seafood & Wild Game Cookbook* calls for fresh chopped parsley. This work also specifies fillets that are 1 inch thick and says that a tablespoon of butter can be added to the hot skillet just ahead of the fish to prevent sticking. Be warned that a tablespoon of butter will smoke something awful and burn almost immediately. Also, I've never had a problem with any blackened food sticking, if the cast iron was hot enough. In most recipes, the trend is to add stuff to the original, and the ingredients list for blackened redfish, already quite long, will continue to grow. It wouldn't surprise me to see monosodium glutamate listed.

In any case, here is my recommendation for blackened fish:

fish fillets (½ to ¾ inch thick)
melted butter
1 tablespoon salt
1 tablespoon Hungarian sweet paprika
½ teaspoon ground red cayenne
1 teaspoon white pepper
1 teaspoon black pepper
1 teaspoon garlic powder
1 teaspoon onion powder
½ teaspoon crushed dried thyme leaves
½ teaspoon crushed dried oregano leaves

Mix the salt, spices, and herbs. Bring the fillets to room temperature. Melt the butter in a pan and coat each fillet on both sides. Sprinkle each fillet liberally with the spice mixture. Heat a cast-iron griddle or skillet as hot as you can get it, and warm some individual serving platters. Prepare bread, salad, cold drinks, and so forth, for serving. Get ready. Using tongs, hold a fillet by one end and lay it out on the superhot griddle. Sizzle a ¾-inch fillet for 2 minutes. Using tongs, flip the fillet over and sizzle the other side for 2 minutes. (Fillets that are only ½ inch thick will require even less cooking, and fillets that are more than ¾ inch thick will require longer cooking.) Pick the fillet up with tongs and place it on a heated serving platter. Serve with melted butter as a sauce. Provide plenty of iced tea or other fire quenchers, such as chilled watermelon chunks.

Variation: After turning the fillet, carefully spoon some melted butter onto the cooked side. Flop the fillet over when placing it on the serving platter, then spoon some butter onto the other side.

EIGHT

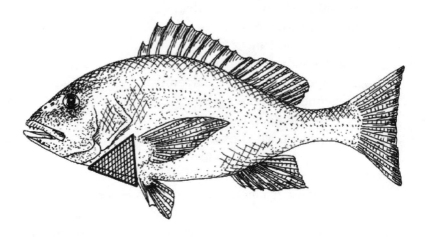

Snappers

All of the snappers make excellent eating and can be cooked by any reasonable method. Often cooked whole, they can be either scaled or skinned. I usually prefer to scale them because the skin often adds to the flavor and color, and helps keep the flesh moist during cooking. All of the snappers have rather large heads with edible throats, a triangular piece of meat defined by the gill flaps and bottom fins. Frequently this meat is sold separately at high prices, but all too often, the sportsman throws it away with the head. The larger snappers also have excellent cheeks and, in general, make very good fish-head stews. The same can be said of the groupers.

Most of the snappers, including the common red snapper, above, have heads not unlike those of largemouth bass. The triangular throat, often thrown out with the head, makes good eating.

Before discussing some of the more common snappers, perhaps I had better add that many people call small bluefish snappers, and that some other fish are marketed as snappers.

Red snapper, *Lutjanus blackfordi.* This popular market fish is also taken by sport fishers from the mid-Atlantic states to South America. A bottom feeder, it is usually taken in depths of 20 to 60 fathoms; as such, it is often a prime target for party boat anglers. Although several species of snappers and groupers have been sold as "red snappers," the real ones have a red skin and are usually marketed whole. They can be cooked by any method, but thanks to their color, they are ideal for baking whole.

Gray snapper, *Lutjanus griseus.* Often called mangrove snapper, this shallow-water species is common in Florida and ranges up the Atlantic to Virginia and south to Brazil. A small snapper, it can attain a weight of about 10 pounds. It makes excellent eating, but it is wary and difficult to catch.

Cubera snapper, *Lutjanus cyanopterus.* Sometimes called Cuban snapper, this species, the largest of the snappers, may exceed 100 pounds. A shallow-water fish, it is sometimes caught in Florida waters. The larger ones should be skinned and cut into fingers, or used in chowders and soups.

Vermilion snapper, *Rhomboplites aurorubens.* This small fish, also called beeliner or night snapper (because it often feeds at night), makes very good eating. The roe is a delicacy.

Other species include the **dog snapper** *(Lutjanus jocu),* **lane snapper** *(Lutjanus synagris),* **mutton snapper** *(Lutjanus analis),* and **schoolmaster** *(Lutjanus apodus).* These are taken mostly in Florida and points south, although some may stray as far north as Cape Cod. All of these and other snappers are good eating and can be used in the recipes given here if they are of appropriate size.

Huachinango

This is one of my favorite dishes for red snappers of about 5 pounds. It can also be cooked with groupers, rockfish, or sea bass of about the same size. Be sure to try this recipe.

red snapper, about 5 pounds, head on
½ cup melted butter
2 medium-large white onions, sliced
2 medium-large tomatoes
2 fresh red chili peppers
2 fresh green chili peppers
1 lemon or lime
1 cup white wine
½ cup red wine
salt and pepper

Scale and gut the fish, then sprinkle it inside and out with salt and pepper. Preheat the oven to 400 degrees. Peel and quarter the tomatoes. Seed and slice the chili peppers lengthwise. Grease a baking pan (just large enough to hold the fish comfortably) with part of the butter. Put the rest of the butter into the pan. Cover the bottom of the pan with pepper slices, then put a layer of sliced onions over the peppers. Place the fish on the onions. Squeeze the juice of a lemon or lime over the fish. Place the tomato quarters over the fish. Add both kinds of wine. Tear off a sheet of aluminum foil, grease the dull side with butter, and place it, butter side down, over the fish.

Bake for 15 minutes. Remove the aluminum foil, spoon some of the pan juices over the fish and tomatoes, and bake for another 15 minutes, or until the fish is done, basting from time to time. Carefully transfer the fish to a serving platter, then top it with onions, peppers, and pan drippings. I usually serve part of the pan drippings, which have a wonderful flavor, over rice. Feeds 6 nicely.

Old Bermuda Snapper

Here's an interesting dish that reportedly came from Bermuda through trade with colonial Virginia. Any sort of good fresh snapper can be used, or perhaps a grouper or sea bass of suitable size.

1 snapper, about 2 pounds
3 cups dry bread cubes
1 cup chopped cucumber, peeled and seeded
juice of 1 lemon
2 tablespoons chopped green onions
2 tablespoons chopped green bell pepper
1 tablespoon chopped fresh parsley
3 tablespoons butter (divided)
¼ teaspoon freshly grated lemon zest
¼ teaspoon dried thyme
¼ teaspoon ground sage
salt and pepper

Scale and draw the fish, leaving the head and tail on, and sprinkle the cavity with salt and pepper. Preheat the oven to 350 degrees. Melt 2 tablespoons of butter in a skillet, then sauté the green onions for 5 minutes or longer. Make a stuffing by mixing the sautéed onion, bread cubes, cucumber, green pepper, parsley, lemon zest, thyme, sage, salt, and pepper. Grease a baking pan of suitable size, then place the fish in it. Stuff the fish with the stuffing mixture. Melt 1 tablespoon of butter, then mix in the lemon juice and baste the fish. Cover the pan with aluminum foil. Bake in the center of the oven for about 50 minutes, basting two or three times with the lemon-butter sauce, or until the fish flakes easily when tested with a fork at the thickest point. Feeds from 2 to 4. I like to allow 1 pound of fish (whole weight) per person.

Cuban Snapper

The Cubans sometimes fry whole fish in very hot oil—without using any batter whatsoever. It is simply delicious. The measures following are for 1 snapper of about 1½ pounds. Increase the measures for additional fish. To do the fish right, you'll need a large, deep fryer with lots of oil in it so that the fish won't lower the temperature too much. Fry one fish at a time. Any of the small snappers will work for this recipe.

1 snapper, 1 to 1½ pounds
peanut oil
juice of 1 lime
2 cloves garlic, crushed
1 teaspoon pepper
½ teaspoon salt

Mix the lime juice, garlic, salt, and pepper. Scale the fish and draw it, leaving the head, fins, and tail on. Score the fish three times diagonally on each side, cutting down almost to the backbone. Rub the fish inside and out with the lime juice mixture, using all of it. Heat the oil in a deep fryer to 400 degrees. Carefully put the snapper into the hot oil. Fry for 3 or 4 minutes, or until the fish is crisply brown. Larger fish will take a little more time; smaller fish, less. Do not overcook. Drain the fish on a brown bag. Serve the fish hot on a bed of Garlic Rice (chapter 27), lining each side with sliced vine-ripened tomatoes and hot Cuban bread.

Servings? I want a whole snapper. Also see the next recipe.

Easy Cuban Red Snapper

Here's another Cuban recipe for red snapper. It can also be made with grouper, rockfish, or other mild fish. Be sure to try this one.

1 red snapper, 3 to 4 pounds
1 can tomato sauce (8-ounce size)
1½ cups shredded cheddar cheese
salt and pepper to taste

Preheat the oven to 350 degrees. Fillet the snapper, then sprinkle salt and pepper on both sides of the fillet. Place the fillets, skin side down, in a greased baking dish of suitable size. Spread the tomato sauce over the fish, then sprinkle with the shredded cheddar. Bake for 20 to 25 minutes, or until the cheese browns nicely. Serve hot with rice and vegetables.

Greek Snapper

Although red snapper is a market favorite, any kind of snapper can be used for this dish. Use small whole fish, allowing one fish per person. The Greek part of the recipe comes from Old World fishing families along the Gulf coast. The distinguishing ingredients are olive oil, lemon juice, and oregano.

> 4 snappers, 1-pound size
> 1 cup olive oil
> juice of 2 lemons
> 2 tablespoons dried oregano
> salt
> chopped fresh parsley

Scale and gut the fish, leaving the head on. Sprinkle the fish inside and out with salt and oregano, then refrigerate for 1 hour. Preheat the broiler and position the rack about 10 inches under the heating element. Mix the lemon juice and olive oil. Grease a broiling pan and arrange the fish in it. Brush on about half of the lemon and olive oil mixture. Sprinkle the top of the fish lightly with salt. Broil for 10 minutes. Using two spatulas, carefully turn the fish. Brush with the remaining half of the lemon and olive oil. Sprinkle lightly with salt. Broil for another 10 minutes, or until the fish flakes easily when tested with a fork. Carefully remove the fish with two spatulas, placing a whole fish on each plate. Spoon the juices from the broiling pan over the fish and sprinkle with chopped parsley. Serve with a huge Greek salad, complete with feta cheese and anchovies, and a loaf of hot, chewy sourdough bread. Forget the ouzo.

Note: The exact cooking time will depend on the thickness of the fish and the distance from the heat. Placing the whole fish too close to the heating element will cause the surface to burn before the inside gets done. If you prefer to cook fillets instead of whole fish, put them skin side down into a heated broiling pan about 4 inches from the heat. Cook for 10 minutes without turning. Snappers much larger than 1 pound should be filleted or butterflied before broiling.

Island Snapper with Lemon Pepper

A number of good snappers haunt the waters of the Caribbean, and all of them are excellent table fare. Scale the fish, leaving the tasty and colorful skin intact.

> small snappers
> melted butter
> lemon-pepper seasoning salt

Grill the fish for a few minutes, preferably quite close to the heat source. Grease the grilling rack well, or use a grilling basket, because the snapper tends to tear apart during handling. Turn the fish with the help of two spatulas. Place the fish on the grill skin side down. When you turn the fish, baste the cooked side with melted butter, then sprinkle it lightly with lemon pepper. When the fish is done, carefully place the fillets on a heated serving platter or individual plates. Then brush the fillets with melted butter and sprinkle on a little more lemon pepper to taste.

Red Snappers and Green Tomatoes

The book and movie *Fried Green Tomatoes* might have popularized this old southern method of cooking tomatoes before they are fully ripe, thereby getting a head start on the harvest. Thanks to the publicity, green tomatoes are now being sold in some markets, and, of course, home gardeners can pull their own as soon as they are almost mature in size but still green.

> 1 pound skinless fillets
> 3 green tomatoes, diced
> 1 medium onion, diced
> 2 cloves garlic, minced
> grated cheddar cheese
> Italian bread crumbs
> olive oil
> salt and pepper

78

Preheat the oven to 350 degrees. Grease a baking dish suitable for serving. Cut the snapper fillets into 1-inch chunks, then sprinkle with salt and pepper. Spread the green tomatoes, onions, and garlic on top. Sprinkle with Italian bread crumbs and grated cheddar cheese, then drizzle the top with olive oil. Bake in the center of the oven for 40 minutes, or until the top browns nicely. If it doesn't brown within 40 minutes, turn on the broiler for a few minutes. Serve hot with rice, steamed vegetables, and sourdough bread.

Fried Snapper Throats

As many fishmongers and some restaurateurs know, snappers have a purely excellent but odd-shaped piece of meat known as the throat. Of triangular shape, it is defined by the bony gill plate and pectoral fins. When the fish is beheaded, this morsel is cut off with the head part. Do not throw it away!

These can be broiled, grilled, or baked, but they are usually fried. Any good recipe will do, and they are often fried along with the fillets or other parts.

Enjoy. Be warned, however, that this piece of fish contains some mean bones. Proceed with caution.

NINE

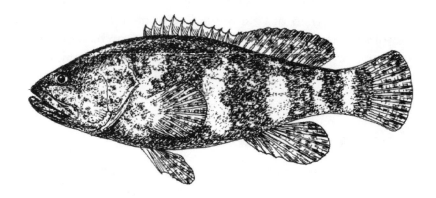

Groupers, Speckled Hines, and Gags

More than 400 species of groupers live in the world's tropical and temperate waters—including 50 that can be caught in Florida. These range in size from the large **jewfish** *(Epinephelus itajara)*, which weighs up to 700 pounds, to the small **speckled hine** *(Epinephelus drummondhayi)*. Some of the groupers, such as the **gag** *(Mycteroperca microlepis)* and the **scamp** *(Mycteroperca phenax)* of the South Atlantic and Gulf coast are important commercially.

The jewfish is the largest of the world's 400 species of grouper. It can weigh more than 700 pounds. All the groupers have large mouths, not unlike freshwater bass.

All of the groupers make excellent eating, with the *Mycteroperca* species being a little better than the *Epinephelus*. They all have big mouths—very similar to the freshwater largemouth bass. In fact, Junior Samples of "Hee-Haw" fame got his start in show business by passing off a partly decayed grouper head as that of a world-record largemouth bass, which he claimed to have caught in a Georgia lake.

The flesh of some groupers tends to be somewhat coarse, making them ideal for chowders. The skin is usually thick and is removed before or after cooking. Large groupers can be filleted, fingered, and deep-fried. The throats are choice eating. Small groupers, such as the abundant **coney** *(Cephalopholis fulva)* of south Florida, are excellent when dressed and cooked like panfish (see chapter 23).

Nassau Grouper with Curaçao

Here's a tasty dish that I like to prepare with the fillets from a 2-pound grouper or perhaps snapper.

> 2 pounds grouper fillets
> 1 cup Coconut Cream (chapter 27)
> ½ cup orange juice
> ¼ cup lemon juice
> ¼ cup curaçao
> 2 tablespoons grated orange zest, divided
> salt and white pepper

Preheat the oven to 350 degrees. In a saucepan, heat the coconut cream, orange and lemon juice, curaçao, and 1½ tablespoons of the grated orange zest. (Grate the orange before peeling it, and do not grate deep enough to get into the bitter white inner layer.) Grease a baking pan of suitable size. Sprinkle the fillets with salt and white pepper, then arrange them in the pan. Pour the hot sauce over the fillets, then bake for 10 minutes. Carefully place each fillet on a plate, spoon some of the pan liquid over it, and sprinkle lightly with a little of the remaining orange zest. Feeds 4.

Fish Flake Fritters

I cooked this dish one night with leftover grouper, which had been baked by another recipe. Any good fish can be used; grouper is ideal because it flakes so nicely. It's a little better to use freshly poached fish instead of leftovers.

> 1½ cups fish flakes (precooked)
> 1½ cups bread crumbs
> 1 can whole-kernel corn (16-ounce size)
> 1 medium onion, minced
> 3 large chicken eggs
> Thai Fish Sauce (chapter 27)
> olive oil
> salt and pepper

If the fish flakes are chunky, mince them with a chef's knife. Mix in the bread crumbs, corn, onion, eggs, 1 tablespoon of Thai fish sauce, salt, and pepper. (Go easy on the salt, as the fish sauce is very salty.) Heat a little olive oil in a skillet or griddle. Shape the mixture into balls, then gently pat flat. Carefully place the patties in the skillet. Cook for a few minutes over medium heat, turning carefully to brown both sides. Since these tear easily, I transfer them directly from the skillet to plates. Set a bottle of Thai fish sauce on the table in case folks want to drizzle some on their servings.

Grouper Sandwich

The grouper sandwich is a favorite item on Florida menus these days. There are many recipes, but part of the success depends on a good, large, fresh hamburger bun and plenty of mayonnaise. Ideally, the fillets should be about 1 inch thick and a little larger than the bun. Fillets from the larger groupers can be cut to size. Ideally, the fillet should weigh at least ¼ pound for a large bun.

4 grouper fillets of suitable size and shape
4 large hamburger buns
¼ cup butter
mayonnaise
lettuce leaves
sliced tomato
thinly sliced purple onion
salt and pepper

Melt the butter in a large skillet (an electric skillet works nicely) and preheat the broiler. Sprinkle the fillets with salt and pepper, then sauté for about 6 minutes on each side, or until lightly browned and cooked through. As the fish cook, spread the inside of the buns with some of the butter from the skillet (use more if needed) and toast inside up under the broiler until crusty and lightly browned. Spread the buns with mayonnaise, and sandwich the grouper fillets. Serve with lettuce, tomato, and onion slices on the side, letting folks add their own fixings. Serve with french fries and cold drinks.

Variations: You can also use grilled or breaded and fried grouper fillets.

Grouper Bisque

The larger groupers, having mild, flaky flesh, are ideal for cooking in fish chowders and chunky soups. This bisque can be made with leftovers, but it's better to poach the fillets right in the soup, then break them up before serving.

1 pound grouper fillets, skinned
6 or 7 green onions with part of tops, chopped
3 cups half-and-half
½ cup sherry
3 tablespoons butter
1 tablespoon flour
salt and white pepper to taste

In a stove-top Dutch oven or suitable pot, melt the butter and sauté the chopped green onions for 5 or 6 minutes. Stir in the flour with a wooden spoon and cook, stirring constantly, for 3 minutes. Add the half-and-half, stirring as you go, and cook almost to the boiling point. Add the sherry. Turn the heat down to very low. Stir in a little salt and white pepper, then add the grouper fillets. Simmer for 10 minutes. Break the fish into pieces. Serve hot in soup bowls with crackers.

Jim's Jewfish Hot Dogs

My older brother was an expert at catching large jewfish from bridges in south Florida. For tackle, he used a shark hook on a chain, attached to a hand rope. In order to play a large fish, he liked to keep quite a length of rope neatly coiled beside him. A main concern here is to avoid getting your foot tangled in the rope, for, as Jim was fond of saying, a large jewfish can snatch your ass off the bridge. Jim enjoyed the challenge—and he also loved jewfish fillets.

For the recipe below, cut the fillets into pieces a little longer than a hot dog bun and a little over an inch square.

> 2 pounds jewfish fillets
> hot dog buns
> mayonnaise
> salt and white pepper
> mild paprika
> water or Court Bouillon (chapter 27)

Steam or poach the fish dog for about 10 minutes per inch of thickness. Also steam the hot dog buns, making them soft but not soggy. Spread each bun generously with mayonnaise, insert a fish dog, sprinkle with salt, pepper, and paprika, and enjoy.

Variations: Fry or grill the fish dogs. Use salsa, catsup, or other condiments, as you like.

TEN

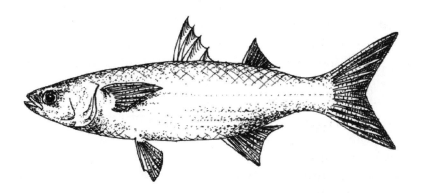

Mullet

Unsung in most parts of the United States, the mullet was appreciated by the Romans and other ancient peoples, and it was even cultivated in ponds by the Egyptians. In culinary literature, mention is made of eating the liver and the trail along with the rest of the fish. Since woodcock was cooked with the trail intact by early European gourmets, the mullet was often called the woodcock of the sea. For that reason, perhaps I should have included it in the chapter with the other seabirds. The mullet, along with the gizzard shad, has a stomach organ that grinds up its food, usually vegetable matter in the water. In Florida, this organ, called a gizzard, is sometimes dressed (split, turned, and cleaned) and cooked along with the rest of the fish.

The mullet, popular in some areas, has an edible gizzard.

There are several kinds of mullet in American waters, some of which live along both the Pacific and Atlantic coasts. These include the **striped mullet** *(Mugil cephalus)*, sometimes called black mullet, and the **white mullet** *(Mugil curema)*, sometimes called silver mullet. Some mullet live in brackish and even fresh water.

The flesh of mullet has a somewhat nutty flavor and is rich in iodine and other minerals. Some are said to have a muddy taste, especially those taken over a muddy bottom or from fresh water. This can be removed by filleting and skinning the fish. In any case, the mullet is best when dressed and iced soon after catching. Although they are often fried, mullet are on the oily side, making them better suited for smoking, grilling, or broiling.

At one time, mullet, being vegetarians, were not commonly caught by hook and line. As ultralight tackle became more popular, however, it was discovered that mullet could be taken on tiny baits, usually on hooks designed for fishing with salmon eggs. Bits of earthworm will sometimes work, as well as dough balls and such vegetable bait as green okra seeds. In some areas, including fresh water, a tiny ball of moss is used. Mullet can also be taken with a fly rod and tiny fly. Since schools of mullet are often seen nosing along, feeding on the surface, they can be caught by casting ahead of the school. Most of the nosing fish, however, are caught by cast net. As I write these words, a school is nosing in a deep pool within 50 yards of my cabin on Florida's Dead Lakes. A local fellow told me that the mullet feed on the moss on the cypress stumps left by a large-scale logging operation decades ago.

Baked Mullet with Wine

I like to cook this recipe with small, very fresh mullet. Other small fatty fish can be used. By small, I mean about ¾ pound.

> 4 dressed small mullet
> ½ cup white wine
> 2 tablespoons butter
> 2 tablespoons diced fresh mushrooms
> 2 tablespoons chopped fresh parsley
> 2 tablespoons finely chopped onion
> 2 tablespoons chopped red bell pepper
> juice of 1 lemon
> salt and white pepper

Preheat the oven to 425 degrees, and grease a baking pan large enough to hold the fish side by side. In a saucepan, melt the butter and mix in the mushrooms, chopped onion, red bell pepper, and parsley. Simmer for 5 minutes. Remove from the heat and stir in the lemon juice and most of the wine, along with some salt and pepper. Pour the sauce over the fish, then bake in the center of the oven for 20 minutes, or until the mullet flakes easily when tested with a fork. Baste twice with the pan juices. Carefully place the mullet onto a heated serving platter. Add the reserved wine to the baking pan and stir it around with a wooden spoon, thereby deglazing the pan. Pour the pan juices over the fish. Serve hot with rice and vegetables.

Lime Mullet

Mullet fillets are ideal for broiling. For best results, place the fish very close to the heat and broil quickly. If you have thick fillets from larger fish, or if you try to broil whole mullet, you'll have to lower the rack and cook for a longer time so that the outside won't burn before the inside gets done. I place the fish on a preheated cast-iron griddle that fits under my broiler; this helps get the bottom of the fish done without burning.

2 pounds mullet fillets
juice of 3 limes (divided)
2 tablespoons butter
salt and pepper
lime wedges

Place the fillets into a nonmetallic container and squeeze the juice of 2 limes over them, turning to coat all sides. Marinate for 30 minutes. Melt the butter in a small saucepan and mix in the juice of the remaining lime. Grease a broiler pan or a cast-iron griddle of suitable size and place it under the broiler, adjusting the racks so that the fish will be about 3 inches from the heat. When the broiler is hot, place the mullet on the broiling pan or griddle, skin side down. Broil for 4 to 6 minutes, or until the meat flakes easily when tested with a fork. Overcook at your culinary peril. When the fillets are done, brush the top with the melted butter and lime mixture, then sprinkle with salt and pepper. Serve hot with lime wedges. A big fruit salad or broiled pineapple wedges go nicely with this dish.

Mullet Breakfast

The Crackers along the Gulf coast of Florida are fond of eating salt mullet for breakfast. My father liked them fried, after freshening them overnight in cool water. Back then, salt mullet was sold in the local stores many miles inland from the coast. These days, salt mullet is more difficult to find, and many salt mullet fans are now giving the fish a light salting the night before. These are usually fried, and most of the Florida people eat them with grits. The following recipe, however, adapted from *The Apalachicola Cookbook*, to which it was submitted by C. M. "Buck" Chauncey, is for poached fish. It's wonderful.

The measures following are for a single serving. Increase as needed.

1 mullet, about 1 pound
1 potato
juice of 1 lemon
1 tablespoon butter
1 teaspoon olive oil
sea salt
pepper

The night before, fillet the mullet and place the pieces in a nonmetallic container. Sprinkle heavily with sea salt and refrigerate overnight. The next morning, wash the fillets in several changes of water. Peel and quarter the potatoes, then boil them in a wide pot until tender. Remove the potatoes with a slotted spoon, placing them on one end of a hot serving platter or to one side of a hot plate. Add the butter and a little pepper to the potatoes. Poach the mullet fillets in the potato water for 15 minutes. Carefully remove the fillets and place them beside the potatoes. Sprinkle with olive oil and lemon juice. Serve hot.

Carolina Mullet

Here's a simple recipe that makes good use of an unusual combination. Be sure to try it on a hot summer day.

2 pounds fresh mullet fillets
1 watermelon
crushed sea salt
bacon drippings
pepper

Sprinkle the fillets liberally with sea salt, put them in a nonmetallic container, and refrigerate for 2 or 3 hours. Preheat the oven to 350 degrees. Drain the fillets, pat them dry with absorbent paper, and fit them skin side down into a greased broiling pan so that they don't overlap. Brush with bacon drippings and sprinkle with pepper. Broil about 4 inches from the heat until the meat flakes easily when tested with a fork. Serve hot with cold watermelon slices.

Mullet Tails with Hominy and Salsa

When I once ate in a restaurant called Ma's in Sopchoppy, Florida, my curiosity got the best of me. I really wanted snapper throats, which I knew well, but instead I ordered mullet tails just to see what was served up. These were merely boneless mullet fillets, but I wasn't disappointed. Fried mullet, both good and inexpensive, is a popular item on rural Florida menus. Often they are served for breakfast, along with grits. I don't like to prepare grits, but I am fond of whole corn hominy, which is available canned these days. Because hominy is on the bland side, I jazz it up with salsa, which can be mild, medium, or hot.

> mullet tails
> peanut oil
> cornmeal
> hominy
> salsa
> salt

Sprinkle the mullet fillets with salt, shake them in a bag with fine stone-ground white cornmeal, and deep-fry them in hot oil (at least 375 degrees) until nicely browned. Drain and heat the hominy. Serve the fish and hominy on plates, with salsa on the side. I merely spoon a little salsa on my helping of hominy, but some people also like it on the fried fish instead of catsup.

Yellow Roe and White

For a long while, yellow mullet roe was widely available in fish markets and country stores in my neck of the woods in the fall, and it was reasonably priced. But the Japanese started buying it up, and these days it's hard to find locally. You have to catch your own.

Most people I know merely salt yellow roe, shake it in flour or cornmeal, and fry it in about 1 inch of hot peanut oil. It can also be successfully poached, broiled, or baked. In any case, the roe should not be cooked too long.

The white roe of mullet—the milt of the male fish—is also a great seafood delicacy. To cook it, merely salt the sac to taste, dust with flour, and sauté in bacon drippings or butter until nicely browned on both sides. I usually cook fresh bacon to serve along with the white roe, then use the bacon drippings for sautéing the roe. Since white roe doesn't dry out as badly as yellow roe, the cooking time is not as critical. Anybody can fry or sauté good white roe.

Any culinary sport who likes brains and eggs scrambled together should try white roe and eggs. The white roe from shad or herring is also very good.

Hot-Smoked Mullet

Smoked mullet is something of a Florida institution. They are usually butterflied and smoked with the scales on. When done, they are served on a plate or platter with the scales down, and the golden smoked meat is pulled off with a fork. There are thousands of recipes for cold-smoking and hot-smoking fish, and most of them will work with mullet because it is so rich in good oil. This recipe works best with a large covered-wagon type outdoor grill fitted with a good vent-control system and a thermometer. It's best to use fish of about 2 pounds, undressed weight.

> 10 pounds mullet, butterflied
> 2 gallons water
> 1 box salt (26-ounce size)
> hardwood chips

If you are using dry wood chips, soak them in water overnight. Chips or chunks from fresh, green wood can also be used, which is what I recommend. Dissolve the salt in the water in a non-metallic container. Put the fish in the brine and refrigerate for several hours. Build a small charcoal or hardwood fire on one side of a large grill, banking it with wood chips or perhaps a small green hardwood log. Close the hood and adjust the draft control, shooting for a chamber temperature of 175 to 200 degrees. Quickly grease the grill and place the fish on it skin side down. Bring the temperature back to 175 to 200 degrees. Smoke the mullet for about 1 hour, or until the surface of the fish is golden brown and the flesh flakes with a fork. No basting is required, but do so if you wish. Just remember that raising the hood releases the heat and a longer cooking time may be required.

E L E V E N

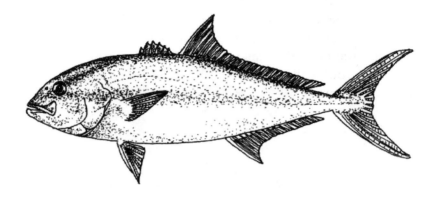

Jacks or Better

When I was a boy, eating an amberjack would have been almost unthinkable. Today they are highly regarded as supermarket fare and rate high on some restaurant menus. When I was a younger man, eating a jack crevalle would have made a laughingstock of an angler, even in the Florida Keys. Today opinions are changing, but slowly. Vic Dunaway said this nicely in his book *From Hook to Table:* "All the jacks have long had the reputation of being very poor table fare—in the States, at least. Actually, they are among the very best of fish, a fact which isn't yet widely known or accepted. They do require a bit of extra cleaning effort, but not much. After being filleted and skinned, the fillets should

---

The amberjack is typical of the family of jacks, which includes the prized pompano and permit as well as some surprising table fare, such as the Atlantic lookdown.

---

be cut in half lengthwise, and the red meat running the length of each piece should be carefully trimmed away—along with some extra bones that lie along that center line. Trimmed fillets may be fried, broiled, or boiled for salad. Delicious!"

I include the pompano and permit in this chapter. If these aren't jacks, they are very close, since all are members of the Carangidae family. My reasoning, however, is that this family of saltwater fishes illustrates two kinds of prejudicial thinking: Some very good fish are generally believed to be trash, and some highly rated fish are simply overrated, especially in terms of price. The pompano is a good fish—but it isn't *that* good. I'll lay even money that a freshly caught lookdown or moonfish, if cooked and served side by side with a pompano, would receive equal or better marks. Yet those fish are considered laughable by many anglers.

In any case, the angler who catches his own fish has the best of both worlds. Here are some Carangidae that are commonly caught in American waters.

Crevalle, *Caranx hippos.* Often called jack crevalle, this fish has often been underrated not only as table fare but also as a gamefish. This species and its close cousins range over all the world's tropical and subtropical seas, and have been seen as far north as Nova Scotia. The fish, generally shunned in the States, is an important market species in Central America and the Pacific. Be warned that the jack crevalle can carry ciguatera poisoning. Usually, it's only the larger fish taken from deep-water reef areas that are suspect.

Almaco jack, *Seriola rivoliana.* Sometimes called falcate amberjack or bonito (and once named scientifically *Seriola falcata),* this Atlantic jack ranges from South America northward to New Jersey. It grows to 12 or 14 pounds.

Bar jack, *Caranx ruber.* Ranging from North Carolina to Brazil, this species weighs up to 12 or 15 pounds. Although white, its flesh is somewhat oily. Excellent when smoked, the bar jack is highly esteemed as table fare in the West Indies. It is also called skipjack.

Blue runner, *Caranx crysos.* This small jack, with an average weight of 1 or 2 pounds, ranges from Brazil to Halifax, with heavy catches made in Florida. It often runs the Gulf Stream and is also taken in the Gulf of Mexico. The blue runner makes excellent eating in spite of bad culinary reviews elsewhere. A similar edible species, the **green jack** *(Caranx caballus),* is caught in California.

Greater amberjack, *Seriola dumerili.* Partly because it can be caught by trolling near the surface, this Atlantic member of the amberjack group is an important charter boat fish in Florida and the Carolinas. It ranges as far north as Cape Cod, and south to Brazil. The meat was long considered to be unfit, but it actually is very good. Some of these fish may be infested with worms (usually near the tail), but these are harmless when cooked. These are large fish, sometimes as much as 6 feet long and 190 pounds, but the smaller fish make better eating. When filleted or steaked, the meat can be broiled, poached, baked, or grilled, provided that it is not overcooked. Smoked amberjack has become popular in recent years—and has long been a delicacy in the Hispanic communities of south Florida. The **lesser amberjack** *(Seriola fasciata)* is sometimes caught from Cape Cod to Cuba, but it is too scarce and too small to be of much importance to anglers.

Be warned that amberjacks taken from tropical waters can carry ciguatera poisoning (see appendix B).

California yellowtail, *Seriola dorsalis.* There is some confusion about the exact scientific classification of this fish, which may be a subspecies, and most anglers know it simply as yellowtail. By whatever name, this cousin of the greater amberjack is a popular gamefish in the Gulf of California and is caught as far north as Los Angeles. It is rather high in oil content and is highly recommended for smoking, grilling, or broiling. Surplus meat is sometimes canned by anglers who catch a few large ones. These fish weigh up to 80 pounds.

Pacific amberjack, *Seriola colburni.* This fine sport fish, which may weigh over 100 pounds, is caught from California to South America. The meat of this species tends to be tough and coarse. The smaller fish make better eating but should not be fried.

Pompano, *Trachinotus carolinus.* The highly touted pompano can be caught from Brazil to Cape Cod. Its flesh is high in oil content, making it ideal for broiling, grilling, or baking. Smaller fish (up to 2 pounds) need not be skinned and are usually cooked whole. Larger fish, which look exactly like permit, should be filleted.

Actually, there are several species of pompano in American waters, and all make excellent eating. The **African pompano** *(Alectis crinitus)* isn't really a pompano but is more closely related to the jacks. It has pretty much the same range as the pompano, however, and is very good eating, except when fried.

Atlantic permit, *Trachinotus falcatus.* This great flats-tailing gamefish, also called great pompano or round pompano, grows up to 50 pounds. It ranges from Brazil to Cape Cod but is most abundant in the waters off southern Florida. With medium oily flesh, it makes excellent eating. Smaller permit look and taste like pompano. Larger permit should be filleted and skinned, and some experts trim out the dark meat. As Vic Dunaway pointed out in *From Hook to Table,* slices from the larger fillets taste like veal and can be used in any veal recipe.

A similar species, the **Pacific permit** *(Trachinotus kennedyi),* ranges from Ecuador to Southern California.

Roosterfish, *Nematistius pectoralis.* This handsome species, a cousin to the amberjack, sometimes swims near the surface with its tall dorsal fin sticking out of the water, hence its name. It jumps several times when hooked and is a popular gamefish in the Gulf of California. It can exceed 100 pounds in weight and 5 feet in length. Although it is often wasted, it is excellent eating.

Atlantic lookdown, *Selene vomer.* This small jack feeds at night and is often caught around lighted boat docks and other such structures in Florida. Growing to about 12 inches in length, it is excellent table fare, having slightly oily but mild meat. This species lives from New England to South America. A similar fish, **Atlantic moonfish** *(Vomer setapinnis),* shares the same general appearance, has compatible habits, and rates high on the culinary scale. Both fish have *vomer* in the scientific name, and often the common names are confused. They can be taken on small jigs and streamer flies. Incredibly, both species are also considered to be trash fish in some quarters.

In summary, I recommend that jacks and Carangidae cousins be broiled, baked, smoked, poached, or grilled. Some of the better ones, such as the lookdown, can be fried. Here are some recipes to try.

Pompano en Papillote

Traditionally, a whole fish of about 1 pound is served to each person, and each fish is cooked separately, in its own bag. It's really best to leave the heads on the fish, unless you are feeding squeamish eaters. If you've got larger pompano, you can cook this dish with fillets, allowing about ½ pound for each plate. Don't whisper my words in the French Quarter of New Orleans, but some of the other small jacks, such as the lookdown, are just as good as pompano in this recipe. In any case, the measures below, designed for 2 servings, can be increased as needed.

> 2 pompano
> 1 cup Fish Stock (chapter 27)
> 1 cup crabmeat
> 1 cup chopped shrimp
> 1 large onion, chopped
> 2 green onions with tops, chopped
> 4 ounces mushrooms, sliced
> ½ cup white wine
> ½ cup butter
> 2 chicken egg yolks
> 1 tablespoon flour
> salt and pepper to taste

Preheat the oven to 450 degrees. In a small bowl, make a paste with flour and a little stock; set aside. Melt the butter in a large skillet, then sauté the fish on both sides, browning lightly.

Put the fish on a heated platter. Sauté shrimp, crab, onion, green onions, and mushrooms, stirring with a wooden spoon, for 4 or 5 minutes. Add the fish stock, then stir in the flour paste, egg yolks, wine, salt, and pepper. Keep warm.

Cut 4 large squares of heavy-duty aluminum foil. Place each fish in the center of a sheet of foil, and spoon half of the sauce onto each one. Cover with another sheet of foil, then fold the edges twice to seal the packet. Place the packets on a cookie sheet and cook in the center of the oven for 25 minutes. Serve hot.

Note: You can also use plastic baking bags or parchment paper for this recipe. If you want a formal presentation, it's best to use a long sheet of parchment paper for each fish. Fold the paper over the fish, cut the ends into a semicircle, and seal. Personally, I like to use brown paper bags, but after I published an article on the subject in *Sports Afield,* the editors received a letter saying that recycled bags are dangerous in that they might explode, catch on fire, or contain toxic substances.

Broiled Pompano

Broiling works best with smaller pompano fillets of less than 1 inch thick. Leaving the skin on the fillets makes them easier to handle.

> 2 pounds pompano fillets
> ½ cup butter
> juice of 1 large lemon
> 1 tablespoon minced fresh parsley
> salt and freshly ground pepper
> lemon wedges (garnish)

Preheat the broiler, adjusting the rack and pan so that the fish will be 4 inches from the heat source. To make a basting sauce, melt the butter in a small saucepan, then stir in the lemon juice, parsley, and a little salt. Bring to a simmer, then steep while the broiler heats up; keep the sauce quite warm. When the broiler is hot (this usually takes about 20 minutes), brush the rack with melted butter or oil. Arrange the fillets skin side down so that they do not overlap. Brush with the basting sauce. Broil for 5 to 10 minutes, depending on the thickness of the fillets, or until the fish flakes easily when tested with a fork. Baste a time or two while broiling. When done, carefully place the fillets on heated plates or a serving platter, skin side down, using spatulas. Baste lightly with the butter sauce, then sprinkle lightly with salt and freshly ground black pepper. Serve hot, garnished with lemon wedges.

Variation: During the last 2 minutes of cooking, sprinkle the fillets with chopped pecans.

Hot-Smoked Amberjack

Amberjack is a favorite for hot-smoking in silo cooker-smokers that have both a water pan and a wood chip pan. These units can be charcoal, gas, or electric heated. The exact cooking times will depend on the thickness of the fillets and on the cooking rig.

> 2 or 3 pounds amberjack fillets
> 2 quarts water
> ¾ cup salt
> ½ cup brown sugar
> ½ teaspoon pepper
> olive oil
> 2 bay leaves
> wood chips

Put the fillets into a nonmetallic container. Mix the water, salt, brown sugar, and pepper. Pour the mixture over the fish. Refrigerate overnight. Rig for cooking, preheating the unit, filling the smoke pan with wood chips, and filling the water pan with water. Add the bay leaves to the water. Grease the racks and place the fillets on them, skin side down. Brush the tops of the fillets lightly with olive oil. Cook and smoke until the fish have a golden color and flake easily when tested with a fork. The fish should be moist and succulent; do not overcook.

Note: The fish don't have to be turned while cooking in a silo-shaped cooker-smoker. If you are cooking on a regular grill, however, you may have to turn the fillets over.

Grilled Yellowtail with Tomato Sauce

The sauce used in this recipe goes with any good poached, broiled, or grilled fish. In this recipe, the amberjack fillet is cooked over an electric grill until done, but a charcoal or gas grill can also be used with or without wood chips for smoke. Allow ⅓ to ½ pound of fillets per person.

> 1 pound yellowtail fillets
> 1 medium to large onion, finely minced
> 1 large tomato, peeled and chopped
> 1 green chili, seeded and minced
> 3 cloves garlic, minced
> 1 tablespoon chopped cilantro, minced
> ½ cup olive oil
> ½ cup red wine vinegar
> bacon drippings
> salt and pepper

In a small bowl, mix a sauce with the onion, tomato, chili, garlic, cilantro, olive oil, and red wine vinegar. Refrigerate until ready to cook. Heat the grill. Grease the racks. Brush the fillets with bacon drippings, sprinkle with salt and pepper, and grill close to the heat for about 5 minutes on each side, or until the fillets flake easily when tested with a fork. Top each serving with the tomato sauce.

Broiled Blue Runner Fillets

Here's one of my favorite recipes for broiling fillets about ¾ inch thick. The average blue runner is just right, and the meat is perfect for broiling.

2 pounds blue runner fillets
½ cup grated Parmesan cheese
¼ cup melted butter
¼ cup mayonnaise
4 green onions with tops, finely chopped
juice of 1 large lemon or lime
salt
Tabasco sauce to taste

Preheat the broiler and a broiling pan. Coat the fillets with lemon juice, setting aside while the broiler heats. Mix the Parmesan, butter, mayonnaise, chopped green onions, salt, and a little Tabasco sauce. Grease the broiling pan and arrange the fillets in it in a single layer, skin side down. Broil about 4 inches from the heat for 10 minutes. Add the Parmesan mixture, spreading it equally over the fillets, and broil for another 2 minutes, or until lightly browned. Serve hot.

Skillet Lookdown

Most of these fish are small enough to fit into a regular skillet. They can be pan-fried (that is, coated with flour or meal and cooked in a little oil), or they can be cooked without a coating, as in this recipe.

skillet-size lookdown
olive oil
fresh lemon or lime juice
salt

Draw the fish, and behead it if it won't fit into the skillet. Heat a little olive oil in a cast-iron skillet and cook the lookdown for 4 or 5 minutes on each side, or until the meat flakes easily, turning once. Sprinkle the fish with a little salt and lemon juice. (I use half a lemon for each fish.) Serve hot.

TWELVE

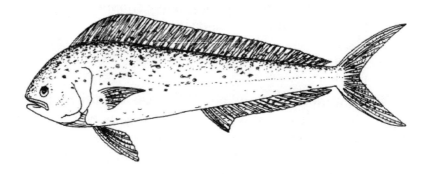

Dolphin

Don't worry. We're not going to eat Flipper. At least not in this book. Whereas Flipper and his porpoise cousins are mammals, we are dealing here with a beautiful gamefish, colored in many shades of blues and yellows and greens, named dolphin, or *Coryphaena hippurus*. In some areas, the dolphin is also called dorado or, possibly to avoid confusion, dolphinfish. In Hawaii, in stateside restaurants, and in most cookbooks, dolphin is called mahi-mahi. It's a rather large fish, growing to more than 70 pounds, but the average catch is 10 or 12 pounds.

Found in all tropical and subtropical seas, the dolphin sometimes follows the Gulf Stream as far north as Prince Edward

The dolphin fish, called mahi-mahi in restaurants, is easily recognized by its high forehead; the male's is almost vertical.

Island. Fast swimmers, they normally haunt the blue waters well off the coast, and often they are attracted to floating patches of sargassum weed, where they feed on flying fishes and other prey. They are also attracted to floating driftwood and debris. Once located, they can be taken on jigs, spoons, plugs, and flies.

The dolphin is a popular gamefish in most of its range and is highly touted as gourmet food far outside its range. It can be cooked in a variety of ways, including frying, and is especially good when baked or broiled. The roe is excellent. The dolphin's flesh is medium oily and firm, but it flakes easily on the grill. I recommend that the skin be left on fillets destined for the grill or broiler; fillets for frying or baking can be skinned. It's easier to skin the fish before filleting.

Regardless of the cooking method, the keys to succulent dolphin are to cover the fish with lots of ice as soon as it is out of the water, avoid overcooking, and call the fish mahi-mahi at the dining table if you're feeding Flipper fans or otherwise squeamish folk.

A smaller species, the pompano dolphin, also a warm-water fish, is perhaps even better as table fare.

Mexican Grilled Dolphin

Here's a wonderful dish of grilled fish and subtropical fruits, which grow in great plenty along the Gulf coast of Mexico. If you like grilled fruit, no vegetables are needed.

> 2 or 3 pounds dolphin fillets with skin
> 6 ripe bananas
> 1 ripe pineapple
> juice of 2 limes
> juice of 1 orange
> 1 cup melted butter (divided)
> 1 tablespoon cayenne pepper (or to taste)
> paprika
> cilantro for garnish

Mix the orange and lime juices. Sprinkle each fillet with cayenne pepper. Put the fillets into a nonmetallic bowl, then pour the citrus juices over them, tossing to coat all sides. Marinate for about 30 minutes. When you are ready to cook, build a hot charcoal fire in one end of a large grill with an adjustable rack. Grease the rack and place it 12 inches above the coals. Quarter the pineapple lengthwise and place the pieces on the grill so that the meat is down. Rub the banana skins with a little melted butter and place them on the grill beside the pineapple. Close the grill. (If you are using an open grill, cover the fruit loosely with aluminum foil.) After 10 minutes, turn the pineapple to grill the other side of the exposed fruit. Grill for another 5 minutes, then move the bananas to one side, away from the heat. Grill the pineapple a little longer if needed for color; they don't have to be completely browned, but the grill marks should show. Then set the pineapple quarters aside.

Brush the fish fillets on both sides with melted butter. Place the fish on the grill, skin side down. Sprinkle with paprika, lower the grill cover, and cook for 10 minutes or so, until the fish flakes easily when tested with a fork. Do not turn the fish. While the fish cooks, place 2 bananas on each plate. Split the skin and butter the banana. Cut the core from the pineapple quarters. Carefully run a fillet knife along the skin, but do not remove the pineapple from the boat-shaped peeling. Slice the pineapple into bite-size chunks and serve it on the skin boat. When the fish is ready, serve it with the fruits. Garnish the plate with a few sprigs of cilantro.

Hawaiian Dolphin

Usually called mahi-mahi, dolphin is a favorite fish (at least for tourists) in our fiftieth state. Here's a good recipe, heavily influenced by Chinese cuisine, that I have adapted from Roana and Gene Schindler's *Hawaiian Cookbook*.

2 pounds dolphin fillets
1 cup chicken broth
½ cup butter
½ cup chopped macadamia nuts
¼ cup red wine vinegar
¼ cup brown sugar
3 tablespoons soy sauce
2 tablespoons cornstarch
1 teaspoon grated fresh ginger root
flour
salt

Sprinkle the fillets with salt, then dust both sides with flour. Heat the butter in a skillet. Sauté the fish on both sides until golden brown. Place the fish on a heated serving platter. Quickly add to the skillet the chicken broth, wine vinegar, soy sauce, brown sugar, cornstarch, and ginger root. Bring to a quick boil, reduce the heat, and simmer for about 10 minutes, or until the sauce thickens. Pour the sauce over the fish, then sprinkle with chopped macadamia nuts. Serve hot.

Dolphin Pizzaiola

For this basic recipe I am indebted to the Bureau of Seafood Marketing, Florida Department of Natural Resources.

2 pounds dolphin fillets
1 can Italian tomatoes (14½-ounce size)
1 can tomato paste (6-ounce size)
¼ cup olive oil
¼ cup grated Parmesan cheese
2 tablespoons chopped chives
2 cloves garlic, minced
1 tablespoon chopped fresh parsley
½ teaspoon creole seasoning
½ teaspoon salt
linguine (cooked separately)

Preheat the oven to 375 degrees. Cut the fillets into ½-inch chunks, then put them into a greased baking dish. Drain the tomatoes, retaining the liquid from the can. Chop the tomatoes, then mix them in a bowl with the juice from the can, tomato paste, olive oil, chives, creole seasoning, garlic, parsley, and salt. Pour this mixture over the fish, spreading evenly. Bake in the center of the oven for 20 minutes. Sprinkle the top with the grated Parmesan, then bake for another 5 minutes. Serve over hot, freshly cooked linguine. Feeds 4 to 6.

Dolphin Fillets in Banana Leaves

Tropical peoples are fond of cooking in banana leaves, and these trees now grow in the warmer parts of the United States. If you don't have banana leaves, try heavy-duty aluminum foil. Fillets from a 4-pound dolphin are just right for this recipe, using a fillet in each banana leaf. I allow a fillet for each person. Use cotton twine to tie the banana leaves, first soaking it in water.

>   2 dolphin fillets
>   2 large banana leaves
>   1 red bell pepper, cut into rings
>   1 green bell pepper, cut into rings
>   2 large onions, sliced
>   1 large tomato, sliced
>   ½ fresh pineapple
>   melted butter
>   salt and pepper

Build a hot wood or charcoal fire, arranging a rack about 2 inches from the coals. Wash the banana leaves and lay them on a flat surface. Using about half of the sliced onion and pepper rings, put down a long layer, just wide and long enough to hold the fillets. Place the fillets, skin side down, on the layer of onions and peppers. Baste the fillets with melted butter and sprinkle with salt and pepper. Place a layer of sliced tomato and pineapple atop each fillet. Add a layer of onion and pepper rings. Wrap the banana leaves around the fillets, fold in both ends, and tie securely with presoaked cotton twine. Place the fillets on the rack over the hot coals. Cook for 25 minutes. Remove from the heat, being careful not to tear the package, and let steam for a few minutes to ensure thorough cooking. Feeds 2 royally. Top the servings of fish with the vegetables and juices from the banana leaf, and serve with rice and steamed vegetables.

THIRTEEN

Sheepshead

Sometimes called the zebra fish or convict fish because it sports five or six vertical bars along either side, the **sheepshead** *(Archosargus probatocephalus)* feeds almost entirely on shellfish. It has strong incisor teeth for cracking mussels, barnacles, clams, and oysters. Although the sheepshead will also feed on crabs and shrimp, its love of the succulent morsels that live inside very hard shells is a good clue to locating and catching the fish. Barnacles and oysters attach themselves to pilings for bridges, piers, and other structures. It follows that sheepshead will feed at these spots, and they can be taken with suitable bait and tackle. If you are fishing from a pier or bridge, fish your bait

Known as a bait stealer, the sheepshead is distinguished by its five or six black stripes. The flesh is sometimes used as a substitute for crabmeat.

very near the bottom, with no slack line, and from time to time very slowly yo-yo the bait as close to the piling as possible.

Successful sheepshead anglers often have different opinions on bait, rigs, and technique, however. If you try to pin them down as to exactly when to set the hook, for example, they have a tendency to mumble. The plain truth is that the fish are difficult to stick with a hook, and successful sheepshead angling requires concentration. Because sheepshead are such a challenge to catch— and make such good table fare—some people more or less specialize in the species, although they will also keep such incidental catches as flounder and pompano.

In addition to its reputation of being hard to catch, the sheepshead is also considered to be difficult to clean. This is not necessarily the case, if you realize that the fish merely has a very thick skin. Using a sharp knife, cut into the fish behind the head and fillet toward the tail—but do not cut through the skin at the tail. Flop the fillet over and work your knife along between the skin and the meat. Then fillet the other side of the sheepshead. It is also possible to skin the fish and then fillet it.

The fish should be kept very cold. Always take an ice chest with you and put the smaller fish (under 5 pounds) directly on ice as soon as they are caught. Larger fish (from 5 to 20 pounds) should be gutted before icing down, and the body cavity filled with ice to promote fast cooling.

If properly handled, the white meat of the sheepshead has a delicate texture and a mild flavor that is hard to beat. The fillets are especially good when they are coated in meal and fried in very hot oil. Also try the flaked meat scrambled in a little butter with chicken eggs and a few chopped green onions. Here are some recipes to try.

Mock Crabmeat

As table fare, the sheepshead stands on its own and shouldn't be considered a substitute for anything. But anyone who has recently priced crabmeat at the grocery store could profit by knowing that lightly boiled or steamed sheepshead makes a very good substitute for crabmeat in a number of recipes for salads, soups, and so on. Skin the fish, fillet it, and boil or steam the pieces for 4 or 5 minutes, or until the fish flakes easily when tested with a fork. Drain the fillets, flake the meat, and use it instead of crabmeat in the recipe.

Sheepshead and Avocados

Here's a wonderful Florida dish, showing Caribbean influence, that I make with the aid of fresh avocados and coconut milk (see chapter 27). It can be made with leftover fish, but freshly cooked sheepshead is perfect.

> 1 pound cooked sheepshead, flaked
> 2 avocados
> ¼ cup butter
> 2 cups thick Coconut Milk (chapter 27)
> 1 small onion (golf-ball size), minced
> 2 tablespoons flour
> 1 tablespoon Pickapeppa or Dat'll-Do-It sauce
> 1 tablespoon chopped fresh parsley
> juice of ½ lemon
> salt to taste
> Parmesan cheese

Preheat the oven to 400 degrees. Cut the avocados in half lengthwise and remove the seeds. Squeeze lemon juice onto the avocados and set aside. Heat the butter in a skillet, add the flour, and sauté for 2 or 3 minutes, stirring as you go. Stir in the coconut milk slowly. Mix in the sheepshead meat, onion, Pickapeppa, parsley, and salt. Fill the avocados with the fish mixture. Sprinkle with freshly grated Parmesan cheese. Place the stuffed avocado halves onto a baking sheet and bake for 15 minutes.

Texas-Style Mock Crab Cakes

Most of our crab cake recipes seem to come from the Chesapeake Bay area and the Northeast. Here's something different from Texas, made with sheepshead.

> 1 pound sheepshead fillets (or see note)
> 1 cup dry bread crumbs (divided)
> ½ cup minced green onions
> ¼ cup chopped pecans
> juice of 1 large lemon
> 1 chicken egg, beaten
> 2 tablespoons softened butter
> 1 tablespoon prepared brown mustard
> 1 teaspoon minced fresh dill weed
> salt
> peanut oil or butter for pan-frying
> lemon wedges (garnish)

Poach the sheepshead fillets for about 10 minutes. Drain and flake the meat. In a large bowl, mix ½ cup of the bread crumbs with the egg, green onions, pecans, lemon juice, butter, mustard, dill, and salt. Mix in the fish. Put the remaining bread crumbs on a plate. Shape the fish mixture into patties, dredge them in the bread crumbs, and pan-fry in a little oil in a skillet or on a griddle. Garnish with lemon wedges. Serve hot.

Note: You can also use the meat from the backbone, rib cages, and head of the fish, saving the fillets for another recipe.

Mock Crab Kabobs

These kabobs can be broiled or grilled, but careful handling is required to hold them together.

> 1 cup flaked precooked sheepshead meat
> 1 cup dry bread crumbs
> ½ cup tomato or V-8 juice
> 1 chicken egg, beaten
> 12 strips bacon, cut in half
> 1 tablespoon finely chopped fresh parsley
> wine
> salt and pepper to taste
> lemon wedges (garnish)

Pour the tomato juice into a bowl, and whisk in the egg. Add the bread crumbs, parsley, salt, and pepper; then stir in the sheepshead meat. Add a little wine if more moisture is needed. Shape the mixture into balls just large enough for the bacon halves to wrap around, overlapping by about ½ inch. Place 3 balls in a line, with the overlapping ends of the bacon on the side, and carefully insert the skewers through the balls one at a time, being sure that they go through the overlapped part of the bacon. After the balls are skewered, flatten them slightly by patting them down with your hand, so that more of the bacon is in contact with the grill. Cook the kabobs over medium heat for about 25 minutes, carefully turning every 5 minutes or so, then increase the heat or lower the rack so that the bacon browns nicely. Garnish with a lemon wedge. Serve the kabobs with rice pilaf and a steamed vegetable or two.

Sheepshead Salad

This salad can be made with leftover fish, but it's really best to poach freshly caught fish. Sheepshead of 2 or 3 pounds are ideal.

1 sheepshead
1 cup diced cooked potatoes
1 medium onion, chopped
1 inner rib celery with tops, chopped
½ red bell pepper, chopped
½ green bell pepper, chopped
¼ cup mayonnaise
1 teaspoon prepared mustard
salt and pepper

Dress the fish and poach for about 15 minutes. Chill and cut the meat into 1-inch chunks. Mix all other ingredients thoroughly, then carefully mix in the fish chunks. Serve on lettuce.

Sheepshead, Wild Rice, and Walnut Sauce

Although this recipe runs a little long, if measured by the list of ingredients, it all goes together easily. I make the sauce after the sheepshead fillets go into the oven. The recipe has been adapted from information from the federally funded Sea Grant program.

The Fish
2 pounds sheepshead fillets
3 slices bacon, chopped
1 cup cooked wild rice
1 cup chopped fresh mushrooms
¼ cup minced onions
¼ cup minced celery, with part of tops
2 tablespoons butter or margarine
salt and pepper

Preheat the oven to 350 degrees. Cook the bacon in a skillet until lightly browned. Add the mushrooms, onions, and celery. Sauté for a few minutes until tender. Stir in the cooked wild rice, along with a little salt and pepper. Place the fillets in a well-greased baking pan of suitable size; 12 by 8 by 2 will be just right. Spoon the wild rice mixture over the fillets, then bake in the center of the oven for 20 minutes. While the fillets cook, prepare the sauce.

The Sauce
2 cups half-and-half
1 cup freshly sliced mushrooms
¼ cup toasted walnuts
3 tablespoons butter or margarine
3 tablespoons flour
1 tablespoon minced onion
½ teaspoon dry mustard
¼ teaspoon dried thyme
salt

Melt the butter in a saucepan, then sauté the mushrooms and onions for 5 minutes. Stir in the flour, mustard, thyme, and a little salt to taste. Slowly add the half-and-half, stirring constantly with a wooden spoon. Cook and stir until the mixture is sauce-thick and smooth. Stir in the walnuts. Serve hot with the sheepshead fillets and wild rice.

FOURTEEN

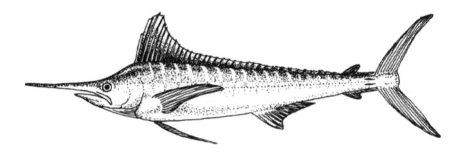

Billfish

All of the large billfish make good eating if they are properly handled and expertly cooked, and some are important commercially. Too often the sportsman is more interested in a stuffed trophy or in showing off the catch back at the dock, just as too many deer hunters want to ride through town with their bucks tied across the hoods of their four-wheelers. If you want good eating, it's best to fillet the fish and ice down the meat as soon as possible after boating or landing the fish. Be very, very careful, however, when handling these large fish.

Blue marlin, *Makaira nigricans.* This great offshore gamefish, growing to 1,000 pounds, roams all the world's temperate and

---

Marlins, swordfish, and sailfish—all large gamefish—are distinguished by their long, pointed bills, hence their other name, billfish.

---

warm seas. On the oily side, its firm flesh is ideal for smoking, and steaks are grilled, broiled, or baked. It is also popular as sashimi. The **black marlin** *(Makaira indica)*, **striped marlin** *(Tetrapturus audax)*, and **white marlin** *(Tetrapturus albidus)* are also excellent eating and are cooked in the same ways.

Sailfish, *Istiophorus platypterus.* This fish can be taken on both the Atlantic and Pacific coasts, sometimes close to shore. Its flesh is very oily and somewhat tough, and it is not as versatile as the marlin and other billfish. It is, however, excellent when smoked or grilled over charcoal or wood coals.

Longbill spearfish, *Tetrapturus pfluegeri.* This species of southeastern and Gulf waters makes good eating, but its flesh is on the dark side and is not as highly regarded as that of the other billfish. There are several similar species, none of which are very abundant.

Swordfish, *Xiphias gladius.* This great fish, sometimes called broadbill swordfish or simply broadbill, frequents the tropical and temperate seas. It makes excellent eating, especially when grilled or broiled.

Here are some recipes that work with billfish. Ordinarily, these fish are first filleted and then cut into smaller pieces. These pieces are called steaks, although this term is easily confused with the steaks made by cutting a whole fish across the backbone. Usually, either cut of meat will work with billfish, provided that the thickness is about 1 inch or less.

Swordfish au Poivre

Since steak au poivre is one of my favorite recipes and the shiitake is one of my favorite mushrooms, I couldn't pass up this dish when I read about it in *Gulf Coast Cooking,* which says it is cooked on Sanibel Island with fresh tuna and other fish of firm texture. It is important that the 4 fillets in the recipe fit into your skillet. It is even more important that they be of the right thickness.

4 swordfish fillets, 1 inch thick and about 6 or
    8 ounces
1 cup fresh shiitake mushrooms, sliced
⅔ cup heavy cream
½ cup green onions, sliced crosswise with part of tops
¼ cup finely chopped red bell pepper
4 tablespoons olive oil
4 tablespoons prepared mustard
2 tablespoons green peppercorns
1 tablespoon coarsely ground black pepper
2 ounces brandy

Rub the top of each fillet with 1 tablespoon mustard, then press the coarse black pepper more or less equally into each side of the fillets. Heat the olive oil in a skillet. Place the fillets mustard side down in the hot skillet and sear for 1 minute. Turn. Add the mushrooms, red bell pepper, green onions, and green peppercorns. Cook for 1 minute. Pour the brandy into the skillet and flame it. Add the cream and cook for 2 minutes, turning the fillets once. Test for doneness and serve the fillets hot. Top with the sauce from the pan.

Billfish Kabobs

Most dishes with pineapple as a major ingredient are usually considered to be Hawaiian, but I want to point out that the pineapple is originally from Central America and the Caribbean, where it is often grilled.

2 pounds swordfish
1 fresh pineapple
2 large onions, quartered
1 large green bell pepper
1 large red bell pepper
½ cup pineapple juice
¼ cup white wine vinegar
¼ cup molasses
¼ cup butter
salt and pepper

Cut the meat into pieces about 2 inches long, 1 inch wide, and 1 inch thick, suitable for stringing up on bamboo skewers. Mix a marinade with the white wine vinegar, pineapple juice, molasses, salt, and pepper. Put the meat into a nonmetallic container, pour in the marinade, toss to coat all sides, and put into the refrigerator for 2 hours. When you are ready to cook, build a hot charcoal fire and remove the fish from the refrigerator. Cut the pineapple into pieces compatible with the fish chunks. Cut the onions and peppers into 1-inch pieces. Drain the fish, reserving the marinade, and string up the pieces on skewers, alternating onion, pepper, fish, and pineapple. Bring the marinade and butter to a light boil in a saucepan, then remove from the heat. Grill the kabobs about 4 inches above the hot coals for 5 minutes on each side, basting from time to time. Serve hot with rice or pilaf. Makes 6 to 8 kabobs.

Broiled Billfish

It's best to use steaks or fillets about 1 inch thick for this recipe. Part of the success depends on using sliced oranges rather than orange sections. Peel the orange before slicing. The slices served on the side should be about ½ inch thick, seeded, and chilled, but those for covering the fillets during cooking should be sliced as thin as you can make them. I like navel oranges because they are easy to peel and usually contain few seeds.

2 pounds billfish fillets
4 large navel oranges
1 large lemon, peeled and thinly sliced
salt and freshly ground pepper

Preheat the broiler. Salt and pepper the fillets, then arrange them on a greased broiling rack. Broil 4 inches from the heat for 5 or 6 minutes. Turn carefully with 2 spatulas, and cover loosely with very thin orange and lemon slices. Broil for another 5 or 6 minutes, or until the fish is firm to the touch. Serve hot with sliced oranges.

Easy Greek Billfish

The Greeks and other Middle Easterners are fond of wrapping food in grape leaves before cooking it. I also like to cook with grape leaves, but sometimes my leaves (from wild grapes) are too small to make a suitable wrap. Hinged grilling baskets simplify the method considerably and also make it easier to turn the fish on the grill. The steaks or fillets should be about ¾ inch thick. If you don't have fresh grape leaves, you can buy canned leaves in ethnic markets and, these days, in many large supermarkets.

2 pounds billfish steaks or fillets
olive oil
grape leaves
2 crumbled bay leaves
chopped fresh parsley
sea salt
freshly ground pepper

Place the steaks or fillets in a nonmetallic container, pour some olive oil over them, sprinkle with sea salt, toss to coat all sides, and marinate at room temperature for 1 hour. Build a charcoal fire in the grill. Open a hinged grilling basket large enough to hold the fish in a single layer. Line the bottom of the basket with grape leaves. Sprinkle on some chopped parsley and crumbled bay leaves. Sprinkle each piece of fish with freshly ground pepper, then arrange the pieces on top of the grape leaves. Add some more parsley and bay leaves. Top the fish with more grape leaves and close the grill. Cook about 4 inches above hot coals for 5 or 6 minutes on each side. Serve hot with lemon wedges, rice, grilled eggplant, and other vegetables or green salad, along with some crusty Greek bread.

Grilled Billfish with Portabellas

This recipe can be made on any grill, using electric, gas, or charcoal heat. I like to cook it on a stove-top grill, such as the Jenn-Air, because I find that the garlic oil flavor doesn't need wood smoke.

    4 billfish steaks, ¾ to 1 inch thick
    1 pound portabella mushrooms, sliced ½ inch thick
    Garlic Oil (chapter 27)
    sea salt

   Brush the steaks and mushrooms on both sides with garlic oil about 30 minutes before cooking; set aside. Preheat the grill and grease the racks. Grill the steaks and mushrooms for 10 to 12 minutes, or until the fish is firm to the touch and nicely browned on each side, turning once. Sprinkle lightly with crushed or ground sea salt.

Grilled Billfish with Onions

If you love onions, be sure to try this recipe. Partly because the aroma from the skillet is wonderful, I like to cook this dish on my stove-top grill in the kitchen instead of on the patio, using the grill for the fish and a skillet for the onion topping. The steaks should be about ¾ to 1 inch thick.

2 pounds swordfish steaks
2 large onions, chopped
8 cloves garlic, chopped
8 ounces fresh mushrooms, sliced
½ cup olive oil, plus a little more
½ cup dry wine
salt and pepper

In a large skillet, heat ½ cup of olive oil on low heat. Add the onions, mushrooms, and garlic. Sauté for 10 minutes, stirring with a wooden spoon from time to time. Add the wine and simmer. As the onion mixture cooks, heat the grill. Brush the fish with olive oil and grill for 5 or 6 minutes on each side, or until firm to the touch, brushing with oil when turned. Sprinkle the fish steaks with salt and pepper. Serve hot, topping each steak with onions and mushrooms.

Smoked Billfish Kedgeree

The British borrowed this fish and rice dish from India, where it is called *khichri*, and in England it is often cooked with the aid of curry powder and smoked salmon. Any good smoked fish can be used, and billfish are excellent when smoked properly. I might add that some anglers have their billfish commercially smoked, but any leftover billfish from a patio hot smoker can be used.

2 cups flaked smoked billfish
2 cups cooked rice, steaming hot
½ cup cream
2 hard-boiled chicken eggs, chopped
1 tablespoon minced fresh parsley
1½ teaspoons curry powder
salt and pepper to taste

Steam the smoked fish for 10 minutes. Mix the rice, cream, parsley, curry powder, salt, and pepper in the top part of a double boiler, with a little boiling water in the bottom half. Carefully mix in the chopped eggs and fish. Serve hot.

FIFTEEN

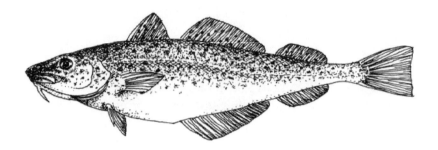

Cods, Hakes,
and Haddocks

Although I must have caught a thousand pounds of codfish from deep-water bays in Newfoundland and thereabouts in the early 1950s, I really can't say it is an important sport fish these days. It doesn't pull very much and is almost always near bottom in rather deep water. It is seldom taken from fishing piers or from the surf. In the Northeast, it can be taken from seagoing boats, and some people in those parts go after it on a regular basis, often with hand lines.

But the cod was once very, very important as a market fish. It still is, although its numbers have been in steady decline. In salted

The Atlantic cod looks much like its cousins the hakes, pollocks, and haddocks.

form, it was shipped to West Africa, the Caribbean, Mexico, and the east coast of South America, as well as to the Midwest. Indeed, some of the best recipes for cooking salt cod come from West Africa, the West Indies, and Latin America, thousands of miles from its deep, cold-water haunts of the North Atlantic. Anyone interested in salt fish should get some good cookbooks from those areas. Of course, some classic recipes were also developed in New England, as reflected in this chapter.

Today, the codfish is still available in salted form, but it is more often found fresh or frozen. It is an excellent table fish, having mild white flesh.

The haddock, a cousin to the codfish, is taken from the same Atlantic haunts, ranging as far south as the Carolinas. It is excellent table fare and a popular market fish. When salted, or first salted and then cold-smoked, it is marketed, usually at high prices, under the name finnan haddie.

Another cousin, the hake, called Poor John in Shakespeare's day, has a more questionable reputation. There are several species, some of which sometimes roam into shallow water and can be taken on a fly rod. It is difficult, at least for me, to tell one hake from another, and, in fact, they all look pretty much like a cod. A true cod, however, has a barbel on the chin and an arch in the lateral line. As a rule, the hakes have a mild white flesh, low in fat. The problem is that hakes tend to be on the soft side and consequently should be eaten shortly after being caught. If they are promptly drawn and iced, they are delicious. They tend to have a slimy feel, however, and should be skinned.

The pollock also makes very good eating. Although they are not highly regarded as table fare by most anglers, the pollock frequents shallower water than the cods and hakes.

Altogether, the cods and hakes comprise some 60 species, mostly in the Northern Hemisphere. Most of these prefer northern waters, but some do not. The southern hake, for example, frequents the Gulf of Mexico. (The lingcod, by the way, is neither a ling nor a cod; it's closer to the rockfish, covered in chapter 16.) In any case, here are some of the more common species taken from American waters.

Atlantic cod, *Gadus morhua.* This popular commercial fish of the North Atlantic ranges as far south as North Carolina. The firm white flesh can be cooked by any method.

Pacific cod, *Gadus macrocephalus.* This close cousin of the Atlantic cod occurs in the North Pacific, commonly ranging south to Oregon and sometimes straying to California waters. Excellent eating, it can be prepared by any method.

Tomcod, *Microgadus tomcod.* This small cod, weighing about 1 pound, is caught from Labrador south to the Gulf of St. Lawrence. This fish sometimes frequents brackish waters. It is excellent eating.

Pollock, *Pollachius virens.* Growing up to 30 pounds and larger, this fish of the North Atlantic ranges as far south as Cape Cod. It can be cooked by any method. Fillets are often fried.

Silver hake, *Merluccius bilinearis.* This hake ranges from Newfoundland to the Carolinas. Like several other hakes, it is important commercially but is not often taken for sport.

Haddock, *Melanogrammus aeglefinus.* This deep-water cousin of the cod ranges from the North Sea to Newfoundland, south to North Carolina. It is an important commercial species and makes excellent eating when fresh.

Here are some recipes that work for all the cods and cousins, including several for salt cod, which is still an important part of several cuisines far removed from the cod's northern haunts.

Salt Fish with Ackee and Cracklings

Captain Bligh brought several fruits to the West Indies, and the breadfruit from the Pacific islands helped cause the famous mutiny on the HMS *Bounty.* From West Africa he brought the ackee, a fruit with a scarlet shell and shiny black seeds. The edible part of this strange fruit is sometimes called vegetable brains because of its appearance. The fresh fruit can be poisonous if improperly handled, so it is usually not exported. But canned ackee is available in some specialty food shops. The recipe also calls for a Scotch bonnet pepper. These are small but very hot. If you can't find one, use any hot green chili.

1 pound salt cod
¼ pound salt pork
6 slices bacon, crisply fried
1 can ackees (19-ounce size)
3 ripe tomatoes, peeled and chopped
2 ripe tomatoes, sliced
2 medium onions, chopped
6 green onions with part of tops, chopped
1 green bell pepper, seeded and chopped
1 red bell pepper, seeded and chopped
1 Scotch bonnet chili, seeded and minced
¼ teaspoon dried thyme
freshly ground black pepper
parsley sprigs (garnish)
whole green onions and chilies, peeled and trimmed
    (garnish)

Soak the salt cod overnight in cold fresh water, changing the water two or three times if convenient. Drain the fish and poach it in water for about 15 minutes, or until it flakes easily when tested with a fork. Drain the fish again, then flake off the meat, discarding the bones. Finely dice the salt pork, then fry it in a cast-iron skillet until the pieces are greatly reduced and quite crispy, leaving the accumulated grease in the skillet. Drain the cracklings on a brown bag. In the salt pork grease, sauté the onions, bell peppers, chili, and green onions for 5 minutes. Add the chopped tomatoes and thyme. Stir in the flaked fish, diced salt pork, and drained ackees. Sprinkle with freshly ground black pepper. Transfer the mixture to a serving platter; garnish with sliced tomato, parsley, whole green onions and chilies, cracklings, and strips of crisply fried bacon. This dish is often served for breakfast in Jamaica.

Salt Cod with Greens

Here's a very unusual West African dish from Burkina Faso, calling for sweet potato greens. That's right. The green leaves of the sweet potato are edible and are eaten in some parts of the world. Dr. George Washington Carver, the black scientist at Tuskegee Institute who did so much for the modern peanut industry, tried to persuade Americans to eat the abundant leaves of the sweet potato. He wasn't successful. If you have your own garden, or know someone who does, try these unusual greens. If not, substitute collards, turnip greens, or spinach. The recipe also calls for whole okra. It's best to get these from your own or a friend's garden, where you can pick them before they get too large. Frozen okra can be substituted.

> 1 pound dried salt cod
> 1 pound sweet potato leaves
> 2 cups whole small-pod okra
> 2 medium tomatoes
> 2 small-to-medium onions, chopped
> 3 cloves garlic, chopped
> 2 hot chili peppers, seeded
> 4 tablespoons tomato paste
> 2 tablespoons peanut oil
> water
> nutmeg

Soak the salt cod overnight in fresh water, changing the water from time to time. In a food processor, puree the tomatoes, tomato paste, chilies, onions, and garlic. Heat the oil in a large cast-iron skillet or stove-top Dutch oven, then simmer the puree for a few minutes. Stir in the okra, and add enough water to barely cover the okra. Simmer for about 10 minutes.

In a large pot, cook the greens in boiling water for 15 to 20 minutes. Drain the greens, then add them, the fish, and the nutmeg to the okra stew. Cover and simmer, but do not boil, for 45 minutes. Serve with rice.

Broiled Scrod

Here's an old Boston dish, dating back to days when small codfish—those less than 3 pounds—were called scrod in parts of New England. The recipe calls for white pepper, which is not as strong as black pepper. For the best results, grind your own white peppercorns in a mortar and pestle.

1 fresh scrod
½ cup salted butter
juice of 1 lemon
1½ tablespoons freshly chopped parsley
salt and white pepper
lemon wedges (garnish)

Fillet the scrod, leaving the skin on, and score each fillet 3 times, cutting about halfway through the flesh. Preheat the broiler and the broiling pan, adjusting the rack so that the fish will be about 4 inches from the heat. Melt the butter in a saucepan, then mix in the lemon juice, chopped parsley, and some white pepper. Simmer for 3 or 4 minutes.

Brush the bottom of the broiling pan with some of the melted butter sauce. Place the fillets in the heated pan, skin side down. Brush heavily with the butter sauce, then sprinkle with salt and pepper. Broil for about 10 minutes, basting after 5 minutes and again toward the end of the cooking period. Carefully remove the fillets, placing them on a serving platter or plates. Spoon the remaining butter sauce over the fillets, dividing it equally. Serve hot, garnished with lemon wedges.

Creamed Haddock

This old Irish dish, very rich and quite filling, goes nicely with new potatoes and string beans.

> 1 pound haddock fillets
> 1 cup half-and-half
> ½ cup butter
> flour
> salt and pepper
> 1 teaspoon dry mustard
> chopped fresh parsley (garnish)

Melt the butter in a saucepan. Dip the fillets in the melted butter, sprinkle with salt and pepper, and shake in a bag with a little flour. Place the fillets in a large well-greased skillet. Mix the half-and-half into the melted butter left in the saucepan, then pour the mix over the fillets. Heat the skillet until the liquid around the fillets starts to bubble. Immediately reduce the heat, then simmer for about 10 minutes, or until the fish flakes easily when tested with a fork. Remove the fillets to a heated serving platter.

Mix the mustard into the liquid left in the skillet. Heat until the liquid starts to bubble. Reduce the heat, then simmer until the sauce starts to thicken. Pour the sauce over the fish, garnish with parsley, and serve hot.

Daniel Webster's Fish Chowder

Arguments will always crop up about what exactly should go into a fish chowder, and whether or not this recipe or that ought to be called New England chowder, Manhattan chowder, or whatever. When all the thousands of recipes are counted and the day of reckoning comes, here's one that will surely be high on the list. I found it in an old book called *Foods of Our Forefathers,* which in turn quoted it from the 1931 edition of *The Cape Cod Cook Book,* by Suzanne Cary Gruver. It has also been printed in other works, including my own *Cast Iron Cooking.*

Here is the recipe, said to be suitable for a large fishing party, in Webster's own words:

"Take a cod of ten pounds, well cleaned, leaving on the skin. Cut into pieces one and a half pounds thick, preserving the head whole. Take one and a half pounds of clear, fat, salt pork, cut in thin slices. Do the same with twelve potatoes. Take the largest pot you have. Try out the pork first; then take out the pieces of pork, leaving the drippings. Add to that three parts of water, a layer of fish, so as to cover the bottom of the pot; next, a layer of potatoes, then two tablespoons of salt, 1 teaspoon of pepper, then the pork, another layer of fish, and the remainder of the potatoes.

"Fill the pot with water to cover the ingredients. Put it over a good fire, let the chowder boil twenty-five minutes. When this is done, have a quart of boiling milk ready, and ten hard crackers split and dipped in cold water. Add milk and crackers. Let the whole boil five minutes. The chowder is then ready and will be first rate if you have followed the directions. An onion may be added if you like the flavor."

By "try out the pork," Webster meant to fry or sauté it until most of the grease cooks out, as when making cracklings. Be sure to try this old recipe in camp or at home. Webster said to use the largest pot you have. A large cast-iron Dutch oven will be suitable. Cod has always been a popular fish in New England, but any good fish of mild flavor will be fine.

Dr. Chang's Codfish

Here's an interesting recipe sent to me by chef Myron Becker, president of Myron's Fine Foods, an outfit that markets gourmet sauces, including 20 Gauge Wild Game Sauce. Becker says he got the recipe from a Dr. Chang of Amherst Chinese foods while Chang was visiting Becker's place on the west coast of Newfoundland. It's best to use cod in the 5- to 6-pound range, cut into steaks 2 inches thick. Becker didn't specify the cooking oil, but the Chinese are fond of peanut oil, and I am too, especially in recipes that call for very hot oil. I use a cast-iron stove-top Dutch oven to cook this recipe.

129

The Fish
cod steaks, 2 inches thick
oil
salt

Heat the oil to 400 degrees. Salt the cod steaks heavily, actu-ally encrusting them with salt. Quickly deep-fry the cod steaks until they are golden and have a salty crust. (Note that no batter or other coating is required.) Do not overcook. Drain and serve hot with Ponzu Sauce, below, or use a dipping sauce of your choice.

To make the Ponzu Sauce, you'll need some Myron's No. 1 Yakitori Sauce. If you can't find this locally, drop a line to Myron's, P.O. Box 862, Wendell, MA 01379. The recipe also calls for Chinese sesame oil, which is made from toasted sesame seeds and has a distinctive flavor. It is available in Chinese food markets and can be found in the oriental section of many supermarkets.

Ponzu Dipping Sauce
1 cup Myron's No. 1 Yakitori Sauce
¼ cup white rice vinegar
1 teaspoon Chinese-style sesame oil
chopped green onions with tops or cilantro

Mix the Yakitori Sauce, rice vinegar, and sesame oil. This mix-ture will keep indefinitely. An hour or so before serving, add the chopped green onions or perhaps some minced cilantro. Serve as a dipping sauce.

Mac's Fried Codfish

Here's a recipe adapted from *The African Heritage Cookbook*, to which it was submitted by Mr. Clarence McKennon of Jamaica, Long Island. (The book, published in New York City, said that this recipe serves 4. I don't hold Mac responsible for that figure, but I doubt that he would be satisfied with one-quarter of a 1-pound codfish. This supports my theory that New York maga-zine and cookbook editors don't eat very much.)

1 pound codfish, cut into chunks
4 tablespoons bacon fat
1 small-to-medium onion, chopped
white cornmeal
salt and pepper to taste
hot sauce or catsup

Sprinkle the fish chunks with salt and pepper, and dredge them with cornmeal. Heat the bacon fat in a skillet, then quickly brown the fish and chopped onion. Serve hot with hot sauce or catsup.

Nova Scotia Hake

Here's an excellent dish from the Nova Scotia Department of Fisheries. The topping complements the bland, white flesh of the hake perfectly. Also try the recipe with fillets of cod or halibut.

2 pounds hake fillets
2 tablespoons butter
½ cup regular mayonnaise
¼ cup minced green onions, with tops
juice of ½ lime
salt and pepper

Preheat the oven to 450 degrees. Grease a shallow baking dish of suitable size to hold the fillets without overlapping. Place the fillets into the dish skin side down. Melt the butter in a small skillet or saucepan, then sauté the green onions for 5 minutes. Stir in the other ingredients, then spread the topping equally over the fish. Bake for 10 minutes per inch of thickness of the fillets at the widest part, plus an additional 5 minutes. The fillets are done when they flake easily when tested with a fork.

Note: If you are using frozen fillets, cook for about 20 minutes per inch of thickness.

Codfish Balls

Although this old recipe was originally made with salt cod, well freshened, I also like it with fresh fish.

> 1 pound fresh cod fillet, diced
> 3 cups diced potatoes
> 1 chicken egg, beaten
> 2 tablespoons melted butter
> 1 cup finely crushed saltine crackers
> salt and pepper
> cooking oil
> water

Put the diced cod and potatoes into a boiler. Cover with water, bring to a boil, reduce heat, cover, and simmer for 15 minutes. Drain. Mash the potatoes, cod, and crushed crackers, mixing well. Add the beaten egg, butter, salt, and pepper. Mix well. Shape the mixture into small patties about ½ inch thick. Heat a little oil in a cast-iron skillet, then fry the patties for about 2 minutes on each side, or until golden brown. Watch carefully to prevent burning. Serve hot. Feeds 4.

SIXTEEN

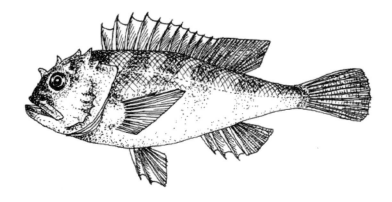

Rockfish

Many East Coast anglers know the striped bass as rockfish, and in the Bahamas groupers are called by that name. But the real rockfish are found, in several species, along the West Coast—and in great numbers. In fact, rockfish of one kind or another make up about half the sportsman's catch in California's salt waters. There are a number of species (250 worldwide, with over 50 along the Pacific coast of the United States), all of which have big mouths like the groupers, snappers, and freshwater largemouth bass—and all make delicious eating, having firm white flesh. The sportsman's catch is usually between 1 and 2 feet long, although these fish grow much larger. They are usually filleted and skinned.

The scorpionfish, a member of the rockfish clan, can be taken along both coasts, but most of the 50 or so rockfish that can be caught in American waters live along the West Coast.

The more important species, plentiful from British Columbia to Baja California, include the **canary rockfish** *(Sebastodes pinniger)*, an orange fish with stripes and bright orange fins; **black rockfish** *(Sebastodes melanops)*, often found in shallow inshore waters; **quillback rockfish** *(Sebastodes maliger)*, caught at depths of 180 to 900 feet; and **yellowtail rockfish** *(Sebastodes flavidus)*, a grayish fish with yellow on the tip of its tail. All of the rockfish are sometimes called rockcods, and, I understand, the black rockfish is sometimes marketed under the name of black sea bass. Further, frozen rockfish fillets are sometimes marketed under the name Pacific ocean perch, and the reddish colored rockfish, such as the **rosy rockfish** *(Sebastodes rosaceus)* or **vermilion rockfish** *(Sebastodes miniatus)*, are labeled red snapper or rosefish. Rockfish are even marketed as ocean perch in the Pacific Northwest!

The **scorpionfish** *(Scorpaena* spp.) is a family of small, ugly rockfish, some of which grow up to 17 inches long. They make excellent eating. One species or another can be taken along both the East and West Coasts of the United States. Oddly, these fish shed their skin from time to time like a snake.

The **sculpins** are kin to the scorpionfish and rockfish, but most of these are too small to be of importance to the angler except as bait (the famous Muddler Minnow fly was invented by Don Gapen to imitate a small freshwater sculpin). The largest of the sculpins, the **cabezon** *(Scorpaenichthys marmoratus)*, grows up to 25 pounds and can be caught inshore along the West Coast from British Columbia to Baja California. Reportedly, the greenish roe can be poisonous, but the fillets make excellent eating.

The **lingcod** *(Ophiodon elongatus)*, ranging from California to Alaska, may or may not be a rockfish, but it looks like one, rather elongated. In any case, it's certainly not a ling or a cod. Weighing up to 70 pounds, this fish makes very good eating, provided you are not put off by the color of its flesh, which can range from white to green to bluish. The lingcod is also called cultus cod or greenling.

In any case, here are some recipes to try with fillets from any sort of rockfish, scorpionfish, or sculpin of suitable size.

Fried Rockfish Fillets

Any good recipe for fried fish can be adapted to rockfish fillets. Although I prefer a sparse dusting with stone-ground cornmeal, here's another recipe you may want to try.

> 2 pounds skinless rockfish fillets
> 1 chicken egg, beaten
> flour
> 1 cup Garlic Oil (chapter 27)
> salt
> lemon wedges (garnish)

Heat the garlic oil in a skillet. Sprinkle the fillets with salt, dip in beaten egg, dust lightly with flour, and fry for 3 or 4 minutes on each side, turning once. Drain on brown paper or paper towels. Serve hot, garnished with lemon wedges.

Steamed Rockfish with Mussels

This recipe can be cooked with steaks from large fish or with fillets ¾ to 1 inch thick. The mussels should be in the shell, well scrubbed. The recipe calls for fish stock. If you don't have some on hand, or don't have the makings, use chicken broth, clam broth, or plain water.

> 1 pound rockfish fillets
> 12 mussels
> 2 large vine-ripened tomatoes, sliced
> 1 large onion, sliced
> ½ green bell pepper, cut into rings
> ½ red bell pepper, cut into rings
> ½ cup Fish Stock (chapter 27)
> ¼ cup dry white wine
> salt and pepper

Arrange the vegetables in the bottom of a stove-top Dutch oven or other suitable pot. Sprinkle with salt and pepper, then pour in the fish stock and wine. Bring to a light boil, reduce heat, and simmer for 15 minutes. Place the fish on top of the vegetables and fit in the mussels. Add a little water if more liquid is needed. Bring to a new boil, reduce the heat, cover, and simmer for 10 minutes. Serve the fish directly from the pot, placing them on individual plates, along with some mussels, and spoon the vegetables and pot liquor on top. Serve with French or tough sourdough bread for sopping. Feeds 2.

Skillet Rockfish

Here's a skillet dish I like to make with fillets, provided that I can cook all the fillets at one time instead of in batches. I've got a square cast-iron skillet that holds them just right.

2 pounds rockfish fillets
1 medium onion, chopped
½ red bell pepper, chopped
½ green bell pepper, chopped
2 tablespoons soy sauce
2 tablespoons sake, sherry, or dry vermouth
2 tablespoons peanut oil
1 tablespoon brown sugar

In a small saucepan, mix the wine, brown sugar, and soy sauce; keep warm. In a large skillet, heat the peanut oil and brown the fillets on high heat, turning once. Carefully place the browned fillets on a heated platter. In the remaining oil (add a little more if needed), sauté the onions and peppers for about 10 minutes. Carefully return the fish to the skillet. Pour in the soy mixture. Bring to a boil, reduce heat to very low, cover, and simmer for 10 minutes. Serve with rice and steamed vegetables.

Rockfish Fillets au Gratin

This recipe makes a very rich dish, so that a small amount of fish goes a long way.

> 1 pound skinless rockfish fillets
> 1 can condensed cream of mushroom soup
>   (12¾-ounce size)
> ½ cup dry Italian bread crumbs
> ¼ cup grated Parmesan cheese
> 2 tablespoons olive oil
> salt and pepper
> water or Court Bouillon (chapter 27) for poaching

Preheat the oven to 425 degrees. Poach the fillets in water or court bouillon for 5 minutes, then carefully place them in a greased baking dish and sprinkle with salt and pepper. In a saucepan, heat the mushroom soup, then pour it over the fillets. Mix the cheese with the bread crumbs, sprinkle the mixture over the fish, then drizzle with olive oil. Bake in the center of the preheated oven for 10 minutes, until the top is nicely browned. Serve hot with vegetables and Italian bread.

Fish 'n' Eggs

This dish always brings back a lot of memories. I first cooked it about twenty years ago. At the time, my wife and I had three children to feed and not a whole lot of money to do it with. But we did have plenty of fish, and I fed them to my family in a variety of ways.

> 2 cups precooked fish flakes
> 6 chicken eggs
> 4 tablespoons butter
> 1 tablespoon chopped parsley
> 1 tablespoon chopped chives
> salt and pepper

Melt the butter in a skillet on medium heat, then sauté the fish flakes for 5 minutes. Beat the eggs slightly in a separate bowl, then pour into the skillet with the fish. Add the parsley, chives, salt, and pepper. Scramble until done. Serves 5 or 6.

Variations: Try adding a few chopped green onions, tops and all. Or add a cup or so of finely chopped ham and, instead of scrambling, cook the mixture like an omelet. A peeled and diced tomato also goes nicely in omelets.

SEVENTEEN

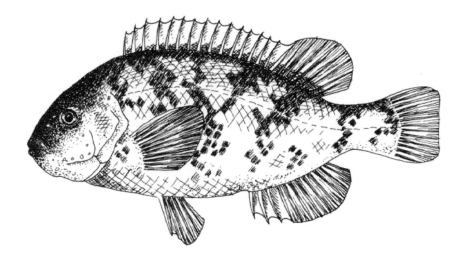

Tautogs, Cunners, and Other Wrasse

This family comprises some 450 species. Most of them live in tropical seas, but some do stray northward. As a group, the wrasse have heavy throat teeth, which they use to crush shellfish and other food. All of these fish make excellent eating—and all are bait stealers, making them difficult to hook. Here are the more common kinds caught in American waters.

Tautog, *Tautoga onitis.* This popular fish with a sort of pretty face is taken from Nova Scotia to South Carolina, being more common in midrange. It is often caught on rocky bottoms and

The tautog has a pretty face, for a fish. Like most of the wrasse, it makes excellent eating but has a reputation as a bait stealer.

mussel beds. Also called blackfish, it averages about 3 pounds, but does sometimes grow to 30. Its white meat makes excellent eating. The tautog is usually filleted and skinned.

Cunner, *Tautogolabrus adspersus.* These bait stealers can be caught inshore from Newfoundland south to the Chesapeake Bay. It's a small fish, growing to about 10 inches. It makes excellent eating, especially when pan-dressed and fried like small trout.

California sheepshead, *Pimelometopon pulchrum.* This wrasse is caught in Southern California. Growing up to 30 pounds, it has mild, firm, white flesh. It is usually filleted.

Hogfish, *Lachnolaimus maximus.* Also called hog snapper, this excellent fish ranges from Brazil to the Carolinas. It grows up to 40 pounds, averaging about 6. Be warned that the larger ones may be poisonous around Cuba and other parts of the Caribbean (see appendix B). On the other hand, they are touted as being the best tasting of the reef fish, having fine-grained white flesh.

Sandy's Surprise

I don't know who Sandy is, but I hereby thank him or her for this recipe, which I have adapted from Vic Dunaway's *From Hook to Table.* The original called for small fish fillets, and I think that cunners of average size (about 10 inches long) are ideal, if you don't mind the work of filleting.

  10 small cunner fillets
  1 pound bay scallops
  8 ounces sliced fresh mushrooms
  1 large tomato, chopped
  1 medium-to-large onion, chopped
  ½ red bell pepper, chopped
  ½ green bell pepper, chopped
  ¼ cup chopped celery
  8 ounces grated Swiss cheese
  8 ounces grated American cheese
  olive oil
  seasoned salt or lemon pepper

Preheat the oven to 400 degrees. Rub the fillets and lightly coat a shallow baking pan with olive oil. Spread the fillets and scallops to cover the baking pan evenly. Sprinkle with seasoned salt. Mix the onion, tomato, celery, bell peppers, and mushrooms, then spread the mixture evenly over the fish and scallops. Mix the cheeses and sprinkle over all. Bake for 10 minutes. Feeds 4 to 6.

Variations: Dunaway says that this recipe can be customized to your taste—or perhaps to available ingredients. Try other vegetables and deep-sea scallops. I also suggest trying frog legs (boned and chopped) or perhaps crawfish instead of scallops, if you've got them.

Tautog and Tomato Soup

Here's a great way to cook a 2-pound tautog, or some other good fish of about that size, or 2 pounds of smaller fish. Fillet the fish, retaining the head, fins, and bony parts. You'll need boneless and skinless fillets.

The Stock
fish head, fins, and bony parts
1 large chopped onion
2 ribs celery with leaves, chopped
2 bay leaves
2 teaspoons salt
½ teaspoon red pepper flakes
water to cover

Put the ingredients into a pot, cover with water, bring to a boil, reduce heat, cover tightly, and simmer for 1 hour or so. Strain out the broth and measure out 2 cups, adding water if you are a little short. Discard the remains, unless you want to gnaw on the head and backbone.

The Soup
fillets cut into 1-inch cubes (from 2 pounds
    undressed fish)
2 cups fish stock
2 cups tomato or V-8 juice
½ cup uncooked rice
¼ pound salt pork, diced
6 green onions with half of tops, chopped
1 tablespoon parsley
½ teaspoon dried oregano
salt
freshly ground black pepper

In a stove-top Dutch oven, cook the salt pork until the oil is fried out and the pieces are crisp. Remove and drain the salt pork pieces. Add the chopped green onions and parsley to the salt pork drippings, stirring for 4 or 5 minutes. Add the fish stock, bring almost to a boil, then add the rice and bring to a boil. Reduce the heat, cover tightly, and simmer for 20 minutes. Add the tomato juice, salt, and oregano. Then add the fish chunks and salt pork pieces, bring almost to a boil, reduce the heat, and simmer for 12 minutes. After adding the fish, do not stir the soup too vigorously, to avoid breaking up the chunks. Ladle the soup into bowls. Serve steaming hot, along with saltine crackers and freshly ground black pepper. It's best to have a pepper mill on the table, giving a twist or two to each serving.

Blackfish with Brown Gravy

This recipe can be made with fillets or steaks from larger fish. The measures below can be cooked in a large skillet with a tight lid. An electric skillet will do.

> 1 pound tautog fillets or steaks
> 2 large potatoes
> 1 large onion
> 2 tablespoons cooking oil (more if needed)
> 2 tablespoons flour
> water
> salt and pepper

Peel the potatoes and onion, then cut them into ½-inch slices. Heat the oil in the skillet and sauté the potatoes until done and lightly browned. Remove and drain on a brown bag. Sauté the onion slices for 5 or 6 minutes, or until lightly browned. Remove and drain. Stir the flour into the remaining oil in the skillet, adding a little more oil if necessary. Cook and stir for 15 minutes, or until the flour browns, stirring with a wooden spoon as you go. Slowly add water, still stirring, until you have a thin gravy. Add the potatoes and onions and increase the heat, bringing to a good bubble. Salt and pepper the fillets or steaks, then place them over the vegetables. Cover tightly and simmer for 15 minutes without stirring. Serve directly from the skillet, being careful not to break the fillets apart.

Hogfish Salad

I love a good fish salad, especially when I've got vine-ripened tomatoes and homemade mayonnaise. This salad can be made from flaked leftover fish, but it's better with freshly poached fish, preferably skinless fillets.

1 pound hogfish fillets
½ cup mayonnaise
½ cup finely chopped celery with part of tops
¼ cup finely chopped onion
¼ cup finely chopped red bell pepper
juice of ½ lemon
2 large tomatoes, sliced
lettuce
salt and white pepper

Poach the fillets for about 8 minutes. Chill, then cut into 1-inch chunks. Mix the mayonnaise, celery, onion, bell pepper, lemon juice, salt, and white pepper. Then mix in the fish chunks. Serve over lettuce leaves, flanked with tomato slices. Feeds 4 for a light lunch.

Baked Wrasse Fillets Paprika

Fillets from any good wrasse, such as the California sheepshead, can be used for this recipe.

2 pounds wrasse fillets
½ cup melted butter
juice of 2 lemons
1 tablespoon grated onion
½ tablespoon Hungarian paprika
1 teaspoon salt
½ teaspoon white pepper

Preheat the oven to 350 degrees. Grease a baking dish large enough to hold the fillets (about 12 by 8 by 2 will do). Arrange the fish in the dish skin side down. Mix the rest of the ingredients, spread evenly over the fish, and bake for 25 minutes, or until the fish flakes easily when tested with a fork. Feeds 4.

EIGHTEEN

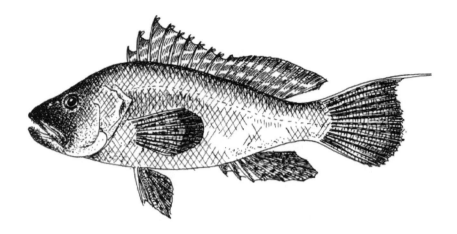

Ocean-Going Basses

Dozens of freshwater and saltwater fish are called bass, and some of the bass species are called something else. The good news is that all of these fish make excellent eating, and most of them have mild white flesh. Typically, the basses have big mouths and, in profile, resemble the snappers, groupers, and rockfish. Here are some American favorites.

Black sea bass, *Centropristis striata.* Ranging from Cape Cod to the Gulf of Mexico, this fish is plentiful and quite popular in the New York area, where they can be caught from docks, piers, or shore, as well as from boats, using artificial baits (usually jigs), clams, or other natural baits. The average catch is from 1 to

A number of saltwater fish are called bass, most with a head and mouth similar to those of freshwater bass. The popular black sea bass, shown here, is easily identified by a long ray on top of the tail.

3 pounds inshore, but they grow up to 5 pounds, with the larger ones usually taken by deep-sea fishers. The flesh is mild, white, and somewhat flaky. They are traditionally used to make sweet-and-sour bass by the Chinese in New York City (see the recipe below). This species is sometimes called blackfish, humpback, or black Will.

Wreckfish, *Polyprion americanum.* Also called wreck bass, stone bass, or wreck grouper, this ocean sea bass is caught on rocky bottoms and near barnacled pilings and shipwrecks. It grows to 100 pounds or better, but the average is about 15 pounds. Its mild, white flesh can be cooked by any method. Do not overcook. When grilling or broiling, baste frequently.

European bass, *Dicentrarchus labrax* (or *Morone labrax).* There is some disagreement among the experts about the scientific classification of this fish. Nonetheless, it is one of the most popular saltwater sport fish in Europe. The flesh is excellent. The American angler won't likely encounter this fish in home waters, but any of the European recipes for this bass can be used for other sea bass of appropriate size.

Giant sea bass, *Stereolepis gigas.* This large Pacific cousin of the jewfish is taken off the California and Mexican coasts and in the Indian Ocean. They can weigh well over 500 pounds. They have mild white meat, low in fat content. It is cooked like jewfish (chapter 9). In fact, *McClane's New Standard Fishing Encyclopedia and International Angling Guide* says they are the same fish, although the text places this fish in "southern Florida and throughout the tropical American Atlantic." Also, McClane's illustration of the jewfish has a rounded or convex tail, whereas the illustration in my 1989 edition of *World Record Game Fishes,* published by the International Game Fish Association, shows the giant sea bass to have a slightly concave tail. Livingston says don't worry about it; you've got a hell of a lot of good eating with either fish.

Striped bass, *Morone saxatilis.* This great anadromous gamefish (often called rockfish, rock bass, or simply rock) of the Atlantic coast has now been stocked successfully along the West Coast and in large inland lakes of mid-America. Growing to over 100 pounds, it has long had a reputation as prime table fare.

Although I feel that the fish is a little overrated, it has firm white flesh, and the smaller ones can be prepared by any method. The larger ones are best cooked in a chunky soup or chowder.

California kelp bass, *Paralabrax clathratus.* Usually called a rock bass, this small fish, seldom weighing more than 5 pounds, makes good eating and is one of the most popular fish with California inshore anglers. Two similar species, the **sand bass** *(Paralabrax nebulfier)* and **spotted bass** *(Paralabrax maculatoasciatus),* also make good eating. The smaller ones can be scaled and pan-dressed, but larger ones are usually filleted and skinned.

Here are some recipes that work especially well with bass, provided that the size is appropriate.

Sweet-and-Sour Sea Bass

For cooking this dish you'll need a fryer long enough to accommodate small whole bass of about 12 or 13 inches. The fryer should also be deep enough to hold sufficient oil to float the cooked fish and to fry at high heat safely. A large, patio-type oblong fryer, usually heated with H-shaped gas burners, is ideal. I also use an oblong fryer designed to work across two burners of my kitchen stove. It is necessary to have lots of oil in the container—at least enough to float the cooked fish—and to heat it to at least 375 degrees.

> 2 bass about 12 inches long
> 2 carrots, sliced
> ½ green bell pepper, sliced
> ½ red bell pepper, sliced
> 3 green onions with part of tops, chopped
> 2 slices canned pineapple
> ½ cup chicken stock
> ½ cup vinegar
> ½ cup sugar
> ½ cup flour
> 1 tablespoon cornstarch
> peanut oil (about 1 gallon for a large deep-fryer)
> salt and pepper to taste

When you dress the bass, scale and gut it, leaving the head, fins, and tail on. Rig for deep frying. While the oil is heating to at least 375 degrees, cut the pineapple slices into wedges. Mix the carrots, green onions, pineapple, sugar, vinegar, chicken stock, and a little salt in a saucepan. (Hold the peppers until later.) Bring the mixture to a boil, turn the heat to low, and simmer for 15 minutes. Then add the cornstarch, cooking and stirring until the sauce thickens. Keep the sauce warm.

Dry the dressed fish with a paper towel. Score the fish three times diagonally on each side, cutting at an angle so that you have flaps of flesh. Sprinkle the bass inside and out with salt and pepper, then roll it in flour to coat both sides. Lower the fish very carefully into the hot oil and fry until it is nicely browned; it will float to the top when it is done if you are using enough oil. Carefully remove the fish and drain it on brown paper.

Quickly heat the sauce almost to a boil. Add the peppers and cornstarch, stirring and cooking for 1 minute. Put the fish onto a separate plate or platter and pour the sauce over it. Serve hot with plenty of rice. This recipe will feed 2 people, and the sauce is intended to be spread evenly over the fish. If you have more people to serve, it's best to cook a fish for each person, and increase the measures accordingly. The Chinese often serve a larger fish in the middle of the table, and each person reaches out with chopsticks to get a bite. Most Americans, however, will do better with individual fish and a fork.

Note: This recipe was adapted from Jim Lee's *Chinese Cookbook,* and a longer version is given in my *Bass Cookbook,* about freshwater basses.

Sea Bass with Garlic

Here's an old fisherman's dish from the Mediterranean coast of Spain. Like so many other distinctive recipes, this one requires only a few ingredients. Don't be put off by the amount of garlic, unless you simply can't stand the stuff, in which case you probably wouldn't have gotten past the title of the recipe anyway. The trick to the recipe is to cook the garlic until it is burnt. It's best to cook the dish in a cast-iron skillet, large enough to hold the fillets in a single layer.

> 1 to 1½ pounds of sea bass fillets
> 20 large cloves garlic
> 1 large ripe tomato
> olive oil
> ½ teaspoon sea salt
> water

Peel the garlic cloves and slice them lengthwise thinly. Cut the tomato into wedges (unpeeled), remove the seeds, and finely chop. Heat the oil in the skillet, add the garlic, and stir with a wooden spatula for 10 to 15 minutes, or until the garlic has turned dark brown. Add the chopped tomatoes. Cook over low to medium heat, stirring with the wooden spatula, until you have a rather dry paste. Stir in 2 cups of water, bring to a boil, and cook until the sauce is reduced by half. Sprinkle the fillets with sea salt, then place them in the skillet. Do not overlap. On medium heat, cook the fish from 3 to 5 minutes on each side, turning only once, or until it flakes easily when tested with a fork. (As a general rule, cook for 10 minutes per pound of thickness.) Serve hot, spooning the sauce over each fillet. The sauce is also good over rice.

Bass Head and Oyster Soup

I found this recipe in J. George Frederick's *Long Island Seafood Cook Book* and I have used it to great advantage, in modified form. I cook it with Apalachicola oysters instead of the fat mollusks of Long Island Sound. Since the Apalachicola oyster tends to be small, I have doubled the measure. In Frederick's text, it isn't clear to me what he finally does with the fish heads or the meat, although he definitely strains the broth and uses it in the soup. Well, I say, don't throw out the heads. If you don't want 'em in your soup, at least flake the meat off the throats and cheeks and add it to the soup.

3 or 4 bass heads (from 2- or 3-pound fish)
water
1 cup milk
2 dozen oysters, and liquid from shells
1 medium onion, sliced
1 carrot, sliced
1 tablespoon fresh parsley, minced
1 tablespoon butter
1 tablespoon flour
6 peppercorns, ground
salt and pepper
mace

Wash the fish heads and shuck the oysters, saving all the liquid from the shells. Put ½ cup of oyster liquor aside and mix the rest (if any) with enough water to make 1½ quarts. Pour the liquid into a large pan, add the fish heads, carrots, onions, peppercorns, and a pinch of mace. Bring to a boil, reduce heat, cover, and simmer for 2 hours. Then remove the fish heads and drain. Strain the broth into another pot. Flake the meat off the fish heads and add it to the new broth. Add the butter, then add the milk. In a small saucepan, dissolve the flour into the reserved ½ cup of oyster liquor, then stir the resulting paste into the soup. Increase the heat and stir until the mixture boils. Add the parsley. Season to taste with salt and pepper. Add the oysters and simmer for 5 or 6 minutes. Serve with plenty of saltine crackers.

Note: This recipe makes a rather thin soup. If you want it thicker, add more flour paste. You can also add diced potatoes and call the dish a chowder.

Barbecued Striped Bass

Here's an easy recipe from Louisiana. You can use any good tomato-based barbecue sauce. For convenience, I usually keep a gallon of Cattleman's brand in my refrigerator (it's cheaper by the gallon). If you have your own favorite homemade sauce, use it.

2 or 3 pounds striper fillets
2 cups Cattleman's barbecue sauce
1 package potato chips, crushed
salt and pepper

Preheat the oven to 350 degrees and grease a large, shallow baking dish. Salt and pepper the fillets, then cut them into bite-size chunks. Dip the chunks in the barbecue sauce, then roll them in crushed potato chips. (The chips crush easily with a rolling pin.) Place the chunks in the baking dish. The chunks should not touch. Bake in the center of the oven for 25 minutes, or until the chips are nicely browned. Serve with Boston baked beans, crusty loaf bread, and iced tea.

Surfside Stripers

Here's an easy recipe for cooking freshly caught saltwater fish beside the sea. Although striped bass are specified, any good fresh fish can be used, and the recipe is especially appropriate for fish of medium fat content.

freshly caught striped bass
cheesecloth
seawater
butter (optional)
pepper (optional)
lemon (optional)

Scale and draw the fish, leaving the head on. Cut a piece of cheesecloth about twice as long as the fish. Wrap each fish. Bring a large container of seawater to a light boil in a suitable container; the oblong fish cookers on double-burner outdoor stoves are ideal. Lower the fish into the water, using the ends of the cheesecloth as handles. Poach the fish for about 10 minutes per inch of thickness, or until the flesh flakes easily when tested with a fork. Remove the fish, unwrap them, and serve them with butter, black pepper, and lemon wedges.

Istanbul Steaks

The Turks, justly famous for their charcoal-grilled kabobs, knew a thing or two about cooking fish by less harsh methods. This recipe is usually made from rather large fish, say 10 pounds or better. Although the list of ingredients calls for 2 pounds of steaks, a greater or smaller amount can be used. I allow at least ½ pound of fillet per person—and want a little more for myself, if there's plenty to go around. The thickness of the steaks is really more important in this recipe than the exact number of pounds to be cooked.

1½ to 2 pounds bass steaks, cut 1 inch thick
1 large onion, minced
juice of 2 lemons
½ cup red wine
½ cup vinegar
½ cup water or Fish Stock (chapter 27)
¼ cup English walnuts, ground
¼ cup white raisins
1 teaspoon salt
½ teaspoon freshly ground black pepper

Put the steaks into a nonmetallic container and sprinkle them with a little salt and the chopped onion. Pour the vinegar over the steaks and marinate for 2 hours at room temperature, turning from time to time. Then put the pieces into a large saucepan or electric skillet and pour in the fish stock or water. Bring to a boil, reduce the heat, and simmer for 10 minutes. (The general rule is to simmer 10 minutes for each inch of thickness. Thus, thinner steaks should be simmered for a shorter period; thicker ones, longer.) Carefully remove the fish steaks and put them onto a heated serving platter. Quickly add the other ingredients to the stock. Stir and simmer until the sauce thickens a little. Pour the sauce over the fish, and garnish with lemon slices and fresh parsley. Serve with rice pilaf, fresh sliced tomatoes, and fried eggplant.

A. D.'s Leftover Striper

I usually like this dish the day after cooking a whole striper of 7 or 8 pounds, but it can be used with almost any cooked fish. It's a little better to use chunks of fish rather than flakes, but either will work.

> 1½ to 2 cups cooked fish chunks
> 1 cup uncooked long-grain rice
> 1 can tomatoes (16-ounce size)
> 1 medium onion, finely chopped
> 4 cups water or Fish Stock (chapter 27)
> 1 tablespoon dry parsley
> ½ teaspoon dry basil
> salt and pepper

Bring the water or fish stock to a boil, then add the rice, onion, parsley, basil, salt, and pepper. Simmer on low heat for 20 minutes. Add the fish chunks and the tomatoes, along with the juice from the can. If you wish, cut the tomatoes into pieces. I prefer the dish on the soupy side, so adjust the water or fish according to taste. Serve hot in bowls, along with crackers.

NINETEEN

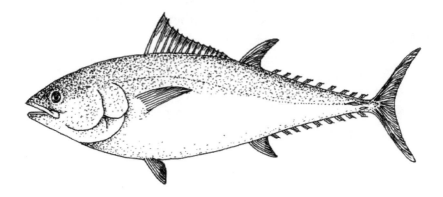

Tunas

Owing largely to the increased popularity of grilled fish and sashimi, fresh tuna has become an important American market fish in recent years. Tunas tend to be bloody fish, especially the bonito, and should be bled, drawn, and iced as soon as possible after being boated. Americans have tended to judge the quality of tuna by the color of the meat—the lighter the better. In some other parts of the world, however, the darkest tunas are prized, and these are gaining favor with the grilled meat set in America.

Here are some species that can be caught in our waters.

Albacore, *Thunnus alalunga.* Also called longfin tuna, the albacore is found in the tropical and temperate waters of both the Atlantic and Pacific. It is especially important as a gamefish

Most of the tunas have a shape similar to the bluefin, above. The finlets between the dorsal fins and the tail are characteristic of the family.

during runs along the West Coast. The albacore is highly prized as table fare and has white flesh. It grows to over 50 pounds but is usually much smaller.

Blackfin tuna, *Thunnus atlanticus.* This relatively small tuna, usually weighing less than 10 pounds, ranges from Cape Cod to Brazil. It makes excellent eating, and grilled steaks taste somewhat like mild beef.

Bluefin tuna, *Thunnus thynnus.* This great gamefish, often the target of fishing tournaments, can weigh 1,000 pounds or better. It is caught in all subtropical and temperate seas, as far north as Newfoundland. This species has rather dark meat, which has long been appreciated in the Orient and is now becoming popular in American restaurants. It is often grilled.

Atlantic bonito, *Sarda sarda,* and **Pacific** or **California bonito,** *Sarda chilensis.* These fish are not highly esteemed in the United States, partly because they are so bloody. But they can be very good if they are drawn and iced immediately after the catch. These are relatively small tunas, seldom weighing more than 10 pounds.

Little tuna, *Euthynnus alletteratus,* and related species. These small tunas, sometimes called little tunny, are often abundant in inshore waters and are frequently taken by sport fishermen. They seldom weigh more than 10 pounds and have dark meat.

Skipjack tuna, *Katsuwonus pelamis.* This fish, weighing up to 30 pounds, is found in all tropical and subtropical seas. The skipjack tunas form large schools—up to 50,000 fish—and are important commercially.

Yellowfin tuna, *Thunnus albacares.* Found in all tropical and subtropical seas, this fish, which can weigh as much as 400 pounds, sometimes follows the Gulf Stream as far north as New Jersey. It has a light-colored flesh and is an important commercial species that is served in many restaurants. It is also popular as sushi and sashimi.

Most of the recipes given here work with fresh tuna. I am also including instructions for canning tuna because the successful angler will likely have a surplus of meat. Properly frozen tuna will keep for 2 or 3 months, however.

Tuna Teriyaki

This dish can be cooked on any grill, but I prefer to cook it over charcoal or, better, over coals from hardwoods such as oak or hickory. It's best to have very fresh tuna steaks, ¾ to 1 inch thick. I allow ½ pound per person, but smaller portions are usually served.

> 2 pounds tuna steaks
> 1 cup soy sauce
> ½ cup sake, dry vermouth, or sherry
> juice of 3 lemons
> 3 green onions with tops, finely chopped
> 3 cloves garlic, minced
> 1 inch fresh ginger root, grated
> ½ tablespoon brown sugar

Dissolve the sugar in the soy sauce and sake, then add the ginger, green onions, garlic, and lemon juice. Place the tuna steaks in a nonmetallic container, pour in the liquid, toss to coat all sides, and refrigerate for 3 or 4 hours.

When you are ready to cook, build a good fire and let it burn down to coals. Position a rack about 4 inches over the coals. Drain the fish. Put the marinade into a saucepan and bring to almost a boil, stirring a time or two. Place the steaks on the rack. Grill for 4 or 5 minutes, basting once. Turn, baste, and grill for another 4 or 5 minutes, or until the fish is medium rare or done to your liking. Do not overcook. Baste on both sides and serve hot with rice, oriental vegetables, and sourdough garlic bread.

Japanese Tuna

The Japanese are notorious for eating raw seafood. The preparation of modern sushi and sashimi, as practiced by restaurant and specialty bars, is a little too ritualistic to be detailed here. Instead, I offer an easy raw fish recipe, which I have adapted from J. George Frederick's *Long Island Seafood Cook Book*. Frederick said to cut the tuna ½ inch thick, but I find that thinner slices work better for people who may be squeamish about eating raw fish. It's best to slice the meat when it is partly frozen.

½ pound tuna steak, thinly sliced
½ cup soy sauce
1 tablespoon freshly grated horseradish
crushed sea salt

Rub some salt into the tuna steak, then let stand for 5 minutes. Cut the tuna into thin slices. Mix the soy sauce and horseradish in a small bowl. To eat, dip the tuna pieces into the sauce with the aid of a toothpick, fork, or chopsticks.

Canned Tuna

This procedure for canning tuna has been adapted from *Recipes with a New Catch*, published by the UNC Sea Grant College Program. Steps 2 and 3 can be omitted but will result in an oilier and stronger-tasting fish.

1. Wash the tuna and cut it into portions that will fit into a pressure cooker.

2. Cook the tuna at 10 pounds of pressure for 2 hours. This precooking helps remove excess oils, thus preventing a strong flavor.

3. Cool the pressure-cooked tuna in the refrigerator for several hours or, if possible, overnight. Proper cooling is essential for firm texture and good flavor.

4. When the fish has been properly cooled, scrape away the skin, remove the backbone, and cut away any streaks of dark meat. Flake into chunks for canning.

5. Pack the chunks into half-pint jars with 4 tablespoons of oil or water, or equal parts of each, and ½ teaspoon salt. Leave 1 inch head space and seal the jars loosely.

6. Process the jars for 80 minutes at 15 pounds pressure.

7. Remove the jars and tighten the tops immediately.

Store the jars until needed. Although this canning procedure should be safe, the UNC Sea Grant recommends that home-canned tuna be thoroughly cooked before eating. I agree.

Poached Tuna

Poached fresh tuna can be served hot or chilled or, better, cut into chunks and used in a salad. Poaching is easy. Fillet the tuna, remove the skin, and cut into pieces small enough to fit your pot and about 1 inch thick.

> 1 to 2 pounds fresh tuna
> 1 quart water
> ½ cup vinegar
> 1 carrot, chopped
> 1 rib celery with tops, chopped
> 1 medium onion, quartered
> 4 cloves
> 2 bay leaves
> salt

In a boiler large enough to hold everything, mix all the ingredients except the tuna. Bring to a boil, then add the tuna. Bring to a new boil, reduce the heat, cover, and simmer for 15 minutes. Carefully remove the tuna pieces. Serve hot with a sauce, steamed vegetables or salad, and bread, or chill for later use, perhaps with the following recipe.

Tuna Salad

Freshly poached tuna makes a very good salad. Use your favorite recipe, or try this one. I like to use the small inner ribs of celery, along with part of the leafy tops.

>1 cup flaked poached tuna
>½ cup diced celery with part of tops
>1 tablespoon chopped red bell pepper
>1 tablespoon chopped fresh chives
>1 tablespoon chopped fresh parsley
>mayonnaise
>salt
>lettuce

Mix the celery, chives, bell pepper, parsley, salt, and mayonnaise to taste. Stir in the tuna and chill. Serve cold over lettuce leaves.

TWENTY

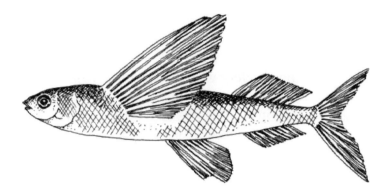

Flying Fish and Other Seabirds

I don't have much preamble for this chapter, but I am sure that some people will be inclined to question whether some of the entries are really birds. Instead of defending my choices, I'll point out that I have left out some notable seabirds and some that claim to be birds but aren't. The famous bombay duck isn't a bird at all; it's a lizard fish caught in the estuary of the Ganges. Also, the great roosterfish is really a jack, covered in chapter 11.

One great seabird, the mullet, has been given a separate chapter. That the mullet is a bird was proven beyond a shadow of a doubt in a court of law in Florida. A fisherman was being tried

Flying fish are delicacies in the Caribbean.

for taking mullet out of season. A slick lawyer successfully argued that the mullet has a gizzard; only birds have gizzards; and, therefore, the mullet is a bird and as such cannot be regulated by the fishing season. I rest my case.

FLYING FISH

A number of species of flying fish (family Exocoetidae) live in the Caribbean and other warm-water seas. Usually, these fish stay in the open water and feed around patches of seaweed. Consequently, they are not often caught by anglers who stay on shore or near land. Nor are they taken by deep-sea bottom fishermen. Because the fish feed on tiny crustaceans found in the seaweed (especially sargassum), the flying fish can be taken by seagoing fly rodders who have successfully matched the briny hatch.

Actually, the flying fish doesn't fly. It can, however, glide for a considerable distance, depending, partly, on its size. (Flying fish grow up to 18 inches, about the length of a pheasant.) The ability to glide no doubt grew from the need to escape from larger dolphins and other fish-eating predators that also feed along the edges of floating seaweed masses. The fish jumps out of the water to escape the charging predator, then sticks out its winglike pectoral fins. Once airborne, the larger specimens can glide as much as 1,000 feet.

The flying fish may also jump and glide just for the hell of it, and there is some evidence that they are attracted to lights above the surface at night. It is a fact that they often fall onto ship decks at night and have even been known to glide into open portholes. Of course, this habit has caused resourceful fishermen to rig lanterns or electric lights over nets at night, thereby catching flying fish, which are delicious table fare, for the market or for their own use. (Anyone who considers fishing in this manner should be warned that large needlefish also jump into and over lighted boats at night, like javelins, so the fisherman might well become the victim. On the other hand, a big needlefish is also a worthy catch from a culinary viewpoint, if you aren't put off by the green bones.) Some skeptics, however, believe that the flying fish aren't really attracted to the light but are merely blinded by it and therefore lose the sense of which way to glide in order to avoid obstacles in the air.

Flying fish have also been occasional targets of bow-and-arrow fishermen and have more frequently been bagged by wing shooters armed with shotguns. In truth, however, this form of wing shooting far at sea is usually enjoyed only by skeet fans aboard yachts. Unfortunately, this sport has not yet developed to the point where trained dolphins are used to flush the flying fish out of the water for the wing shooter's benefit!

In any case, the flying fish is one of the tastiest creatures of the ocean. It is ideal when filleted and fried, perhaps first smeared with a little Jamaican jerk rub. Also try the following island recipe.

Flying Fish Pie

The flying fish is quite popular in the Caribbean, and it is cooked in a number of ways. Here's something special from Barbados, which I have adapted from *The Complete Book of Caribbean Cooking*, by Elisabeth Lambert Ortiz.

The Filling
1½ pounds flying fish fillets
2 pounds yams or sweet potatoes
1 large onion, thinly sliced
1 large tomato, peeled and thinly sliced
2 hard-boiled chicken eggs, sliced
4 tablespoons butter, divided
salt and freshly ground pepper
salted water

The Sauce
2 chicken egg yolks
2 tablespoons vegetable oil
2 tablespoons melted butter
½ cup dry sherry
1 tablespoon Worcestershire sauce

Peel the yams, boil them in salted water until they are tender, cool, and slice them thinly. Preheat the oven to 350 degrees. Heat 2 tablespoons butter in a skillet. Sprinkle the fillets with salt and pepper, then sauté them for 2 or 3 minutes on each side, turning carefully with a spatula. Cut the fillets in half crosswise. Grease a deep baking dish that is suitable for serving. Place half of the fillets on the bottom, cover with layers of half the onion, half the tomato, half the sliced egg, half the yams, in that order. Repeat the layers, ending with the yams, and then drizzle on the rest of the butter.

To make the sauce, whisk the egg yolks, then mix in the oil, melted butter, Worcestershire sauce, and sherry. Mix well, then pour the sauce over the pie filling. Place the baking dish in the center of the preheated oven. Bake for 30 minutes, or until the top is golden brown. Feeds 4 or 5.

Note: If you use sweet potatoes, bake them in the oven until they are done, let them cool, peel and slice them, sauté in butter until lightly browned on both sides, and use in layers as directed above.

GOOSEFISH

The goosefish *(Lophius americanus)* is also called monkfish, bellyfish, frogfish, or sea devil. The last part of the scientific name, *americanus,* is difficult for me to understand, because this species is not often eaten in America, although it is highly prized in Europe. These big-headed, many-toothed fish are also called anglerfish because they use a flap of skin on their long, flexible dorsal spines as a fishing lure.

In the Western Atlantic, the goosefish can be caught from Newfoundland to North Carolina. It doesn't have much meat for its size (up to 50 pounds), but what's there is very good. The fish should be skinned and filleted. If you've got a big goosefish, be sure to cut out the cheeks from the sides of the head. They're gourmet fare.

A. D.'s Skillet Goosefish

Here's a good recipe to use whenever you suspect that your guests might not approve of your offering. It makes lots of gravy for serving over rice.

1 pound goosefish fillets
1 can mushroom soup (12¾-ounce size)
1 large onion, sliced
1 large tomato, sliced
1 cup water
¼ cup chopped fresh parsley
2 tablespoons butter
salt and pepper to taste
rice (cooked separately)

Melt the butter in a large skillet. Sauté the onions on medium-high heat until browned. Mix the water into the soup, then add the mixture to the skillet, stirring about. Add the tomato slices, parsley, and fish fillets, along with some salt and pepper. Bring to a light bubble, reduce heat, and simmer for about 10 minutes, or until the fish flakes easily when tested with a fork. Serve the fillets and gravy hot with lots of rice, French-cut green beans, and crusty bread.

Catalanian Goosefish with Almonds

Here's a dish from the Mediterranean coast of Spain, where the goosefish or monkfish grows. The recipe has been adapted from *The Catalan Country Kitchen,* by Marimar Torres. The recipe calls for fish stock (see chapter 27), which is a standard ingredient in some Old World cuisines. It can be made from the goosefish head and bony parts. See the poaching section of appendix A for instructions. Be warned that saffron is expensive stuff.

2 pounds goosefish fillets
¾ cup toasted whole almonds
¼ cup toasted sliced almonds
½ cup dry white wine
½ cup Fish Stock (chapter 27)
3 large red bell peppers, cut into strips
3 large cloves garlic, minced
2 tablespoons olive oil
½ teaspoon salt
½ teaspoon white pepper
½ teaspoon saffron threads

Preheat the oven to 350 degrees. Place the goosefish fillets into a well-greased pan, bake for 15 minutes, cut into medallions, and set aside, reserving the juices in the baking pan.

Heat the olive oil in a skillet. Sauté the garlic and peppers over low heat for 20 minutes. Grind the whole almonds in a food mill, then add them to the skillet, along with the wine, stock, pan juices, salt, pepper, and saffron. Cook over medium heat for 5 minutes. Puree the skillet contents in a food processor, then return it to the skillet. Add the fish medallions, heat through, sprinkle the sliced almonds on top, and serve hot.

PARROTFISH

Several species of many-colored parrotfish can be caught in the Western Atlantic. Perhaps the **queen parrotfish** *(Scarus vetula)* is the best known, found in the Caribbean and Florida waters. Excellent eating, the parrotfish is said to taste like lobster when poached. Try it—but be warned that the innards of parrotfish may be poisonous.

SEA SQUABS

Fillets of puffers or blowfish are often sold as sea squab or sea chicken, partly because of the texture and flavor of the meat, although some people will argue that the flavor is more like frog legs, and partly because the backstrap, when crisply fried, resembles a drumstick. Because the innards of some of the puffers are deadly poisonous, great care should be taken not to rupture any of the innards when skinning and dressing the fish. I have read that the skin and the roe, as well as the other innards, are poisonous.

Also known as blowfish, swellfish, or globefish, all of the puffers can inflate themselves with either water or air when alarmed. These fish come in several species, three of which are found in the Atlantic. The **southern puffer** *(Sphaeroides nephelus)* grows to about 14 inches in length. It lives off southern Florida and throughout the Gulf of Mexico. It is often toxic and should not be kept for food, as the poison is usually fatal. The **smooth puffer** *(Lagocephalus laevigatus),* also known as rabbitfish, ranges in the Atlantic from Cape Cod to Argentina. The tail is considered a delicacy, but the innards may be poisonous. It grows to 7 pounds. The **northern puffer** *(Sphaeroides maculatus)* ranges from Florida to Cape Cod. It grows to about 14 inches in length. It is probably safe to eat, provided that it is skinned and dressed properly.

The **porcupinefish** *(Diodon hystrix),* sometimes called spiny puffer, is similar to a puffer in that it puffs up when alarmed. This strange fish has sharp spines that stick out when it is inflated, which make it difficult to handle and dress. The porcupinefish is, however, very good eating—but, again, the innards have been reported to be poisonous.

Other species of puffers live in temperate and tropical waters. In Japan, the famous *fugu* is prepared, by trained chefs, from puffers, and at one time the Japanese used puffer innards to commit suicide. In Hawaii, the word for puffer is maki-maki—deadly death.

The bottom line is that all the puffers may be poisonous to a degree, from harmless to deadly. According to A. J. McClane, fishing authority, an old Japanese folk song goes, "I want to eat fugu, but I don't want to die." I feel the same way. I will eat northern puffers if I catch and clean them, but I'll have to pass on the rest.

166

Sea Squab Sesame

I recommend olive oil in the ingredients below, but you can substitute peanut oil or other cooking oil. If you try the olive oil, remember that it is cheaper by the gallon.

> 2 pounds skinless puffer fillets
> juice of 3 lemons
> olive oil
> flour
> ¾ cup sesame seeds
> salt and pepper

Pour ½ inch of olive oil into your skillet and turn the heat to medium-high. When the oil is hot, salt and pepper the fillets and shake them in a bag with flour. Shake off the excess flour, then dip the fillets in the lemon juice, roll them in the sesame seeds, and fry in the hot olive oil for a few minutes, or until nicely browned, turning once. Drain on a brown bag. Serve hot. Allow ½ pound of fillets per person, more or less.

Before eating a puffer, read the comments above and make sure you know what you are doing.

SEA ROBINS

Several species of these small fish are caught, in season, along the Atlantic coast. Being bottom feeders, they are often caught by anglers fishing for other species. Shrimp and cut fish make good bait. Although one government publication said that "relatively small" 6/0 and 8/0 hooks work best, you'll do a thousand times better with a size 2 or 4, I say. The sea robins are seasonal fish, staying in deep water during winter and shallow during summer. One of the more common sea robins, *Prionotus carolinus,* ranges from Nova Scotia to the Georgia islands. The larger sea robins grow up to 16 inches long, but many are much smaller. Because of the large head and fins, fillets tend to be small compared with the overall weight of the fish; a 1-pound fish might yield ¼ pound of fillets. All of the sea robins are excellent eating, although some anglers believe them to be poisonous. Others hold these fish to be far too ugly for table fare.

The sea robin has a large, bony head, complete with spines, and large fins and tail. The large pectoral fins resemble wings, and that's where the name sea robin comes from. Although the fish will sometimes swim toward the surface and glide back down, apparently for the fun of it, they are not flying fish. Instead, the "wings" are used to stir up the bottom mud as the fish feed.

The same government publication that recommended size 6/0 or 8/0 hooks said that sea robins are called grondin in Europe and are a key ingredient in the classic French bouillabaisse. The French, however, are a little fussy about what is or isn't a classic bouillabaisse. I can only hope that the following won't strain our diplomatic relations.

East Coast Bouillabaisse

This recipe calls for several kinds of shellfish, and the exact selection should depend on what you have available. I recommend the following mix, however, if convenient.

1½ pounds sea robin fillets
½ pound eel, skinned and cut into 2-inch segments
12 large shrimp or freshwater crawfish
12 fresh mussels (in the shell)
12 fresh clams (in the shell)
crab legs or stone crab claws, cracked
2 large vine-ripened tomatoes
1 large onion, chopped
1 leek, chopped with part of top
4 cloves garlic, minced
¼ cup chopped fresh parsley
1 quart Fish Stock (see chapter 27) or water
1 cup white wine
½ cup olive oil
2 bay leaves
salt and pepper
paprika
saffron (if you can afford it)
hot French bread, the chewy kind

Heat the oil in a large pot, then sauté the onion, leek, tomatoes, and garlic for 5 minutes. Add the fish stock and parsley. Bring to a boil. Then add the eel, clams, mussels, and crab claws or legs. Simmer for 5 minutes, then add the crawfish. Simmer for another for 5 minutes, then add the sea robin fillets, wine, bay leaves, salt, pepper, paprika, and saffron. Simmer for 5 minutes. Serve hot in large, wide bowls. Have ready plenty of hot French bread for dunking into the bouillabaisse. Feeds 4 to 6.

TWENTY-ONE

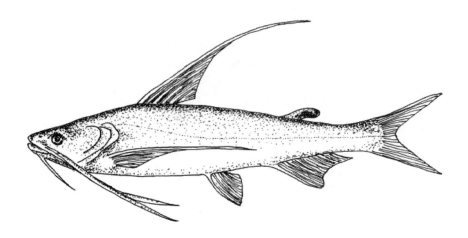

Catfish and Eels

CATFISH

The largest cats, weighing up to 400 pounds, are taken from fresh water in the Amazon Basin, Eastern European rivers, and Asia. Only two of the dozens of species of catfish are commonly caught in our salt water, and both of these are taken on the East Coast or in the Gulf of Mexico. Both species have unusual breeding habits. The male fish carries the fertilized eggs in his mouth, and continues to carry the young fish for two or three weeks after they hatch.

The **gaff-topsail catfish** *(Bagre marinus),* as the name implies, has a long dorsal fin that resembles a sail. It grows to 5 or 6 pounds,

Despite its slimy skin, the gaff-topsail catfish makes very good eating.

ranging from Cape Cod south and throughout the Gulf of Mexico. It makes excellent eating and will hit jigs or plugs. It is often taken in brackish water and will sometimes run up rivers. In fact, a river rat of my acquaintance, who runs trotlines (baited with crawfish) more or less commercially, often catches them on low water in the Apalachicola River, calling them sailcats. Because his customers won't eat them (if they know what they are), he considers them nuisances—along with eels, skates, and rays. Nevertheless, these catfish are excellent eating. They do, however, have a rather slimy skin.

The **sea catfish** *(Arius felis)*, sometimes called hardhead, has the same general range as the gaff-topsail. It does, however, prefer salty water and is seldom caught in brackish bays or tidal rivers. It has a bad reputation as table fare, but it is edible and may well be as good as any catfish if properly handled and cooked—and is surely better than those farm-raised catfish that are so highly touted. The hardhead grows to 3 pounds.

Both the gaff-topsail and the hardhead have sharp spines at the dorsal and pectoral fins. Through a complicated defense mechanism, these spines can release a poison into your flesh. Although the poison is not fatal to humans, it can cause a painful wound.

Saltwater cats similar to the gaff-topsail and the hardhead live in the Pacific, but generally in tropical waters. Other catfish, however, may sometimes be caught along with the gaff-topsail. In fact, Texas lists the blue cat in saltwater records, with the saltwater record coming from Galveston Bay.

In any case, here are some recipes for catfish.

Catfish Amandine

This is an easy dish to prepare, if your fillets fit nicely into the pan. I use a large, round (13-inch) skillet and 4 fillets of about ½ pound each. A square electric skillet might hold the fish a little better. In addition to the skillet, you'll also need a heated serving platter large enough to hold the fish. The suggested cooking times are for ½-pound fillets; larger, thicker fillets may require further cooking.

4 catfish fillets, ¼ to ½ pound each
½ cup olive oil
½ cup butter (real butter, not margarine)
½ cup flour
¼ cup white wine
1 small package sliced almonds
juice of 1 lemon
1 teaspoon white wine Worcestershire sauce
salt and pepper
lemon wedges (garnish)
fresh parsley (garnish)

Heat the olive oil in the skillet. Salt and pepper the fillets, then shake them in a bag with the flour. Sauté on medium heat for about 5 minutes on each side. When the fillets are nicely browned and done, carefully put them onto a heated serving platter. Pour off the olive oil, add the butter, and heat it until it begins to brown. Quickly stir in the lemon juice, wine, and white wine Worcestershire sauce. Add the almonds. Stir and cook for a minute or two, until the almonds brown lightly. Remove the skillet from the heat and spoon the almond sauce over the fillets. Garnish with lemon wedges and fresh parsley. Serve with rice pilaf and vegetables. Feeds 2 to 4.

Cayenne Catfish

My good ol' boy buddies really like fried catfish fillets seasoned with cayenne. If you crave hot stuff, increase the measure of cayenne. If you or your guests don't care for it, reduce the measure. Or, better, fry two batches—one hot and one mild.

2 pounds catfish fillets
2 cups stone-ground fine white cornmeal
2 tablespoons cayenne pepper
oil for skillet frying
salt

Mix the cornmeal and cayenne in a bag. Heat about ½ or ⅝ inch of oil in the skillet, depending on the thickness of the fillets. (The oil should almost cover the fillets, but not quite.) Salt the fillets and shake them in the cornmeal. When the oil is very hot—almost to the smoking point—fry the fillets, a few at a time, until browned on both sides, turning once. Do not overcook. Drain well on a brown bag. Serve hot with hush puppies, french fries, and green salad.

Variation: I served up the last batch of catfish I cooked with heated canned hominy topped with mild salsa. The meal was delicious and lower in fat. Also see the next recipe.

Texas Cats

Cook this easy but very tasty recipe with the aid of commercial picante sauce, which can be mild, medium, or hot. This sauce is available in most supermarkets. It's best to have a wide skillet so that all the fillets fit without overlapping. Although I like cast iron, large electric skillets will work.

> 1 to 2 pounds catfish fillets
> 1 jar picante sauce (26-ounce size)
> ¼ cup peanut oil
> salt
> rice (cooked separately)

Salt the fillets. Heat the oil very hot, just short of smoking, and cook the fillets for 2 minutes. Turn and cook for another 2 minutes. Add the picante sauce and simmer for 6 minutes. Allow ½ pound of fillets for each person. (I can eat a little more.) Serve over rice.

Pine Bark Stew

I've seen several recipes called pine bark stew, although I have never figured out why. I suspect that the dish is from North Carolina—Tarheel country—and that the original called for catfish. Further, I suspect that the pine bark was used as a sort of shallow

173

bowl or curved plate to hold the stew for eating. In any case, the last version I saw called for skinless sea trout (weakfish). I'm going back to catfish, the salt water kind, preferably fillets of the gaff-topsail.

> 2 pounds catfish fillets
> ¼ pound salt pork, diced
> 1 can tomatoes (16-ounce size), chopped,
>   along with the juice
> 1 large potato, diced
> 1 medium onion, diced
> 2 pods dried red pepper, whole
> salt to taste
> boiling water

Finely dice the salt pork, then cook it in a stove-top cast-iron Dutch oven until the pieces are crispy and most of the oil has cooked out. Add the onions, sautéing for 4 or 5 minutes, stirring as you go. Add the diced potatoes, then cover them with boiling water. Add the salt and red pepper. Simmer for 10 minutes. While waiting, cut the fish fillets into 1-inch pieces. Add the fish, simmer for 10 minutes, and carefully stir in the diced tomatoes, along with the juice from the can. Remove the pot from the heat and let it set for a few minutes. Serve the stew hot in bowls—or on pine bark—along with crackers or hot bread.

Neapolitan Catfish

Here's a dish I adapted from Vic Dunaway's *From Hook to Table*. It will work with whole fish or fillets. The directions apply to fish of about ¾ to 1 pound when dressed. Larger fish will require an increase in baking time.

3 pounds dressed catfish
1 large can tomato sauce (15-ounce size)
1 cup grated Parmesan cheese
3 cloves garlic, minced
1 tablespoon olive oil
1 tablespoon chopped fresh basil
½ teaspoon sugar
salt and pepper

Preheat the oven to 350 degrees. Grease a baking pan of suitable size to hold the fish without overlapping. Sprinkle the fish with salt and pepper, arrange in the pan, and bake for about 30 minutes, or until the fish flakes easily when tested with a fork. Meanwhile, heat the olive oil in a skillet, simmer the garlic for a few minutes, and add the tomato sauce, sugar, and basil. Simmer for 5 minutes. Spoon the sauce evenly over the fish, sprinkle with Parmesan cheese, and bake for an additional 5 minutes. Serve hot. Feeds 4 to 6.

EELS

Several species of eels spend all or part of their lives in salt and brackish water. The **American eel** *(Anguilla rostrata)* is perhaps the most widely know in culinary circles, along with the **European eel** *(Anguilla vulgaris)*. The young of both species are born in the Sargasso Sea in the Atlantic Ocean, then make their way to the rivers of North America or Europe, depending on the species.

The **conger eel** *(Conger oceanicus)* is often caught at night in eel pots and crab traps. It is a smaller cousin to the European conger *(Conger conger)*, an important food fish in Europe. The smaller American variety, sometimes called sea eel or silver eel, was once marketed on the East Coast. They are best when smoked or stewed. The European species is often used in bouillabaisse.

The **spotted cust-eel** *(Otophidium taylori)* can be caught on the Pacific coast. Although usually small, it grows to a length of 5 feet. Cust-eels are very important in the seafood cookery of South America, where they are called *congrios,* and they are the most highly prized seafood of Chile and Peru.

Although often called moray eels, the **morays** (family Muraenidae) aren't true eels, but they are close enough to be included in this chapter. There are more than one hundred species, all with thick, scaleless skin and bad teeth. The spotted moray is marketed in the West Indies; reportedly its meat is white and has a pleasant taste. It is often smoked, but be warned that these fish can carry ciguatera poisoning if caught from warm coral reef waters.

The **sea lamprey** *(Petromyzon marinus)* isn't an eel either, but it can be cooked in the same ways. It is considered a delicacy in parts of Europe and can be taken in American waters from Maine to Florida.

When preparing eels for cooking, remember that the skin is quite slippery. Some people grasp them with a dry cloth or sheet of paper, and others put them in salt to deslime them. They are usually skinned, which is easy if you secure the head, cut a circle around the fish, grasp the skin with pliers, and pull straight back. Eels are often cut into lengths for cooking, but they can also be filleted.

The flesh of most eels is quite oily and does not lend itself well to frying. Granted, they are often fried, but that's simply not the best way to go. If you do fry, fillet the eel and cook it a little longer than usual. The eel is perhaps at its best when hot-smoked between 165 and 180 degrees for 4 hours, more or less, depending on size.

Here are some recipes to try.

Japanese Grilled Eel

Most of the oriental peoples love eel, and the Japanese marinate them in a mixture of soy sauce and sake. After marinating, the eels can be broiled or even sautéed quickly on a griddle. But cooking them over hot coals is the best way to go. The Japanese celebrate the hottest day of the year with grilled eel. According to Waverley Root, author of *Food*, the politicians have themselves photographed at the eel feast, much like American politicians at a Texas barbecue; also according to Root, the Japanese consume 865 tons of eel on that single day! So, if you get tired of barbecued pork or beef on July 4, try the following recipe:

eels
soy sauce
sake, sherry, or dry vermouth
butter
brown sugar

The eels can be cut into segments and broiled, or they can be skinned and filleted. The pieces are merely arranged on the grill. The fillets, after marinating, can be threaded onto skewers, ribbon fashion. My choice often depends on the size of the eels and who will be eating them. I can stomach one whole, even when it is shaped like an S or an L, but other people may be a little finicky about eating anything that suggests a snake.

In any case, dress the eel while it is very fresh. Mix a marinade with equal parts of soy sauce and sake. Put the eels into a non-metallic container and pour in the marinade. It is not necessary to cover the eels with the marinade. A cup of marinade will be plenty for 2 pounds of eels. Toss the pieces to cover all sides. Marinate for 2 hours, tossing from time to time.

When you are ready to cook, build a charcoal or wood fire and let it burn down to coals. Remove the eels from the marinade. Pour the leftover marinade into a saucepan. Add a little butter and heat. When the coals are right, put the eels on the grill about 6 inches above the heat. Baste with the marinade sauce. Grill for about 5 minutes, or longer for large eels that have not been filleted. Mix some brown sugar into the sauce, then baste the eels on the cooked side. Cook for 4 minutes (or longer), then turn and baste. Turn every minute or so until the eels are nicely browned and done. The oil in the eel permits some leeway, but of course the eels should not be cooked too long over high heat.

You can also cook this recipe with indirect heat if you have a larger covered grill. Simply put the eels on one side of the grill and the fire on the other side. Cover and cook for several hours, with or without smoke, or until the eels are done.

Irish Stewed Eels

The Irish used eels in soups and stews, and this recipe is an old one called *eascain stobhach* in Gaelic.

> 4 pounds small or medium eels
> 1 tablespoon chopped fresh parsley
> 1 tablespoon chopped chives
> 2 cups thin white sauce (below)
> salt and pepper

Skin the eels and cut them into 4-inch lengths. Put the pieces into a saucepan with water, bring to a boil, cover, and simmer for 5 minutes. Drain off the water and drain the eel pieces. Make a white sauce (below) and pour about 2 cups over the eels. Stir in the chives, parsley, salt, and pepper. Heat until bubbly—but do not boil—and stew for 45 minutes, stirring from time to time with a wooden spoon. Add a little water if necessary. Serve hot.

White Sauce

Make a thin white sauce by melting ¼ cup butter in a skillet and stirring in ¼ cup flour, as when making a roux. Stir in 1½ cups whole milk and ½ cup water, along with a little salt and white pepper. Heat and stir for a few minutes, but do not boil.

All manner of stuff can be added to the recipe, but I like to keep it simple. The last time I made eel stew I added some wild onions and part of their green tops instead of the chopped chives and parsley. I wouldn't hesitate to try ramps, and the milder green onions (sometimes called spring onions or scallions) can be used to advantage.

Basque Elvers

Small eels—4 inches or less—are considered delicacies in many parts of the world. They are much more popular in Europe, and the recipe below is from Spain. I don't know how the small eels, or elvers, are caught, but I have seen them by the thousands in American streams. Sometimes they are stumped by a hydroelectric or other dam across the stream and will try somehow to get over it. I have seen them trying to climb the dam on the Chattahoochee River at Fort Gains, Georgia. Farther downstream, I have seen them climbing out of the river on the riprap at the base of the dam. A nearby bait dealer sometimes sells these for high prices—and he catches them in a trap placed within a few feet of the anglers' walkway!

In any case, if you can get some small eels, be sure to try this recipe. I cut off their heads and gut them but leave the skin intact. If you can't get the eels, try small sand lances, smelts, or other fish. (The fish are usually thicker than eels and must be cooked longer.)

> 1½ pounds elvers
> ½ cup olive oil
> 4 cloves garlic, halved
> 2 small fresh chili peppers, seeded and sliced
> salt

Heat the olive oil in a cast-iron skillet or wok, then sauté the garlic and chili peppers for a few minutes to flavor the oil. Wash the eels and pat them dry with paper towels. Salt the eels, then quickly stir-fry them in the hot oil. Serve hot. Eat bones and all.

See also whitebait, chapter 23.

TWENTY-TWO

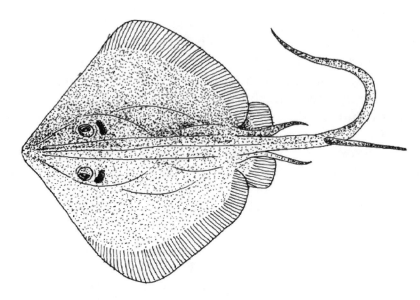

Skates and Rays

The skates and rays are perhaps the most underused edible fish that saltwater anglers encounter. Part of the problem is that people are afraid of these things—and with good reason: Some can deliver an electric shock, and others (the stingrays) have sharp spines on the tail.

There are three kinds of electric rays on the East and West Coasts. These use an electric current to stun their prey, but the shock is not fatal to humans.

The **Atlantic torpedo** *(Torpedo nobiliana)* can be encountered from Key West to Nova Scotia. It can grow to 100 pounds but is usually around 30. Its shock has been measured at 220 volts. The

The skates and rays are easily recognized. Some have stingers located near the base of the tail and should be handled carefully.

Pacific electric ray *(Torpedo californica)* is similar to the Atlantic torpedo but is a little smaller. The **lesser electric ray** *(Narcine brasiliensis)* grows to about 15 inches and generates 37 volts. It ranges from North Carolina south to Brazil, and also lives in the Gulf of California to South America. It makes excellent eating.

Several species of stingrays have one or more spines sticking out of their tails, between the tip of the tail and the body. Contact with these can be quite painful. Never grab any skate or ray by the tail to land it, unless you are certain of your catch. If you land a stingray, carefully cut the wings off and discard the rest. The large **spotted eagle ray** *(Aetobatus narinari),* weighing up to 500 pounds, has large, poisonous tail spines that can cause severe pain or even death; it is, nonetheless, edible. The **bluntnose stingray** *(Dasyatis sayi)* is small but very common in shallow water, ranging from Cape Cod to Brazil, and is especially common in the Carolinas, coastal Georgia, and Florida. The small **round stingray** *(Urolophus halleri)* ranges from California to Panama. There are other sting-rays, all of which have one or more spines located somewhere between the tip of the tail and the body. I don't see that exact identification is too important for the angler unless you have an interest in such matters, in which case you should consult books dealing with identification of fishes. My guess is that anyone wanting a stingray to eat would use the same caution as with a rattlesnake destined for the table, whether it be an eastern dia-mondback or a timber rattler.

Here are some other species of interest, included partly because some of them don't look like a skate or ray, and partly because they can be excellent eating.

Sawfish, *Pristis pectinata.* Believe it or not, this unusual ray with a long, flat, saw-toothed snout makes excellent eating. It is usually hooked in shallow water or in deep pools near land, and sometimes in brackish water or large rivers. Although more common in Florida, it ranges the East Coast to Long Island and south to Brazil. Similar sawfish live in the Pacific. These things grow up to 18 feet long and can be very dangerous, so be careful if you are successful in beaching one. The smaller ones are low in oil content and are delicious when cooked by any method. The larger ones are higher in oil content and are more suited for grilling, broiling, baking, or smoking. They are usually steaked without skinning.

Atlantic guitarfish, *Rhinobatos lentiginosus.* Found along the Atlantic coast to North Carolina, this warm-water ray grows to 2 feet or better in length. It is more elongated than most rays; in fact, it is shaped like a guitar, as the common name implies.

Barndoor skate, *Raja laevis.* This large skate, weighing up to 40 pounds, makes good eating and has been marketed as scallops. It grows in the Atlantic from Newfoundland to the Carolinas.

Atlantic manta, *Manta birostris,* and **Pacific manta,** *Manta hamiltoni.* These large rays can have a wingspan of 22 feet and a weight of over a ton. They are edible, but the smaller ones make the better table fare.

Many other species of skates and rays may be encountered in American waters, and all of them are edible in the sense that the meat won't poison you. I haven't eaten all of them, but I would certainly try any skate or ray that I landed, and would be especially happy to see a small one. In the past, large skates and rays caught by commercial fishermen have been cut into mock scallops and marketed as the real thing. A law forbids this practice, but my guess is that some restaurants don't always obey the letter or the spirit of the law. (I have received red snapper when I ordered trout.) If in doubt, note that the fibers in a scallop muscle will run longitudinally, whereas a mock scallop stamped from a skate or ray will have fibers that run crosswise. I'm not passing judgment here, and I would rather have a "deep-sea scallop" cut from a freshly caught skate than the real thing soaked in water and iced in a market for many days. If you want to convert a skate to scallops, get a punch designed for cutting holes in gasket material or use a pipe, or perhaps a cookie cutter, of suitable diameter.

It is best to put the meat on ice as soon as the fish is caught, and some people recommend bleeding. To accomplish both, simply cut the wings away from the body and put them on ice. Later, you can skin the wings and cut them into chunks or scallops or whatever. Small wings can be cooked whole, but it's usually best to cut them up. Each wing contains a layer of carti-lage in the center, and you can cut "fillets" from the top and bottom of each wing. If you prefer, you can leave the cartilage in, then pull the meat away at the table. With small skates, try grind-ing the wings in a sausage mill, cartilage and all. The outer perimeter of the wings is mostly cartilage and is usually trimmed away.

The body of the skate or ray can also be eaten and can be cooked like a roast. If you like, remove the innards and ice the body with the wings. Skinning can come later. The upper part of the tail, by the way, also contains some good meat—but beware the spines on the stingrays.

When championing skates and rays, a booklet called *Recipes with a New Catch*, published by the Sea Grant College Program, says that prior to cooking, the meat should be soaked for several hours in a solution of ½ cup white vinegar or 1 cup salt to 1 gallon water. I don't think this is necessary with small skates or rays that have been properly iced, but suit yourself.

French-Fried Skate with Liver

The French have a number of ways to prepare skate, often with the aid of complicated sauces. My old edition of *Larousse Gas-tronomique* says that skate gains from being slightly "high," although not high enough to alter the smell. This means that the meat is aged for a few days before cooking. Suit yourself, but I say it's better to ice the fish as soon as possible and to let it get high in the refrigerator.

The Skate Wings
skate wings, skinned and chunked
milk
flour
oil for deep frying
salt
fried parsley (garnish)
lemon wedges (garnish)

183

Boil and chill enough milk to cover the skate. Put the skate chunks into a nonmetallic container, cover with the cold milk, and refrigerate for several hours. Rig for deep frying, heating the oil to 375 degrees. Drain the skate chunks and dust lightly with flour. Deep-fry a few at a time until nicely browned. Drain and salt to taste. Serve hot, garnished with fried parsley and lemon wedges.

If you also want to eat the liver, which is delicious, cut it into pieces, soak it in milk, and fry it along with the chunked wings. The French, of course, have a different recipe for the livers, set forth below, if you want to take the trouble.

The Liver
skate liver
white wine
olive oil
lemon juice
chopped parsley
salt and pepper
oil for deep frying
flour
fried parsley (garnish)
lemon wedges (garnish)

Poach the skate liver in white wine for a few minutes. Cool and cut the liver into slices. Marinate the slices in olive oil, lemon juice, chopped parsley, salt, and pepper for 1 hour or so. Rig for deep frying. Drain the liver slices, dust with flour, and fry until nicely browned. Serve hot, garnished with fried parsley and lemon wedges.

Deviled Ray

Here's a good recipe I have adapted from *Recipes with a New Catch,* published by the UNC Sea Grant College Program.

> 2 cups minced ray or skate
> 2 cups bread crumbs
> 2 chicken eggs
> ¼ pound butter, melted
> 1 medium onion, minced
> 3 tablespoons mayonnaise
> 2 tablespoons Worcestershire sauce
> juice and zest of ½ lemon
> 1 tablespoon chopped fresh parsley
> Fish Stock (chapter 27) or chicken broth
> salt and pepper
> paprika
> crab shells or clam shells

Preheat the oven to 350 degrees. Mix the bread crumbs, onion, eggs, mayonnaise, lemon juice and zest, melted butter, Worcestershire, salt, pepper, and parsley. Stir in the minced ray and enough stock or broth to make the mixture the consistency of bread dough. Stuff this mixture into clam or crab shells, sprinkle with paprika, and bake in the center of the oven for 20 to 30 minutes, or until slightly browned. Feeds 2 to 4.

Skate or Ray Salad

Here's an excellent way to cook and eat skate or ray. I always leave the skin on the fish until it is cooked, drained, and cooled. Then it can be removed easily with a fork.

The Meat
2 pounds skate or ray wing
1 quart water
2 ribs celery with leaves, chopped
1 medium-to-large onion, chopped
juice of 1 lemon
1 tablespoon chopped fresh parsley (optional)
2 bay leaves
salt

Put the water into a pot, then add all the ingredients except the skate or ray. Bring to a boil, then add the skate, bring to a new boil, cover, reduce the heat, and simmer for 25 minutes. Remove the skate, drain, and cool. Discard the stock and vegetables. Using a fork, pull the skin from the skate wing and cut the meat into bite-size chunks. Chill until you are ready to proceed.

The Salad
skate chunks (above)
1 cup chopped celery with tops
½ cup mayonnaise
½ cup chopped onion
2 hard-boiled chicken eggs, chopped
2 tablespoons pickle relish
salt and pepper
lettuce leaves
tomato wedges or cherry tomatoes

Mix the mayonnaise, onion, celery, eggs, relish, salt, and pepper. Gently stir in the skate chunks. Serve on lettuce leaves surrounded with tomato wedges or cherry tomatoes.

A. D.'s Skate Burgers with Salsa

One of the best ways to cook skates and rays, in my opinion, is to grind them in a sausage mill, shape the meat into patties, and cook them like hamburgers. The patties can be served on buns, or on a plate along with vegetables, rice, salad, and other parts of a complete meal.

When grinding, it's best to cut the skate or ray into chunks that feed nicely into the grinder. Partly frozen meat is easier to grind. I grind the meat first, then prepare the salsa before cooking the patties.

The Burgers
1 pound skate
bacon drippings
1 small-to-medium onion
salt and pepper
1 or 2 chicken eggs, if needed
flour, if needed
salsa (below)

Cut the skate into chunks and brush with bacon drippings. Peel and chop the onion. Mix the skate and onion, adding a little salt and pepper. Grind the mixture in a sausage mill, using a ⅛-inch wheel. Shape part of the mixture into a patty, handling it very carefully. Heat about 1 tablespoon of bacon drippings on a griddle or in a skillet, then cook the patties for about 5 minutes on each side or until done, turning once. Do not overcook. If the patty has held together properly, proceed with the rest of the batch. If the patty has torn apart, you may need some binder to help hold things together. In this case, whisk an egg or two and stir it into the remaining ground meat, along with a little flour. When all of the patties have been cooked, top with salsa and serve hot.

The Salsa
¾ cup chopped fresh tomato
¾ cup mango cubes (½-inch dice)
¾ cup finely chopped onion
¼ cup red bell peppers, chopped
¼ cup green bell peppers, chopped
¼ cup chopped fresh cilantro
2 cloves garlic, minced
1 fresh jalapeño, seeded and minced
1 tablespoon olive oil
1 teaspoon fresh lemon juice
½ teaspoon salt

Heat the oil in a skillet, then sauté the onion, peppers, garlic, and cilantro for 5 or 6 minutes. Stir in the rest of the salsa ingredients, then simmer for a few minutes. Keep hot until the patties are cooked.

TWENTY-THREE

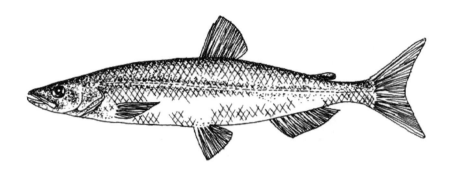

Panfish

Almost any fish small enough to be cooked in a skillet could properly be called a panfish, and some of these, such as grunts and perches of various sorts, are treated in other chapters. Many of the saltwater panfish are similar in size to the bluegills and other freshwater bream; that is, they are hand-sized with spiny fins. These are usually fried whole. Then you pull out the top and bottom fins and related spines, and eat them like corn on the cob. You can leave the rib cages on the cleaned backbone, or salvage the meat if you've got the time.

If you aren't in the habit of eating small, whole spiny-rayed fish, remember that each hard fin bone or spine that sticks up will have a similar bone that goes into the flesh. When pulling

Smelt and some other small fish make delicious table fare.

out the fin, make sure that the spines also come out. Be warned that some very bad advice has gotten into fish cookery literature. Some magazines and books advise you to remove fins and tails with scissors or kitchen shears. Don't do it. If you cut off the fins, you can't pull out the spines and will likely end up with a mouthful of bones. (For more information on bony fish, see chapter 25.)

In any case, here are some panfish that make good eating but are not covered in other chapters.

WHITINGS

Although the whitings seldom grow over a foot long, some of them are called kingfish, even by scientists. The **northern king-fish** *(Menticirrhus saxatilis)* can be caught from Maine to Florida. The **minkfish** *(Menticirrhus focaliger)* lives only in the Gulf of Mexico. Others are called southern kingfish and, sometimes, sea mullet and Virginia mullet. By whatever name, the whiting is sometimes quite plentiful, and some coastal people are reported to prefer it over all other saltwater fish.

With the whitings, the species really doesn't make much difference (but note that the silver hake is sometimes marketed under the name whiting). All of them live near the shore and are caught over a sand bottom. They have small mouths and are best taken with bait on small hooks and light tackle. Although the flesh tends to be on the soft side, they can make very good table fare if they are eaten right away.

I am partial to whiting fillets dusted with fine stone-ground cornmeal and fried in very hot peanut oil right on the beach where the fish are caught, but these fish can be cooked in a number of ways. Here's a special recipe to try.

Whiting with Whatyagot

I like to cook this dish with small, thin, white fillets, stuffed, rolled, and baked. Whiting fillets are almost perfect. If you don't have a few shrimp on hand, feel free to use steamed crawfish, crab, lobster, or even fish flakes, especially from a flaky fish that resembles crab or lobster, such as sheepshead.

> 2 pounds whiting fillets
> ½ cup minced cooked shrimp
> 1 cup milk
> melted butter
> 2 tablespoons flour
> 1 small (golf-ball size) onion, minced
> ¼ cup minced celery with part of tops
> salt and pepper

Preheat the oven to 350 degrees. Heat 2 tablespoons of butter in a saucepan or small skillet. Sauté the onion and celery for 2 or 3 minutes. Stir in the flour with a wooden spoon. Slowly add the milk, stirring until the mixture thickens. Take the pan off the heat, then stir in the shrimp, along with a little salt and pepper. Sprinkle each fillet with salt and pepper, then spread with some of the filling. Roll the fillets, secure with round toothpicks, and fit into a greased baking pan. Brush liberally with melted butter, and bake for about 40 minutes or until the center of the fish is opaque, basting twice. If in doubt, cut into a roll before serving. Feeds 4 to 6.

SMELTS

Smelts are circumpolar, and one sort or another can be caught in the North Pacific, Atlantic, and Arctic Oceans and in fresh water. Some are anadromous, that is, they swim up freshwater streams to spawn. All the smelts are small fish. Although on the oily side, they make delicious eating provided that they are kept on ice. They are often beheaded, drawn, and deep-fried. The smaller ones can be eaten bones and all if they are crisply fried. Some are taken primarily in fresh water. The following are some of the species that can be taken in salt water, usually with some sort of net. The **capelin** *(Mallotus villosus)*, like the California grunion, spawns on the beach. It is a rather arctic species but can be taken in Maine.

Eulachon *(Thaleichthys pacificus)*, also called candlefish, is an oily smelt that was once fitted with a wick and burned like a candle. In Alaska, it is called hooligan. They are delicious eating but tend to be soft. Smoked eulachon are popular, but the size of the catch is regulated these days. The **surf smelt** *(Hypomesus pretiosus)* is caught in the surf from Alaska to California. The **whitebait smelt** *(Allosmerus elongatus)*, a Pacific species, is taken as far south as San Francisco. As its name implies, it is sometimes used as whitebait (covered later in this chapter). The **rainbow smelt** *(Osmerus mordax)*, occurring in the North Atlantic, Pacific, and Arctic Oceans, is often caught with small minnows, worms, and other bait in New England harbors and estuaries.

Foolproof Campfire Smelts

I hate recipes that tell you to wrap fish or other victuals very tightly in aluminum foil, put the package over hot coals, and cook for 10 minutes—or until the fish flakes easily when tested with a fork. Of course, the hard part is undoing the hot package to make the test. And what happens if the fish is raw? Can you reseal the hot package? If so, how? A recipe writer doesn't want to deal with these questions and usually doesn't point out the problem. Nonetheless, the disclaimer on the cooking times is almost always necessary, simply because some fires are hotter than others and some fish are larger than others. On the other hand, I have never had the recipe below fail me with what I call cigar fish, which include smelts, stunted yellow perch, and channel catfish under 7 inches long. I do, however, insist on having top-quality heavy-duty aluminum foil for cooking. Some of the thinner stuff tears too easily, letting out the steam and juices.

> 2 or 3 pounds dressed smelts
> 4 to 6 pieces thin bacon
> 1 large onion, cut lengthwise into boat-shaped slices
> 8 ounces sliced fresh mushrooms
> ½ cup chopped fresh parsley or watercress
> salt and pepper

Build a good fire with charcoal or wood and let it burn down to coals. Tear off a suitable length of aluminum foil for each person. Allow ½ pound of fish and a strip of bacon for each. Cut the bacon strips in half and place the pieces in the center of the aluminum foil, lengthwise. Top the bacon with smelts. Add some onions, mushrooms, and parsley. Sprinkle with salt and pepper. Seal the package by folding the aluminum foil lengthwise, then making a fold in the fold. Seal both ends in the same manner. When all the packages are ready, place them on a rack above hot coals or put them directly onto a sparse bed of coals that have been raked from the fire. Cook for 8 minutes. Remove the packages from the fire and let them sit for 4 minutes. Steam should have built up inside the sealed foil and will help cook the fish. One of the packages will probably have sprung a leak and you'll be able to see some steam escaping. If not, punch a small hole in one with a fork tine. If you see steam, you're OK. If not, open the package and try flaking the meat with the fork. If it pulls off the bone easily, you're ready to eat. If not, you're on your own.

The method above is about as foolproof as this way of cooking can get. But I'll have to admit that I like to live dangerously, and after the hoboes have cooked for about 4 minutes, I turn them over for a few seconds to allow some of the bacon drippings to run to the top of the fish. Then I turn them back over to finish cooking.

Alaskan Hooligan Fry

Hooligan is the corrupted form of eulachon, the name of a small, smeltlike fish that runs in great numbers in some of our rivers each spring. According to *Alaska* magazine, ". . . these fish are extremely oily and must be cooked just right or the oil will make them unpalatable. Be sure to prepare plenty of these, since people will no doubt eat more than you expect.

"Use either freshly dressed or completely thawed frozen hooligan. Wipe dry. Coat the bottom of a heavy frying pan with vegetable oil. Place the pan over medium heat and heat the oil to almost smoking hot. While the pan is heating, the fish should be dipped in slightly beaten egg, then in cracker crumbs, dry bread crumbs, flour, or cornmeal (any combination will do). Prepare enough fish for one panful at a time. Put them on to fry and cook quickly. (You may need to raise the heat.) Speedy cooking prevents the little fish from becoming soft and ensures a good crisp crust. When the fish are put on to fry, set the oven to 350 degrees and place a good-sized baking pan inside. The oven should be hot by the time the first panful of fish is fried. The hooligan may then be placed in the pan and kept hot. This step in the preparation should not be omitted because it also helps to dry the fish somewhat and gets rid of their excess fat. Hooligan are so fatty that if fried and served without this 'drying off' they will be too oily for most people to enjoy.

"Fry as many fish as you wish and transfer each successive panful to the baking pan in the oven. Between each frying, pour excess fat out of the frying pan. Leave the fish in the oven for 15 minutes after putting the last ones in. Serve on a large platter surrounded by lemon wedges and sprigs of parsley. Hot rolls and coleslaw should accompany fried hooligan."

Smelts with Anchovy

Here's a Swedish method of preparing small sardines with a bit of salt anchovy. Use it for smelts and similar edible cigar-sized fish.

> 2 pounds fresh smelts or sardines
> 1 small can anchovies with juice
> 3 tablespoons butter
> 3 tablespoons bread crumbs (divided)

Preheat the oven to 375 degrees. Butter a baking dish and sprinkle the bottom lightly with part of the bread crumbs. (The baking dish should be just large enough to hold all the fish.) Fillet the fish and lay them out, skin side down. Place about half an anchovy fillet crosswise on the large end of each fillet. Roll each sardine fillet around the anchovy, then fit them into the baking dish. Sprinkle the remaining bread crumbs and the juice from the anchovy can over the fillets, dot with butter, and bake in the center of the oven for 15 minutes, or until golden brown. Serve hot with boiled new potatoes and plenty of green salad.

OTHER PANFISH

Here are some other tasty panfish that the saltwater angler might encounter.

Pinfish, *Lagodon rhomboides.* These little fish, usually 8 inches long or less, but occasionally growing to 14 inches, are among the most plentiful of inshore saltwater fish. They range from Cape Cod to the Yucatán and are sometimes called sailor's choice or Canadian bream. The **spottail pinfish,** *Diplodus holbrooki,* and several cousins, sometimes called spotted bream, are also plentiful in pretty much the same range. They are usually a little smaller but make good eating. All of the pinfish can be scaled, gutted, and cooked like freshwater bluegills and other bream.

Sea bream, *Archosargus rhomboidalis.* Several small, edible saltwater fish are commonly called bream from one coastal locale to another, but only one is so named. The sea bream is caught mostly in Florida and southward, but it does stray up the Atlantic coast. It grows to a foot in length, but most are hand-sized. They are similar in habits to the pinfish.

Porgy, *Calamus* spp. Several species of porgies are quite plentiful in southeastern coastal waters and in the Gulf of Mexico. Most of these panfish have firm white flesh, tasty but rather bony. Usually they run about a pound and as such are cooked like other panfish. The larger ones can be filleted or scaled and baked whole like a snapper or smoked. The **scup** *(Stenotomus chrysops)* is commonly called porgy in the Northeast, and it (or a similar species) ranges south to the Gulf of Mexico. Although this species is often treated as trash, even in some books about fish, it makes good eating if it is quickly iced and properly cooked.

Squirrelfish, *Holocentrus ascensionis.* This small reef fish ranges from Florida to Brazil, preferring shallow waters. It makes good eating but is difficult to clean because of its many spines and sharp gill plates.

Mojarra, family Gerridae. About ten species of this small panfish can be caught in American waters. They grow to 10 inches long, but most are less than 8. Mojarras are very common in Florida and often invade the bonefish flats in large schools. They are sometimes called shad. Although small, they are very good when scaled, drawn, and cooked like freshwater bluegills and other bream.

California grunion, *Leuresthes tenuis.* At spawning time— always at night within a few days of a full moon and always on a falling tide—this small cigar-shaped fish actually leaves the water to lay eggs in the sand. At this time, they are picked up by hand by anglers, and the event is something of a jubilee in parts of Southern California. Grunion make excellent eating and can be cooked like smelt.

WHITEBAIT

The epicures of Victorian England relished tiny fried fish, and the tradition still continues here and there today. I know a fellow in Maine, for example, who enjoys whitebait. At its best, fried whitebait is very fresh and quite small—an inch or so. Ideally, several species are cooked in one batch. Most any sort of small fish will do. My friend in Maine likes the **sand lance** *(Ammodytes americanus).* The **Atlantic silverside** *(Menidia menidia)* is also used extensively, along with the fry of various herrings, smelts, sticklebacks, whitings, and elvers.

The nice thing about whitebait is that the small fish don't have to be scaled or cleaned. That's right. They are fried whole, heads, guts, and all. Partly because the fish aren't drawn, it's best to have live or at least very fresh fish.

> 1 pound whitebait
> flour
> oil for deep frying
> salt
> lemon wedges

Rig for deep frying at 375 degrees with a small-mesh basket. Dry the fish roughly with paper towels, then dust them with flour. Fry in a mesh basket for 30 seconds, and drain on brown bags. (Don't cook too many at a time, or the temperature of the oil may drop too low.) Sprinkle with salt and serve with lemon wedges.

TWENTY-FOUR

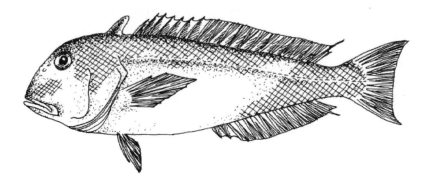

A Mixed Catch

I first called this chapter A Mixed Stringer, a common term that indicates a mixed catch. I changed the wording, however, because it's usually not a good idea to put saltwater fish (or any other kind) on a fish stringer (or in a live well) if they can be put into an ice chest or box with plenty of ice. In any case, this chapter contains a number of excellent saltwater fish for the table, most of which are thrown back or out on the bank as trash fish.

TRIGGERFISH

When I was a kid, I sometimes went deep-sea fishing on a party boat in the Gulf of Mexico. Typically, about twenty-five of the men

Tilefish can be cooked by any method or used to make an excellent sashimi.

in our town would pool their money, rent a boat for the day, and drive down in a caravan of cars. At the end of the day, all the catch was taken off ice and piled on the dock, where it was every man for himself. The first to go were the red snappers, then the groupers. The odd-looking triggerfish were always left on the dock. The captain of our boat tried to tell us that we were leaving the best fish, but we thought he was joking. He wasn't.

Several species of these odd-looking warm-water fish, family Balistidae, can be taken in American waters, sometimes as far north as Massachusetts. They have very tough skin with platelike scales, making them difficult to dress, but once filleted and skinned, they make excellent table fare. The firm, snow-white meat of the **queen triggerfish** (*Balises vetula*) is said to have a texture similar to frog legs. If you like sashimi, be sure to try triggerfish. Also try the fillets fried.

WAHOO

Also called oahu fish, the wahoo (*Acanthocybium solandri*) can be found worldwide in tropical and temperate seas. It's a very fast fish, clocked at over 50 miles per hour, and it can weigh over a hundred pounds. It is kin to the mackerels, but its flesh is not at all oily. Fine-grained, white, sweet, and somewhat dry, it can be cooked by any method but should not be overcooked. Steaks or fillets to be broiled or grilled should be basted.

Broiled Wahoo

This recipe works with steaks or fillets about 1 inch thick or less. Thicker fillets must be cooked longer and farther from the heat.

> 2 pounds wahoo steaks or fillets
> ¼ cup butter
> 2 tablespoons soy sauce
> juice of 1 lemon
> freshly ground black pepper

Mix the soy sauce, lemon juice, butter, and black pepper in a saucepan and warm. Preheat the broiler. Dip the wahoo fillets in the basting sauce and place them about 4 inches from the heat. Broil for about 5 minutes on each side, or until the fish flakes easily when tested with a fork, basting twice.

TRIPLETAIL

Found in both the Atlantic and Pacific, this odd species *(Lobotes surinamensis)* is also called buoy bass, because it likes to hang around buoys or floating debris, as well as black fish. It was given the name tripletail because its top and bottom fins trail back and look like tails. By whatever name, it weighs up to 50 pounds and has snow-white, mild, delicate flesh. Usually filleted and skinned, it can be prepared by any method.

TILEFISH

Found in rather deep water from Nova Scotia to the Gulf of Mexico, the tilefish *(Lopholatilus chamaeleonticepsis)* is sometimes taken by party boat anglers using heavy sinkers and bottom-fishing rigs. They grow to 50 pounds. The tilefish makes excellent eating, and its firm, mild flesh can be cooked by any method. It is sometimes eaten as sashimi. The flesh, which is firm but tender, has been compared to lobster or scallop. Sometimes a Pacific species has a butter flavor, but this is rare.

Sautéed Tilefish Fingers

Fillet and skin the fish, then cut the meat into fingers about ¾ inch thick and 3 or 4 inches long. Salt and pepper the fingers, then dust them lightly with flour. Heat some olive oil in a skillet. Sauté 5 or 6 whole cloves of garlic until lightly browned. Remove the garlic, then sauté the fish fingers for 7 or 8 minutes, turning once. Carefully transfer the fingers to a serving platter or individual plates. Add a little water to the skillet, bringing to a quick boil and scraping up any bits of fish or flour from the bottom. Pour the pan sauce over the fish. Serve hot, along with the garlic cloves, garlic bread, and a huge green salad.

SNOOK

This great southern gamefish can be taken consistently in south Florida and southeast Texas, but the snook *(Centropomus undecimalis)* is more plentiful along the lower Gulf coast of Mexico and Central America. It is highly prized as table fare, and many of the Mexican and Mayan recipes work well with it. There are several related smaller species, all good eating. The snook can weigh up to 50 pounds but are usually much smaller.

The snook should be filleted and skinned. (If not skinned, it may have a slightly soapy taste.) It can be cooked by any method. For frying, cut the fillets into fingers.

Snook with Adobo Sauce

Here's a great Mayan recipe that doesn't require hard-to-find ingredients. Ancho chilies are widely available, but any dried red chilies about 2 or 3 inches long can be used. Longer hot chilies can be used in reduced numbers. Of course, there is a great deal of difference in the hotness of the various chili peppers, but in most authentic Mexican recipes the chilies are seeded and cored before they are used, which removes most of the heat, leaving a nutritious and flavorful pepper. As a general rule, the smaller peppers are hotter than the larger ones. In any case, be sure to wash your hands thoroughly after seeding hot chili peppers; the oil can burn your skin and can be dangerous to your eyes and tender parts. Some chefs wear gloves. Start making the sauce an hour or so before you are ready to cook the fish, as the dried peppers have to soak in water for some time.

The Sauce
6 ancho chili peppers
3 large tomatoes
1 medium onion, chopped
1 clove garlic, chopped
1 teaspoon sugar
½ teaspoon salt
10 peppercorns
½ teaspoon dry thyme
¼ teaspoon cumin seeds
¼ teaspoon dry oregano
½ inch cinnamon stick
⅛ teaspoon cloves

Wash the dried chili peppers in cold water, then open them and carefully remove and discard the pith and seeds. Put the peppers into a bowl and cover them with hot water. Soak for an hour. Then remove the peppers, chop them, and set aside. Save the water in which the peppers were soaked. In a mortar and pestle, grind the cloves, cinnamon stick, peppercorns, and cumin seeds; I grind these separately and dump them into a small mixing bowl. Stir in the sugar, salt, thyme, and oregano. Peel and chop the tomatoes. (Purists will also want to remove the tomato seeds, but I seldom go this far.) Put the chopped tomatoes, onions, garlic, soaked chili peppers, and ground and mixed dry ingredients into a blender. Add the pepper water a little at a time and puree the mixture. The sauce is not yet complete, but stop at this point and proceed with the fish.

The Fish
1 snook of about 5 pounds
½ cup olive oil
flour
½ cup freshly grated Parmesan (or other hard cheese)
1 stick frozen butter
salt and pepper
sauce mix from above
½ teaspoon lemon juice for sauce

Preheat the oven to 400 degrees. Dress the snook whole, with or without the head and tail; sometimes this will depend on preference and sometimes on whether the snook is small enough to fit into your cooker. (If your cooker is not wide enough, you can cut the fish in half to cook and put it back together for serving.) Heat the olive oil in an oblong cast-iron fish cooker. Sprinkle the fish with flour, then sauté it on both sides until it is nicely browned. Carefully remove the fish, putting it into a baking pan or roaster of suitable size. Stir the sauce into what's left of the olive oil in the cooker. Simmer the sauce, stirring as you go, for 5 minutes or so. During the last minute, stir in the lemon juice, salt, and pepper.

Pour the sauce over the snook. Sprinkle with the Parmesan cheese, then grate some of the frozen butter over it. Bake for 45 minutes, or until the fish flakes easily when tested with a fork.

A 5-pound snook (undressed weight) will feed 5 people. Serve with rice, sliced tomatoes, sliced avocado, and perhaps steamed chayote.

SALMONOIDS

The salmons and trouts are very important fish to some anglers and to the commercial fish trade. But most anglers catch them in fresh water, sometimes far from the ocean, and more and more the commercial fish are from farms. Charter boats and private boats do take lots of salmon from salt water in some areas of Northern California and the Northwest.

Small trout are at their best when sautéed in butter. (Anyone seriously interested in trout cookery should take a look at my *Trout Cookbook.*) Salmon are best when poached, grilled, or smoked, or perhaps salted and eaten raw. Generally, I lean to simple recipes for both trout and salmon. Here's one of my favorite salmon recipes.

A. D.'s Grilled Salmon

Build a hot fire of hardwood or charcoal. Cut the salmon into 1-inch steaks. Cut a lemon in half and melt a little butter. Stick the exposed part of a lemon half into the melted butter, then baste a steak, squeezing the lemon just a little. Do each steak the same way, on both sides, and sprinkle lightly with salt. When the fire has burned down, grill the steaks about 4 inches from the coals for 4 or 5 minutes on each side, basting once or twice with the squeezed lemon and butter.

SABLEFISH

Found in deep water all along our Pacific coast, the sablefish *(Anoplopoma fimbria)*, also called coalfish, blackcod, or butter-fish, grows up to 40 pounds, but the average catch is between 2 and 20. The flesh of the sablefish, rather high in oil content and somewhat buttery or soft in texture, is best when smoked, but it can also be grilled or broiled successfully. Smoked sable-fish is sometimes marketed as smoked Alaskan cod.

NEEDLEFISH

These slimjims (family Belonidae) are edible, if you don't mind the green bones. The larger ones—the houndfish grows to 5 feet in length and over 10 pounds in weight—are dangerous because they often make long jumps, flying through the air like javelins, especially when frightened by a light. There are several species, all of which stay near the surface. They can be caught on flies, plugs, and live bait, and tend to walk on their tails when hooked.

The needlefish is commonly eaten in Europe, where it is some-times called garfish, and *hornfisk* is a Scandinavian delicacy. It is also very popular in Malta. Any European recipe calling for garfish can be used for needlefish caught in American waters, if the size is appropriate. They are usually skinned and cut into sections like eels.

STURGEONS

The sixteen species of sturgeons (family Acipenseridae) all provide excellent caviar, and most of them are tasty when smoked. These are usually large fish, covered with bony scutes. Some of the sturgeons are strictly freshwater fish, but most of them live in salt water and run up rivers to spawn. Most of these are caught in fresh water, however, so they are not of much importance to the saltwater angler. Also, angling is restricted in some areas for some endangered species. In any case, the smaller sturgeons make the best eating, and they are delicious when properly smoked.

COBIA

Often called ling, crabeater, black salmon, black kingfish, or sergeant fish, the cobia *(Rachycentron canadum)* of the Atlantic ranges from the tropics to Cape Cod. Like the tripletail, it is fond of buoys and floating debris. It can weigh as much as 100 pounds, with 30-pounders being common. It makes delicious table fare and is said to have a lemon taste (which explains why it is also called lemonfish) and to resemble chicken or frog legs. Cobias are usually filleted and skinned. The meat tends to be dry, so it should not be overcooked. Baste frequently when baking, broiling, or grilling cobia.

Grilled Cobia with Kumquat Sauce

The sauce for this dish should be made with kumquat marmalade. If this is not readily available, substitute orange marmalade (preferably made with the bitter Seville orange). The cobia steaks should be about ¾ to 1 inch thick.

205

2 pounds cobia steaks
1 cup fresh orange juice
juice of 1 lemon
1 medium onion, chopped
½ cup kumquat marmalade
2 cloves garlic, minced
⅛ teaspoon hot pepper sauce (such as Tabasco)
salt

Mix the orange juice, lemon juice, onion, garlic, and pepper sauce. Place the cobia steaks in a nonmetallic container or large Ziploc bag, pour in the marinade, and turn to coat all sides. Marinate in the refrigerator for several hours.

Start a charcoal fire and let it burn down to coals, or preheat an electric or gas grill. Drain the fish, reserving the marinade, and sprinkle lightly with salt. Place the marinade into a small pan. Bring to a light boil, reduce the heat, and stir in the marmalade. Simmer for about 5 minutes, stirring about, until the mixture thickens into a sauce. Keep hot. Grill the fish about 4 inches from hot coals for about 4 minutes on each side. Do not overcook; cobia tends to dry out quickly. Place the steaks on heated plates, topping with a spoonful of sauce. Serve the rest of the sauce in a bowl. Feeds 4 to 6. Serve with rice and steamed vegetables or salad.

BUTTERFISH

This Atlantic species *(Peprilus triacanthus)* is common along the northeast coast south to Florida. The average weight is 1 pound or less, although they do grow to baking size. The butterfish, as the name implies, is on the fatty side—but deliciously so. They are great for broiling, grilling, or smoking, and, being quite thin, they work in recipes for pompano or flounder.

In spite of advice to the contrary in some other books, these fish can be fried successfully. In *Coastal Carolina Cooking,* one of the local cooks, Sarah Latham of Belhaven, says that pan-fried butterfish taste better than any other fish she has ever eaten. You can use any good frying recipe, but Sarah salts and peppers the fish, dips it in egg, coats it with cornmeal, and pan-fries it in 1 cup of shortening over medium heat in a skillet.

If you are fortunate enough to land a larger butterfish, try the following recipe.

Grilled Whole Butterfish

When dressing the fish, scale and draw it, leaving the head on. Make two diagonal slashes on each side, cutting down to the backbone. It's best to put the fish in a grilling basket to facilitate turning.

> 3- to 4-pound butterfish
> ¼ cup olive oil
> juice of 1 large lemon
> salt and pepper

Build a charcoal fire or preheat the grill. When the coals are ready, brush the fish inside and out with a mixture of olive oil and lemon juice. Cook the fish about 8 inches above the heat for 10 minutes on each side, basting from time to time. The fish is done when the meat along the backbone is opaque; check by inserting a fork into one of the diagonal cuts. Sprinkle with salt and pepper and serve hot. Feeds 2 to 4.

Variation: If you don't have a lemon handy, squeeze the juice from a mild onion and use it instead. For juicing an onion, I cut it into small pieces and squeeze them with a heavy-duty garlic press.

BARRACUDAS

Several barracudas can be caught in American waters. All of these have tasty flesh—but be warned that the **great barracuda** *(Sphyraena barracuda)* can sometimes carry ciguatera poisoning (see appendix B). Although ciguatera is not often fatal, it is a very serious matter. Of the 300 tropical marine fish suspected of carrying ciguatera, the great barracuda tops the list, but only the larger barracudas taken from deep water are afflicted. My rule of thumb is to keep any barracuda of less than 5 pounds taken from inshore Florida waters—but some experts recommend that you do not eat *any* barracuda caught in Florida. The great barracuda, by the way, grows to 100 pounds. It is a rather tropical species, ranging from Florida to Brazil, and is also found in the tropical Pacific south of California. It is also called cuda or sea pike.

The other barracudas are safe to eat. The **Pacific barracuda** *(Sphyraena argentea)* and three related species can be caught along the Pacific coast from Alaska to Baja California. They weigh up to 12 pounds and make delicious eating, and the roe is also very good and commonly eaten. The **guaguanche** *(Sphyraena guachancho)*, growing to about 20 inches long, makes very good eating and is considered a delicacy in parts of the West Indies. It is taken from Florida to Brazil, and occasionally farther up the Atlantic coast. The **northern sennet** *(Sphyraena borealis)* is caught along the coast of New England south along the Atlantic, where it merges with a similar species called **southern sennet** *(Sphyraena picudilla)*. These small barracudas, growing up to a length of 15 inches, are excellent eating.

All of the barracudas are easy to dress and are usually skinned and filleted. Some people cut away any red meat, but this may not be necessary. Mild and lean, barracudas can be cooked by any method but should not be overcooked.

ATLANTIC SPADEFISH

The Atlantic spadefish *(Chaetodopterus faber)*, also called angelfish, is almost as deep as it is long. It ranges from Cape Cod to Brazil and is often caught on rocky bottoms or around wrecks and pilings. Growing to 20 pounds and having a firm texture, spadefish make excellent table fare. They should be filleted and skinned, then fried, broiled, or grilled.

Grilled Spadefish Fillets

This recipe works best for fillets about 1 inch thick. For easy turning, use a hinged grilling basket.

2 pounds spadefish fillets
½ cup melted butter
½ cup soy sauce
black pepper

Rig for grilling, using either a folding grilling basket or a well-greased rack. Mix the melted butter, soy sauce, and black pepper. Baste the fillets well, then grill 4 inches above the coals for 10 minutes, turning once and basting several times. Serve hot.

OTHER EDIBLE CATCHES

Atlantic saury, *Scomberesox saurus,* and **Pacific saury,** *Cololabis saira.* These small, slim fish resemble the needlefish and make very good table fare. The Japanese commercially exploit the Pacific saury, which ranges across the North Pacific rim to California.

Atlantic cutlassfish, *Trichiurus lepturus.* This strange creature, with a body like an eel and a head like an alligator, grows in the Atlantic from Cape Cod to Argentina, as well as in the Indian Ocean and the Western Pacific. It also has a cousin that can be caught from Southern California to Peru. It grows up to 2 pounds in weight and a yard long. The cutlassfish is eaten in Japan but not often in America. Try it. At times it is very abundant in some American waters. The meat is firm, white, and toothsome and can be cooked by any method.

Inshore lizardfish, *Synodus foetens.* This edible species, caught along the Atlantic from Canada to Florida, is also called sand pike.

Oyster toadfish, *Opsanus tau.* This ugly creature, also called mud toad or oyster cracker, has nice sweet flesh. It can be caught along the Atlantic seaboard.

Ocean pout, *Macrozoacres americanus.* Caught from the Gulf of St. Lawrence to the Delaware Bay, this eel-like fish has sweet white flesh. Weighing up to 12 pounds, it is also called yellow eel, muttonfish, or congo eel.

Pricklebacks, family Stichaeidae. There are a number of these eel-like fish in the Pacific and Atlantic Oceans. They are sometimes called rock eel or monkeyface eel, but they are not true eels. Most are small, but a few, such as the rock blenny, grow up to 2 feet, and some of the deep-sea pricklebacks are larger. They have a good flavor and should be skinned.

Atlantic wolffish, *Anarhichas lupus,* and **spotted wolffish,** *Anarhichas minor.* These fish of the North Atlantic are sometimes taken as far south as New Jersey. The spotted wolffish is sometimes called spotted catfish and has been marketed under the name ocean catfish. The Atlantic wolffish is good table fare, having firm white flesh, and is popular in parts of Europe. It grows up to 5 or 6 feet long.

TWENTY-FIVE

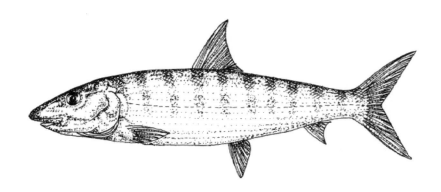

Ladyfish and Other Bony Fare

Several saltwater fish are quite bony but can nevertheless make excellent eating if you know a trick or two. Many of the small panfish, discussed in chapter 23, are considered bony but don't present a problem if you understand how to eat them. The bones are in predictable places, and you simply learn to eat around them, making this a matter of experience as much as a matter of cooking. Other fish, such as the shad and bonefish, have tiny, hidden intermuscular bones that are difficult to avoid at the table unless the fish is prepared properly.

Bonefish and other bony species, such as herrings and shad, can make good eating if properly prepared.

There are several ways to soften or otherwise negate small bones in fish. Here's my summary:

1. *Removing the bones.* There are people who claim to be able to bone a shad, but I have never actually met such a person. I have seen several articles on the subject, complete with photographs, but these were impossible to follow. Also, I have in hand a forty-four-page booklet, published in California, called *How to Catch, Bone & Cook a Shad.* The booklet sets forth thirty-two photographs, explained by detailed captions. After puzzling over it for an hour, I confess that I don't have the head for following the procedure, although I majored in mechanical engineering in college. Frankly, I feel that a shad would spoil before I could bone it by these procedures. Somewhat amused and somewhat in despair, I wrote to a well-known shad angler, Charles Waterman, asking him whether he actually knew anyone who could bone a shad and have enough left to eat. He didn't give a direct answer but did say he couldn't follow articles on the subject. I'm not saying it can't be done. I am saying that *I* can't do it. Even if I could, I probably couldn't communicate the process to the reader.

2. *Gashing.* A good many people claim to be able to gash a fish in such a way as to negate the intermuscular bones. This may or may not work, depending on the species and on who is doing the gashing. I have not had much success with this technique, except by cutting the fillets into thin strips—about like thick bacon—and frying until crisp in hot fat. In any case, all gashing depends on reducing the length of the bones and on getting hot grease into the gashes, thereby making the fish crisp. If you are serious about gashing, first try to determine the lay of the bones in the species you are dealing with, then determine how to gash the fish in order to cut the bones into several pieces. There can be a big difference in gashing crosswise, lengthwise, or diagonally.

3. *Hot frying.* If small fish are fried crisply enough, they can be eaten bones and all. The smaller the fish, the more successful this technique is. Cutting the fish down to the backbone will help, and hot frying may be the real secret to the gashing technique above.

4. *Grinding.* I have successfully ground bony fish in a sausage mill, but this is really no guarantee. A lot may depend on the grinder and on the wheel being used. I prefer a wheel with ⅛-inch holes. The ground meat can then be shaped into patties or balls and sautéed, fried, poached, baked, or whatever. There are a number of recipes, such as the one set forth later under Ladyfish, but you may not need many ingredients. The best patties, to me, are simply ground fish, salt, and pepper. The problem is that such a simple patty may not hold together very well, in which case such binders as chicken eggs and flour may be required. I often make patties with ground fish, dredge them with flour or fine cornmeal, and fry in about ½ inch of hot oil. Also try shaping ground fish, with a little salt, around a flat skewer and grilling over a fire.

5. *Pickling.* Here's a recipe that softens intermuscular bones so much that you can't detect them. Fillet the fish and cut them across the grain into bite-size pieces from ½ to ¾ inch wide and thick and 2 inches long, just right for topping a cracker.

> 2 pounds bony fillets
> 4 cups water
> 2 cups salt
> onions
> pickling spices
> wine vinegar

Dissolve the salt into the water in a nonmetallic container. Add the fish pieces. If they are not completely submerged, weight them down with a plate or saucer or block of wood. Leave the fish in the brine for 2 days in a cool place.

Rinse the fillets well in cool water and sterilize four 1-pint jars. Put 1 tablespoon of pickling spices into the bottom of each jar. Cover the spices with thin slices of onion. (Or you can tie the spices in a piece of cheesecloth or use a cloth parts bag or old-fashioned tobacco sack if you have one.) Add a layer of fillets, another slice of onion, and so on, until the jar is almost full, ending with onions. Fill the jars with a mixture of half wine vinegar

213

and half water. Tap the jars all around with your finger to free the air bubbles. Then cap the jars and refrigerate. The bones will be dissolved and the pickles ready in 3 or 4 weeks. The pickles will keep for several months. Eat the pickles with saltines or use them in salads.

6. *Salting.* There are several ways to salt fish, all of which will soften the bones. I have covered this subject at some length in my book *Cold-Smoking and Salt-Curing Meat, Fish, and Game* and can't do justice to the subject here. Essentially, however, all you need to do is to keep enough salt on the fish for a long enough period of time. For softening the bones in a few fish, I recommend filleting them and laying them out on a sloping wooden plank, skin side down. (If the fillets are thicker than 1 inch, cut them into steaks or fingers.) Salt the pieces heavily on both sides. Tilt the board so that the liquid can drain off. Add more salt as needed. After about 3 days, rinse the fish in several changes of fresh water (called freshening) or, better, soak overnight. Dust the fillets with flour and deep-fry in very hot oil, or use in any recipe that calls for salt fish. Alternatively, you can soak the fillets in a brine (4 cups salt to 1 gallon water) for several days.

7. *Canning.* Proper canning will greatly soften the bones in fish, as demonstrated in commercially canned salmon and sardines (which, in some cases, are really herrings). I recommend that home-canned meats be thoroughly cooked before eating. Anyone who is serious about canning should obtain a good book on the subject from a bookstore or public library. Also see the canning instructions for tuna in chapter 19.

8. *Slow cooking.* Wrap the fish or fillets in aluminum foil, sealing with double folds, and bake at 350 degrees for 6 to 8 hours. The long, slow cooking (steaming, really) will soften the bones. Also, see slow-cook recipes later for shad.

9. *Pressure cooking.* Cut the fish into chunks and place them on a rack in a pressure cooker over a little water. Cook at 10 pounds pressure for 5 minutes per pound. This will soften small bones.

So much for techniques, which, by the way, also apply to bony freshwater fish such as suckers and chain pickerel. Here are some important saltwater bony fish, along with a few recipes.

LADYFISH

The ladyfish *(Elops saurus)* lives in the warmer parts of the Atlantic and Pacific and is especially plentiful in parts of Florida. It is often taken near the shore in bays and estuaries, where it readily hits artificial lures. Ladyfish grow up to 8 or 9 pounds, but 1- and 2-pounders are the average catch. Why they are often called ten-pounder nobody knows. In addition to being bony, the ladyfish has soft flesh, but it firms up nicely when cooked.

Fried Ladyfish

If small pieces, or fingers, of ladyfish fillets are fried crisply, the bones seem to disappear. The key here is in having thin pieces—no thicker than 1 inch—and in getting the oil quite hot—at least 375 degrees. I prefer peanut oil and a light dusting of cornmeal instead of a thick batter, but other recipes will work with ladyfish fingers, such as the one below.

> 2 pounds ladyfish fillets
> 1 can tomato sauce (8-ounce size)
> 1½ cups flour
> ½ cup grated Parmesan cheese
> salt and freshly ground black pepper
> peanut oil for deep frying
> cocktail sauce (optional)
> lemon wedges (optional)

Rig for deep frying at 375 degrees. Salt and pepper the fillets, then cut them into fingers. Mix the flour and Parmesan in a small bag. Dip the fingers into tomato sauce, then shake them in the bag with the flour mixture. Deep-fry the fillets a few at a time for 3 or 4 minutes. The fish is done when it floats on top of the oil, but I like to brown bony fish for a few more seconds. Serve with cocktail sauce and lemon wedges, along with french fries and coleslaw, or whatever you normally serve with fried fish.

Ladyfish Cakes

Skin and fillet the fish, cut the fillets crosswise into fingers, and grind the meat in a sausage mill fitted with a ⅛- or 3⁄16-inch wheel.

> 1 cup ground fish
> ¼ cup cracker crumbs
> ¼ cup seasoned Italian bread crumbs
> 1 small onion, diced finely
> 1 chicken egg
> salt
> pepper
> butter or margarine

Combine the ground fish, crumbs, onion, and egg. Salt and pepper to taste. Shape the mixture into patties about ¾ inch thick. Heat the butter in a skillet and fry the patties. Brown on both sides. Serves 2 for a light lunch.

BONEFISH

Also called banana fish, silver ghost, phantom, ladyfish, and grubber, several species of bonefish *(Albula* spp.) frequent shallow-water flats in tropical and subtropical waters. I may be forever banned from the Florida Keys and the Bahamas, where sport-fishing interests will urge you to release all bonefish, and I will surely be laughed out of Taylor's Barber Shop, but I have to point out that the bonefish is considered choice eating in some parts of the world. The meat is white, firm, and nutty in flavor. The roe is also very good. Try baking the bonefish like a shad, or broil it and pick out the bones. The latter suggestion comes from Vic Dunaway's *From Hook to Table,* which says that when the fillets are broiled, a great many of the bones will arch up from the meat and can be picked away.

SHAD

The **American shad,** *Alosa sapidissima,* is an anadromous species that can be caught, in season, from Florida to Maine. They have also been stocked along the West Coast. The meat is very good, if you can beat the bones. There are other species of shad, such as the **hickory** *(Alosa mediocris,* also called roe herring, hick, or tailor shad), that are not as highly rated as table fare. Try pickling them or bake them at 300 degrees for 3 or 4 hours. All of the shads produce excellent roe.

Stuffed Connecticut Shad

At one time, cooking shad from the Connecticut River was something of a tradition. This time-tested recipe, one of my favorites, has been adapted from *Old-Time New England Cookbook,* by Duncan MacDonald and Robb Sagendorph.

> 1 freshly caught American shad of about 5 pounds
> 6 strips smoked bacon
> 1 cup fresh cracker crumbs
> 1 cup hot water
> ¼ cup melted butter
> 1 medium onion, minced
> 1 teaspoon sage
> ½ teaspoon pepper
> ½ teaspoon salt

Preheat the oven to 400 degrees. Scale, gut, and dry the shad, leaving the head on if your pan is long enough to accommodate the whole thing. Mix the cracker crumbs, melted butter, onion, sage, salt, and pepper; then stuff the shad, sewing the belly opening shut with cotton thread or twine, or securing it with round toothpicks. Place the stuffed shad on a well-greased rack in a baking pan. Add the water. Lay the bacon over it, being careful not to overlap the strips. Pin the ends of the bacon down with round toothpicks. Bake the fish in the center of the preheated oven for 10 minutes. Reduce the heat to 350 degrees and bake for about 35 minutes, or until the fish flakes easily when tested with a fork, basting from time to time with the pan juices. Serve hot. I allow about 1 pound of shad undressed weight per person. Also see the following recipe for slow-baked shad.

Baked American Shad

Here's another recipe designed for softening the small bones by long cooking. Be warned that the same recipe may not work for other bony fish, some of which are dry and flaky as compared with the rich, oily flesh of the American shad.

> 1 whole American shad, 3 to 5 pounds
> 6 strips bacon
> 1 tablespoon wine vinegar
> salt and pepper
> lemon slices (optional)
> water

Scale and gut the fish. Preheat the oven to 200 degrees. Find a pan of suitable size and shape to hold the shad. Pour in about a quart of water and the wine vinegar. Bring the water to a very light boil, then reduce the heat and poach the fish for 20 minutes. Drain the fish (saving some of the liquid) and sprinkle it lightly inside and out with salt and pepper. Place the fish on a rack in a roasting pan and put it into the oven for 5 or 6 hours. Remove the pan and preheat the broiling pan. Leaving the fish on the rack, cover it with strips of bacon. Put it under the broiler and cook until the bacon is crisp. Garnish with lemon slices and feast.

Sow Shad Soup

Here's a good recipe to try whenever you want to use the fillets from a roe shad for other purposes. Fillet the fish as usual for another recipe, saving the head, backbone, fins, tail, and roe for this soup. Although a 5-pound fish is specified in the ingredients list, the size isn't all that critical, and two or more smaller fish can be used provided that they have roe.

> soup makings from a 5-pound roe shad
> 8 ounces fresh mushrooms, sliced
> 4 slices bacon
> 1 cup red wine
> 2 quarts water
> 1 large onion, chopped
> 1 rib celery, chopped
> 1 tablespoon chopped fresh parsley
> 2 tablespoons flour
> 2 bay leaves
> ½ teaspoon thyme
> 4 peppercorns
> salt
> freshly ground black pepper

Heat the water in a pot or boiler, then add the fish head, backbone, tail, and fins, along with the onions, celery, bay leaves, parsley, wine, peppercorns, salt, and thyme. Simmer for 1 hour or thereabouts on very low heat. Strain and measure the liquid, then reduce by boiling to 4 cups. From the solid contents of the pot, separate the fish head and backbone, discarding the rest. With a fork, pull the meat from the head and backbone, setting it aside.

Fry and drain the bacon in a large skillet, and set it aside to drain. Sauté the mushrooms for a few minutes, then set aside to drain. Measure out 2 tablespoons of bacon grease, heat it in a stove-top Dutch oven, add the flour, and cook for 3 or 4 minutes, stirring constantly. Slowly add all the fish broth, then simmer for 5 or 6 minutes, stirring as you go.

Poach the roe in a little water, but do not boil, for 10 minutes, or until cooked through, depending on size. Cut the roe sacs in half to check for doneness. Remove the roe from the sacs, putting it directly into the broth. Add the sautéed mushrooms, flaked fish, and a little pepper. Heat through, then serve immediately in bowls, with the strips of bacon and plenty of bread on the side.

HERRINGS

The **Atlantic herring** *(Clupea harengus harengus)* and a very similar subspecies, the **Pacific herring,** along with other herrings,
are very important commercially but are not of much importance
to most sport fishers. Most of the fish sold as sardines in America
are really herrings. All of the herrings are oily and are often smoked.

For hundreds of years, salt herrings have been very important
in Europe. Salting is still one of the more popular ways of dealing
with the bones. In *Coastal Carolina Cooking,* for example, Katherine
Taylor says to gut the fish and pack them in brine in large jars.
Before cooking, freshen the fish in fresh water for 6 to 8 hours,
then fry them until they are quite crisp. Eat them bones and all.

As a rule, fresh herrings are not highly regarded in America
as table fare, even by people who love canned sardines or kippers.
In *The Frank Davis Seafood Notebook,* Davis said of the skipjack
herring: "Too bony, too oily, and too bloody for any recipe. Not
even a good trash fish!" I'm not so sure. And there are some sur-
prises. The flesh of menhaden (a herring that is sometimes called
porgy, buker, or bughead) is usually used for making cat food and
chicken feed, but its roe is delicious. Try it with scrambled eggs.
The **alewife** *(Alosa pseudoharengus,* also called river herring,
branch herring, goggle eye, grayback, or forerunner herring), once
important commercially, is bony and none too good, but it can
be canned, salted, smoked, or pickled. Its roe is excellent.

I might add that anyone who catches lots of herrings, perhaps
with the aid of some sort of net, might want to look into Scandinavian recipes.

Salt Herring with New Potatoes

The Scandinavian people eat raw salt herrings and other fish,
just as the Mexicans eat seviche and the Japanese eat sashimi. If
you are so inclined, try the following recipe. If you are opposed
to eating raw fish, read this recipe anyway, then take a close look
at the stuff served at smorgasbords.

salt herrings
dill sprigs
sour cream
chopped chives
boiled new potatoes (cooked separately)

Freshen the salt herrings overnight in fresh cold water. Skin and wash the fish, then carefully cut it crosswise into ½-inch slices. Rearrange the slices on a platter to resemble a whole fish. Sprinkle with chopped chives and dill. Mix some chopped chives with sour cream, chill, and serve with the fish, along with boiled new potatoes.

Flemish Herring Roe

The people of Belgium are very fond of seafood, and here's a good recipe from that country.

½ pound herring roe
1 tablespoon prepared Dijon-style mustard
mild paprika
melba toast
salt water

Bring some water to a boil, add a little salt, and poach the roe for about 10 minutes, or until the berries are opaque all the way through. Drain. Place the roe on a small plate or in a shallow dish. Remove the skin and break up the berries. Stir in the mustard. Sprinkle with paprika. Serve hot on melba toast.

TWENTY-SIX

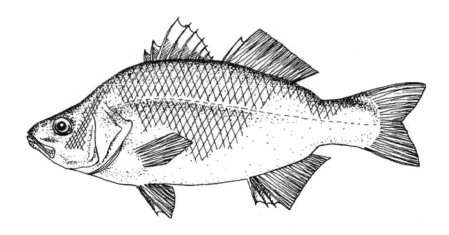

Perches

In an article about fish cookery, a large New York fishing and hunting magazine made reference to a fatty fish like perch. Fatty? What perch? Millions of anglers call bluegill and similar hand-sized freshwater panfish perch, though these certainly are not fatty. The crappie is often called white perch or speckled perch, but it is not fatty either. The dozens of surfperch on the Pacific coast are not fatty. The saltwater silver perch is not fatty. The yellow perch is not fatty. Nor is the Sacramento perch or the Rio Grande perch. I occasionally see some "Nile perch" for sale in my local supermarket, and they are not fatty (but they are probably tilapias and not real Nile perch). I'll have to conclude that the magazine author was talking about the ocean perch, which

---

White perch is one of the very best fish for the table.

---

is fatty but is seldom caught by sport fishermen. In short, I don't think the guy who wrote the article knows very much, if anything, about the sportsman's catch. He doesn't even speak the lingo.

In any case, here are some perches that may interest the saltwater fisher—some of which might even be found in the marketplace. Unless otherwise indicated, they all have lean white flesh, not at all fatty.

WHITE PERCH

This popular panfish *(Morone americana)* is caught in very large numbers in New England, ranging as far north as Nova Scotia and south to North Carolina. They live in fresh and brackish water, as well as salt water. The average catch is 8 or 9 inches—perfect for pan frying. On a culinary scale of 1 to 10, this fish would rate a 10 from me but might be rated lower by critics who can't handle the bones.

White Perch with Black Beans

The Chinese are fond of cooking with the aid of fermented beans, called *dow see,* available in Chinese markets and some super-markets. This recipe should be cooked with relatively small fish, and white perch are ideal. When you dress the white perch, leave the heads on. This recipe works with most small, white-fleshed fish or fillets. Larger fish can also be used, provided that the steaming time is increased. Allow 15 minutes for the first inch of thickness, plus 8 or 10 minutes for each additional inch.

2 pounds dressed white perch
¼ cup peanut oil
6 green onions
4 tablespoons soy sauce
2 tablespoons fermented black beans
2 tablespoons sake, sherry, or dry vermouth
1 tablespoon minced fresh garlic
1 teaspoon grated fresh ginger root

Trim off the roots and the top third of the green onions. Split the onions several times lengthwise, making a bundle of fine strands. Cut the strands into 1-inch segments. Rig for steaming. Heat the peanut oil in a skillet or wok, then add the black beans. Stir for 2 minutes, then stir in the green onions, soy sauce, wine, garlic, and ginger. Reduce the heat but keep hot. Place the fish on a deep plate. Pour the sauce over the fish. Put the plate in the steamer for 15 minutes. Serve with rice and Chinese vegetables.

Manhattan Indian Fish Chowder

I don't want to stir up the Yankees again, but the plain truth is that Indians were making good fish chowders and clam chowders long before the squabble about whether such a dish ought to include tomatoes. I hold that any American vegetable can be used in this recipe, which would include potatoes, Jerusalem artichokes, corn, and, yes, tomatoes. Even American squash or pumpkin is allowed, although I bar zucchini on the grounds that it's an Italian corruption of an original American vegetable. Suit yourself.

> 2 pounds dressed white perch (or other good fish)
> 4 medium potatoes, diced
> 4 ears corn (if available fresh)
> 4 tomatoes (vine ripened, if available)
> salt and red pepper flakes
> water

Dice the potatoes, shuck the corn, and cut the corn off the cob. Simmer these in 6 cups of water for 30 to 40 minutes. (Do not boil. The Indians heated the water with hot rocks, so remember that proper simmering can be accomplished at below 212 degrees.) Add the dressed perch (whole) and the tomatoes, along with some salt and a few flakes of red pepper. Simmer for 8 to 10 minutes, or until the fish flakes easily with a fork. Carefully remove the fish and pull all the meat off the bones. Put the flaked meat back into the chowder and stir. Serve hot.

SURFPERCH

Dozens of surfperch and perchlike fish are taken along the Pacific coast, and some are called seaperch (below). The **black perch** *(Embiotoca jacksoni)* is taken in California and Baja California waters, usually near rocky coasts and pilings. The small **kelp perch** *(Brachyistius frenatus)* is taken along the Pacific coast, usually in kelp along rocky shorelines. They grow to about 8 inches. The **pile perch** *(Rhacochilus vacca)* is quite plentiful along the California shore and is frequently taken by anglers. The small but plentiful **shiner perch** *(Cymatogaster aggregata)* grows to about 8 inches, ranging from Alaska to Baja.

The **opaleye** *(Girella nigricans)* has similar perchlike habits, looks like a perch, and is often called blue-eyed perch, Catalina perch, or button perch, as well as blue bass. Whether or not it's really a surfperch may be open to question, but doesn't really matter to most anglers or cooks. The **halfmoon** *(Medialuna californiensis)* is similar to the opaleye and is often called by one perch name or another.

Most of the small surfperch are pan-fried or deep-fried, but they can be cooked by other methods, as in the following recipe.

Russian Surfperch

I have adapted this recipe from Kira Petrovskaya's *Russian Cookbook,* where it was called *okoon v smetane.* The directions called for 6 or 7 small perch (or any small, white-meat fish). Hand-sized surfperch are ideal. These should be scaled, drawn, and beheaded.

> 6 or 7 perch
> 1 cup sour cream
> ½ cup Fish Stock (chapter 27)
> 1 medium onion, chopped
> ½ cup chopped fresh parsley
> 4 tablespoons flour
> butter
> salt and pepper
> boiled potatoes, cooked separately

Preheat the oven to 400 degrees. Roll the perch in flour, and sauté them in butter for 2 minutes on each side. Put the fish into a baking dish and sprinkle with salt and pepper. Quickly sauté the onion in the skillet. Add the fish stock and sour cream. Dissolve 1 tablespoon of flour in water and add the paste to the sour cream mixture. Bring to a quick boil. Reduce the heat and simmer until the sauce thickens. Pour the sauce over the fish and bake in a hot oven for 10 to 15 minutes. Sprinkle parsley over the fish and serve, along with hot boiled new potatoes and perhaps sauerkraut.

SEAPERCH

A number of fish are called seaperch. Some of these are surfperches (above) of the Pacific coast, such as the **island seaperch** *(Cymatogaster gracilis);* **pink seaperch** *(Zalembius rosaceus);* **rainbow seaperch** *(Hypsurus caryi);* **rubberlip seaperch** *(Rhacochilus toxotes),* considered to be the best of the commercial surfperch; the beautiful **striped seaperch** *(Embiotoca lateralis);* and **white seaperch** *(Phanerodon furcatus),* an important commercial species in California. The ocean perch is also called seaperch.

SILVER PERCH

The silver perch *(Bairdiella chrysura),* actually a small drum, is plentiful along parts of the Atlantic coast, as far north as New York, and in the Gulf of Mexico. It can be taken in brackish water and sometimes even in fresh water. Growing to about 12 inches in length, it makes excellent eating. A related species, *Bairdiella icistius,* sometimes called the Gulf croaker, was stocked successfully in California's Salton Sea.

SAND PERCH

The sand perch *(Diplectrum formosum),* actually a small sea bass, is caught from Virginia to Florida and around the Gulf of Mexico to Texas. They seldom grow over 12 inches in length. Good eating.

OCEAN PERCH

The ocean perch *(Sebastes marinus),* also called rosefish, red perch, red fish, sea perch, or Norway haddock, is a fish of open water and great depths, important commercially but seldom encountered by sport fishers. They grow to 5 pounds, but 1 pound is average. Ocean perch are on the oily side and have a strong flavor. They are not at their best when fried. It's best to bake or broil them. This species is technically a rockfish, the only Atlantic member of that clan. They are usually orange or red, or somewhere in between.

YELLOW PERCH

The **yellow perch** *(Perca flavescens),* a freshwater species, can sometimes be caught in large numbers in salt or brackish water estuaries from the Carolinas to Canada. Although small, these make delicious eating.

TWENTY-SEVEN

Sauces and Go-withs

In this chapter I am including a few sauces and condiments that are frequently served with fish, along with some ingredients that are often used in recipes. Cooking oils for frying fish are discussed in appendix A.

Fluffy Rice

Broiled and grilled fish are often served with rice of one sort or another. If you buy wild rice or perhaps a blend of wild and cultivated rice, it's best to follow the directions on the package. For this recipe, use ordinary long-grain rice.

> 1 cup long-grain rice
> 2 cups water
> salt
> cooking oil

In a pan with a tight-fitting lid, heat the water to a boil along with a little oil and salt. Add the rice and bring to a boil again. Reduce the heat, cover tightly, and cook on very low heat for exactly 20 minutes. Do not peek during the cooking time. Remove the pan from the heat, dip the bottom into a larger pan of cold water, and remove the top. Serve hot.

These measures will make enough rice for 2 to 4 people as served with fish. Double the recipe if more is needed.

Garlic Rice

Melt 4 tablespoons of butter in a skillet. Sauté 2 cloves of crushed garlic for 2 minutes. On low heat, stir in 1 cup of long-grain rice and stir continuously until the butter has been absorbed. Do not brown the rice. Quickly add 2 cups of chicken stock, along with a little salt and white pepper. Reduce the heat to very low and cook for 20 to 25 minutes, or until all the stock has been absorbed.

A. D.'s Skillet Hush Puppies

If you've got a favorite recipe for hush puppies, use it. If not, you may want to try mine. You'll need some stone-ground cornmeal, preferably white. I don't really measure the ingredients, which vary a little from one batch to another, depending on the meal and perhaps the humidity.

> stone-ground cornmeal
> hot water
> oil
> salt and pepper

Put some meal into a bowl. Stir in a little salt and pepper, along with a little oil. Slowly stir in enough hot water to make a mush. Let this sit for about 30 minutes. Then stir again, adding a little water as needed. The consistency should be right for dropping the mixture from a large spoon. Heat ½ to ¾ inch of oil in a skillet. The oil should be medium hot, well below the smoking point. Drop in a spoonful of hush puppy mix. It should flatten a little from its own weight, making a patty about 2 inches in diameter. Adjust the consistency if necessary, adding more water if the mixture is too stiff or a little more meal if it is too soupy. Fry a few at a time until nicely browned on both sides, turning once. Drain on a brown bag. Serve hot.

Variation: Add some minced onion to the hush puppy mix.

Toasted Garlic Bread

Here's a bread that I like with any grilled or broiled fish, and especially with the fatty species such as mackerel.

> 1 large loaf French, Italian, or sourdough bread
> ¼ cup olive oil
> 4 cloves garlic, crushed through a press
> 2 tablespoons mayonnaise

Slice the bread on a diagonal, making each piece about 1 inch thick. Preheat the broiler. Mix the oil, garlic, and mayonnaise. Arrange the bread on a rack about 4 inches from the heat source. Brush the tops with the olive oil mixture. Broil until lightly browned. Turn, brush, and broil until the other side is browned to your liking. Watch closely to prevent burning.

Garlic Oil

I like to use garlic-flavored oil for sautéing and stir-frying, as well as for making toasted garlic bread. Although any good cooking oil can be used, I prefer olive oil or peanut oil. Simply fill a jar with peeled garlic cloves, cover it with oil, and set aside for a few weeks. Of course, the garlic can also be used.

A quicker method, which can give a distinctive burnt flavor, is to sauté some sliced garlic in oil until it browns. This oil can be used immediately for stir-frying or sautéing.

A. D.'s Tabasco Oil

Fill a small jar with a mixture of fresh red, green, and orange tabasco peppers. Cover with olive oil. After a week or so, use the oil sparingly to flavor stir-fry oils.

Lemon Relish

This recipe, designed to go with the Louisiana Shark recipe in chapter 1, is also good with other fish. Here's what you need to make about a cup of relish:

½ cup sour cream
¼ cup crushed pineapple, drained
2 tablespoons green bell pepper, finely chopped
2 tablespoons peeled lemon, diced
1 teaspoon grated lemon rind (zest only)
1 tablespoon onion, finely chopped
1 tablespoon light brown sugar
¼ teaspoon dry mustard
¼ teaspoon celery salt
⅛ teaspoon ground cloves

Mix all the ingredients in a small nonmetallic bowl and refrigerate before serving. Grate only the yellow part of the lemon rind.

Amandine Topping

This topping is usually served with trout, and especially with speckled trout in New Orleans. But try it with any good fried, sautéed, or broiled fish.

1 cup slivered almonds
1 cup salted butter
juice of 1 lemon
½ teaspoon black pepper, freshly ground

Melt the butter in a cast-iron skillet and heat it until it turns slightly brown. Add the almonds and cook for 1½ minutes, shaking the skillet as you go. Remove the skillet from the heat. Add the lemon juice and pepper, stirring with a wooden spoon. Put the skillet back on the heat for 1 minute. Serve the sauce hot over the fish. These measures will be enough for 4 small whole fish or fillets.

Jalapeño Salsa

Any good salsa goes nicely with grilled, broiled, or poached fish. Also, those Americans who insist on eating catsup with their fried fish ought to try salsa instead. There are hundreds of good salsa recipes and commercial mixes. Here's one of my favorites, especially if I've got vine-ripened tomatoes from my garden.

> 1 large tomato, peeled and chopped
> 1 medium-to-large onion, chopped
> 1 jalapeño pepper, seeded and minced
> 3 tablespoons olive oil
> ½ tablespoon wine vinegar
> salt and pepper to taste

Heat the oil in a small skillet and sauté the onion for 4 or 5 minutes. Add the chopped tomato, jalapeño, salt, and pepper. Cook on low heat, stirring as you go, for 5 minutes, or until the sauce begins to thicken. Stir in the wine vinegar. Serve with fish.

Note: Any hot green pepper can be used instead of the jalapeño. Just remember that some of these things are very hot. The seeds and inner pith should be removed before mincing. Wash your hands after working with hot peppers.

Shrimp Sauce

> 1 can condensed cream of shrimp soup
> (10¾-ounce size)
> ½ cup finely chopped cooked shrimp
> ¼ cup milk
> salt and white pepper to taste

Mix all ingredients, heat to a simmer, and pour over baked, broiled, or pan-fried fish.

Oyster Sauce

Here's a good sauce to make whenever you have fresh oysters to spare. When you shuck them, be sure to catch and save all the liquor from the shell. I like it over grilled or broiled fish.

    2 dozen small oysters with their liquor
    ½ cup scalded milk
    2 tablespoons butter
    2 tablespoons flour
    1 tablespoon white wine
    1 tablespoon chopped parsley
    juice of ½ lemon
    salt and pepper

Heat the oyster liquor and wine in a saucepan. Add the oysters and stew for 2 or 3 minutes. Remove and chop the oysters. In a small pan, melt the butter and stir in the lemon juice, flour, and parsley. Add this mixture to the oyster sauce. Stir in the scalded milk and minced oysters. Bring to a boil, remove from heat, and stir in some salt and pepper. I like lots of freshly ground black pepper. Serve hot over broiled or grilled fish.

Meunière Sauce

    1 cup salted butter
    juice of 2 lemons
    2 tablespoons minced fresh parsley
    salt and pepper to taste

Heat the butter over low heat in a small skillet until it begins to turn brown. Quickly remove the skillet from the heat and stir in the parsley, lemon juice, salt, and pepper. Stir for a minute, then return the skillet to the heat for a minute. Remove the skillet from the heat, but keep warm until you are ready to serve the fish.

Hot Pepper Jelly Sauce

The jelly used in this recipe can be made at home, but these days it is available in specialty shops and some supermarkets. Jalapeño jelly will do just fine.

> ½ cup hot pepper jelly
> 2 tablespoons white wine vinegar
> 2 tablespoons white wine

Melt the jelly in a saucepan, then stir in the vinegar and wine. Cool to room temperature and serve with fish patties.

Tartar Sauce

> 1 cup mayonnaise
> 2 tablespoons finely chopped salad pickles
> 2 tablespoons minced green onions
> 1 clove garlic, minced
> 1 tablespoon finely chopped fresh parsley
> 1 teaspoon prepared yellow mustard

Mix all ingredients in a serving container. Refrigerate for an hour or so before serving.

Tomato Sauce

In a pinch, canned tomatoes can be used for this recipe, but I prefer vine-ripened fresh tomatoes, if available. To peel the tomatoes easily, immerse them in boiling water for about 10 seconds, then slip the skins off.

3 large tomatoes, peeled and chopped
1 large onion, finely chopped
2 cloves garlic, minced
¼ cup butter
1 teaspoon fresh thyme, minced
salt and pepper

Melt butter in a skillet, and sauté the onion and garlic for 5 minutes. Add the chopped tomatoes, thyme, salt, and pepper. Bring to a light bubble, reduce the heat, and simmer uncovered for 30 minutes.

Egg Sauce

Egg sauce is good with grilled or broiled fish, in which case it should be made with fish stock.

1 cup Fish Stock (page 240)
3 tablespoons butter
3 tablespoons flour
2 chicken egg yolks

Beat the egg yolks in a bowl. Melt the butter in a saucepan and stir in the flour with a wooden spoon. Then gradually stir in the fish stock. Remove the pan from the heat. Slowly stir the contents of the pan into the egg yolks, stirring as you go. Pour the mixture back into the pan. Heat for about a minute, but do not boil. Serve hot with grilled, broiled, or poached fish.

Horseradish Sauce

This sauce is especially good with poached fish, and it makes use of part of the poaching liquid (or fish stock). It is made from fresh horseradish roots, which are more widely available in supermarkets and from many home gardens these days.

> 1 cup grated horseradish root
> 2 cups Fish Stock (page 240)
> 1 cup butter
> 1 cup whipping cream
> 1 cup soft bread crumbs
> 3 yolks of hard-boiled chicken eggs
> 1 tablespoon creole or Dijon mustard
> salt
> Tabasco sauce

Bring the fish stock to a boil in a saucepan, add the horseradish, and simmer for 20 minutes. Stir in the butter, cream, and bread crumbs. Season with salt and a little Tabasco sauce. Bring almost to a boil, then turn off the heat. Mash together the egg yolks and prepared mustard, then stir the mixture into the sauce. Serve hot over poached or steamed fish.

Easy Red Horseradish Sauce

> 1 cup bottled catsup
> 1 tablespoon grated horseradish (or to taste)

Grate the horseradish, then slowly mix it into the catsup, tasting as you go. Serve with deep-fried fish.

Dill Sauce

> 1 cup sour cream
> juice of 1 lemon
> ½ teaspoon chopped fresh dill weed
> ½ teaspoon salt

Mix all the ingredients and refrigerate. Serve cold over chilled poached fish.

Green Peppercorn Sauce

This wonderful sauce is good with grilled or broiled fish and is especially good with hot-smoked fish. The green peppercorns, available in spice markets, are packed in water.

> 8 ounces sour cream
> 2 tablespoons green peppercorns, crushed
> crushed sea salt to taste

Mix all the ingredients in a small serving bowl, cover, and refrigerate for at least 1 hour. Serve chilled.

Maître d'Hôtel Sauce

> ¼ cup butter
> juice of 1 lemon
> 1 tablespoon minced fresh parsley
> ½ teaspoon salt
> ⅛ teaspoon white pepper

Soften and whip the butter in a bowl. Stir in the salt, pepper, parsley, and lemon juice. Serve at room temperature with fried fish. You can also use this sauce as a baste during the last few minutes of grilling or broiling.

Onion Sauce

½ cup butter
juice of ½ lemon
½ cup minced green onions with half of tops
salt and pepper

Heat the butter in a skillet. Sauté the minced green onions for 5 minutes. Stir in the lemon juice, salt, and pepper. Serve warm over poached or broiled fish.

Basic White Sauce

1 tablespoon butter
1 tablespoon flour
1 cup half-and-half
salt and white pepper

Melt the butter in a saucepan. Stir in the flour, but do not brown. Remove the saucepan from the heat. Stir in the half-and-half, blending well. Add a little salt and white pepper.

Fish Sauce

The people of Southeast Asia use fish sauce in recipes and as a table sauce. Made by salting down anchovies or other fish and catching the drippings, it is called *nuoc mam* in Vietnam, *Nam Pla* in Thailand, *tuk trey* in Cambodia, and *patis* in the Philippines. Several brands of fish sauce can now be purchased in some of the larger American supermarkets and specialty shops. It has a long shelf life.

Anchovy Butter Sauce

Here's an excellent spread or thick sauce for use on poached or broiled fish. I use anchovy paste because it is convenient for squeezing out a small amount.

¼ cup butter, softened
1 teaspoon anchovy paste
juice of ½ lemon
½ teaspoon brandy
2 or 3 drops Tabasco sauce

Mash the butter in a small mixing bowl until soft. Stir in the rest of the ingredients. Serve at room temperature.

Caviar Butter

½ cup butter, softened
¼ cup black caviar berries
juice of 1 lemon

Whip the butter until it creams. Mix in the caviar and lemon juice. Turn into a mold, and chill until you are ready to serve.

Court Bouillon

After poaching the fish in the court bouillon, the liquid can then be used as fish stock for making various sauces. Boiling vegetables in water yields a liquid for poaching fish. The first three ingredients of the court bouillon recipe below are set forth in equal measures. Any mix of these yielding a full cup will be satisfactory, but I prefer to go heavy on the celery if I have a choice.

⅓ cup chopped onion
⅓ cup chopped celery
⅓ cup chopped carrots
1 tablespoon chopped fresh parsley
2 bay leaves
6 cloves
6 peppercorns
3 tablespoons butter
½ cup red wine vinegar
2 quarts water

Put 2 quarts of water into a stock pot and turn on the heat. In a skillet, heat the butter and sauté the carrots, celery, and onions. Add the skillet contents and the rest of the ingredients to the boiling water. Bring to a new boil and simmer for 30 minutes. Strain the liquid and use immediately or store in jars, refrigerated. If you freeze the court bouillon, consider using plastic containers instead of jars.

Fish Stock

Never throw out a head or backbone left from filleting a fish. Both can be used to make fish stock, which is used in a number of recipes and can also be used as a soup or the base for a soup. Make up a batch of stock whenever you clean fish.

> 4 pounds fish heads and bony pieces
> 2 quarts water
> 2 cups dry white wine
> 1 medium onion, chopped
> 1 rib celery with green top, chopped
> 1 carrot, chopped
> ½ cup chopped fresh parsley
> 3 bay leaves
> 10 peppercorns

Put all of the ingredients except the wine into a pot, and bring to a boil. Cover, reduce the heat to very low, and simmer for 1 hour. Then strain the liquid and put it back into the pot. Add the wine and simmer until the volume is reduced by half. This recipe makes about 4 cups of stock. Use it immediately, refrigerate it for several days, or freeze it.

Coconut Milk and Coconut Cream

The coconut is now used in one way or another in the cuisine of most parts of the world, and coconut milk is a very important ingredient in many African and Indonesian recipes.

Crack the coconut, remove the meat in chunks, and grate it into a suitable container. Pour over the grated meat an equal volume of hot water. Cool, then squeeze out the liquid and strain it. This is coconut milk. You can repeat the process several times, but the liquid will become weaker as you go. To make coconut cream, let the strong coconut milk stand for several hours, then skim off the rich top layer.

To make 1 cup of coconut milk, start with 1½ cups of grated meat and 1½ cups of hot water.

If you don't have a fresh coconut, substitute unsweetened desiccated grated coconut, available in packages or perhaps frozen. Also, you may be able to find canned or frozen coconut milk in a supermarket or specialty food store or by mail. (I was surprised to find a good supply of canned coconut milk at a Dixie Dandy store in Wewahitchka, Florida, near my cabin on Dead Lakes.) But be warned that the cream of coconut with piña colada recipes on the back is usually too sweet.

APPENDIX A

How to Cook Fish

Although the chapters in this book should be pretty much self-contained, some pointers and advice can apply to cooking fish by any recipe. Being something of a stickler for technique, I believe that attention to details can be more important than exact ingredients. Soggy fried fish, for example, isn't going to suit my taste, no matter how many spices the batter contains.

SKILLET FRYING

This is my favorite way to fry a few fish for four or five people. I use a cast-iron skillet, which can be heated to a high heat. By high, I mean at least 375 degrees, preferably hotter, just under the smoking point. I use peanut oil because it takes the heat well without burning, but olive or other oils, such as canola, can also be used. Peanut oil, however, can be used over and over, provided that it is properly strained and stored after use.

I like to have the fish about half covered with oil, or a little more. With most fillets and small fish, this means putting about 1 inch of oil in the skillet, or a little better. When the fish are put in, there will be some displacement, so don't put in *too* much oil. Having the hot oil bubbling too high in the skillet is dangerous and can lead to a fire, especially when using gas heat.

While the oil heats up, salt the fish and shake them in a bag with fine stone-ground cornmeal or perhaps flour. Personally, I don't use any kind of milk or egg or other goo with the coating, as a thick batter soaks up lots of grease, but suit yourself. Immersing the fish in very hot oil also keeps the fish from absorbing too much oil and seals in the juices.

Do not crowd the skillet. Turn the fish gently with short tongs or perhaps with the aid of a spatula. When both sides are nicely browned, take the fish up carefully and place onto absorbent paper to drain. Do not pile pieces of fish atop each other during the initial draining. Any absorbent paper can be used, but I prefer a brown bag. I also take the fish to the table on the brown bag, unless we've got snooty guests. Hush puppies and french fries can also be drained on a brown bag, but there is a limit to how much stuff one bag will hold. If this is a problem, I sometimes heat up a long cast-iron griddle across two stove burners. After draining the fish and other fried stuff on a brown bag, I transfer them to the heated griddle. An electrically heated serving platter can also be used. In any case, proper draining is very important to good fried fish.

PAN FRYING OR SAUTÉING

This method works better with small fish or fillets cooked on low heat in a little butter or oil. How much oil? Enough to barely cover the bottom of the skillet. Maybe 2 tablespoons. If you cook more than one batch of fish, you may have to add more oil. If you're using butter, it's best to change with every batch because butter tends to turn too dark during the cooking. A thin dusting of flour is all you need for sautéing, and some recipes require no coating at all.

This method is really ideal when cooking for one or two people. Some griddles, however, will permit cooking for larger crowds.

The fish are turned once. A sauce is used with some recipes, such as Trout Meunière in chapter 2. For convenience, I prefer to make the sauce in the skillet, using the oil and juices left after cooking the fish, along with a little flour and other ingredients. Some other people insist on cleaning the skillet and heating a fresh batch of butter or oil. If you want to use the skillet without cleaning out the dredgings, as I do, it is important to cook the fish on low heat without burning the butter or oil. It helps to have good heat control and a heavy skillet such as cast iron.

DEEP FRYING

The secret to successful deep frying is to heat lots of oil in a pot of suitable size and shape. For best results, the oil should be at least 375 degrees, and preferably hotter. A good deep-frying thermometer will help you. Note that the high temperature should be pretty much maintained. This requires that only a small or moderate amount of fish be added to the oil at a time. Too much fish will lower the temperature too drastically. Having a good thermometer immersed in the oil will help you know when to turn the heat up or down.

I prefer peanut oil because it has a high smoking point and doesn't flavor the fish or absorb odors. It can be reused if it is strained; I run mine through coffee filters. Olive oil is also good, and the price gets better by the gallon.

In any case, you need lots of oil with plenty of depth to it. Having hot, deep oil makes frying almost foolproof because a piece of fish will float when it is done. I usually let each piece stay in for a few seconds after it floats, then take it out with tongs or a slotted spoon or strainer. This piece-by-piece approach keeps me busy and allows me to place each fish individually on brown bags to drain instead of dumping them all out from a pot-fitted strainer. Proper draining (discussed under Skillet Frying) can be very important. The done-when-it-floats approach also allows me to cook the larger pieces longer than the small ones.

Deep frying is ideal for feeding fried fish to a large crowd. It is also ideal for cooking fish that have been heavily coated with batter.

BROILING

Broiling is a method of cooking fish under the heat as distinguished from grilling it over the heat. An electric oven with a heating element in the top works better than a gas oven, in my opinion. Proper broiling is easy—but it's also exacting and not foolproof. The general rule is to cook the fish as close as possible to the heat without burning the surface before the inside gets done. Consequently, the thicker the fish, the farther it must be from the heat.

Thin fillets work better than whole fish, except that they are difficult to move without tearing. The good news is that thin fillets don't necessarily have to be turned. I often start the fillets cooking on a cast-iron griddle on top of the stove, and then put the whole works into the oven, thereby cooking both the top and bottom. Small whole fish can be broiled successfully, but these have to be turned over. Most broiling pans have a rack across the top so that the fish juices and basting liquid are contained below. Some of these racks are wire and some are sheet metal with slots. Fish tend to stick to either kind, making it difficult to turn the larger fish. If your hinged grilling rack fits under your broiler, use it for fish that have to be turned. Here are a few more tips on broiling fish.

1. *Choose the highest temperature setting.* On most modern electric kitchen stoves, the heat is controlled thermostatically. Unless you have reason to do otherwise, turn the heat to broil or the highest setting. Then you can lower the rack with larger fish. This method works better than cooking it closer on a lower heat.

2. *Preheat the broiler.* Allow about 20 minutes for the broiler to heat to maximum.

3. *Leave the oven door open while broiling.* If you shut the oven door, you are baking as well as broiling. Besides, I like to see and smell and hear my fish broiling.

4. *Get thin fillets close to the heat.* The sliding racks in most electric ovens are adjustable. For small fillets, put the rack in the topmost position, then put your broiling pan on it. For thin fillets, you may have to put some sort of spacer under the broiling pan in order to get the fish closer to the heat. Two inches isn't too close for thin fillets. A disgruntled woman once told me that broiling too close to the heating element makes a mess in the oven, causing the grease drippings and basting liquid to pop and spatter. I don't deny it.

5. *Baste.* Most fish should be basted, usually with butter or oil, a time or two while broiling. Often a leftover marinade is used for basting. Some people, however, object to using leftover marinade toward the end of the cooking period because it contains uncooked fish juices and blood. Think about it. In any case, an oily baste keeps the surface of the fish from drying out, adds flavor, and helps in

browning. How often you baste depends on the recipe, but thin fillets usually need only one treatment about halfway through cooking. Don't baste too often, however, lest you cool the fish too much for proper broiling.

6. *Watch your business.* If you have to scrape your toast every morning, remember that broiling fish is a full-time job. This is especially true of thin fillets very close to the heat.

GRILLING

Grilling fish over hot wood coals, in addition to providing excellent eating, seems to satisfy a primitive yearning in man. These days, grilling can also be accomplished quite successfully over gas-heated lava rocks or electric heat. Although grilling seems at first to be very close to broiling (cooking under the heat), there is a difference. Grilling is more of a hands-on kind of cooking, where the cook stands over and watches the process as he goes. Perhaps more important is the fact that smoke and vapor rise from the heat, from wood or wood chips, and from drippings from the fish or the basting liquid. The smoke adds flavor and aroma, and the drippings add sizzle.

Although the arena for grilling is still pretty much the patio, the same techniques and most of the same recipes can be used in camp or in the kitchen. That's right. A number of modern grills can be used indoors, and I am very fond of using the built-in grill on my electric stove. It's very handy day or night, rain or shine.

In my opinion, all true grilling is done on a rack directly over an open fire or coals. This includes cooking on a spit or kabob skewer. Some grilling techniques involve a hood that covers the fish or meat. The hoods come in handy for adding more smoke to the flavor, or for cooking large fish by the indirect method— that is, by using a large grill with a covered hood and putting the fire in one section and the fish in the other. This can be compared to cooking in an oven with the advantage of some smoke for flavor. (Smoking is covered under a separate heading.)

In direct grilling, the rule of thumb is that the smaller the fish, the closer it should be to the heat, within reason. The larger the fish, the farther away it should be from the heat. In both cases, the idea is to get the inside done at the exact time the outside is nicely browned. It's not hard, but it requires constant attention and some common sense. Actually, each time you grill fish is a new experience in cooking. In any case, here are some tips to consider.

1. *Use good fuel.* If you use charcoal, consider getting the real stuff instead of using pressed briquettes. It's more expensive, but it burns better and gets hotter. Also, it isn't stuck together with additives. If you use briquettes, it's best to avoid the self-starting kind, which contain even more additives. I'll admit to using the liquid starting fluid from time to time, and I find it very handy to have, but I really prefer to start a fire with the aid of twigs, paper, or some such kindling.

If you've got the time, consider building a hardwood fire and letting it burn down to coals. Green wood, although hard to start burning, makes good coals and provides wonderful smoke. When grilling for a large crowd, consider using hard coal instead of charcoal, if you can find it these days. Coal burns long and hot.

2. *Let your fire get hot.* Always allow plenty of time for your fire to get hot, be it wood, charcoal, briquettes, gas-heated lava rocks, or an electric coil and grate. My stove-top unit has an electric coil over a cast-iron grate and requires 30 minutes to get at its best.

3. *Grease your rack.* I like to grease my grilling rack before building the fire, then again just before I put the fish or meat on for cooking. Bacon grease is my favorite, but any good cooking oil will do. A new rack should be greased and heated a time or two over a hot fire to break it in and season it.

4. *Spare the wire brush.* My wife says that my opinion on this step is wishful thinking, but I like to think that failure to clean the grate after grilling on it prevents rust and promotes seasoning.

5. *Baste—but not too much.* Although many saltwater fish are on the oily side and therefore don't require as much basting as a cod or such fish with dry, white flesh, a good basting with oil or butter will help keep the surface moist and aid in browning. A little oil on the surface of the fish also helps it absorb last-minute additions of salt and pepper and perhaps herbs. Be warned,

however, that basting can be overdone, especially with thick tomato-based sauces, which tend to burn if applied too early during the grilling process.

6. *Get gear that works.* The price of a piece of grilling gear does not necessarily indicate how useful it will be to you. Spatulas are especially useful to me for grilling fish; in fact, I like to have two spatulas when turning fillets, one for the bottom and one for the top. But the metal in some spatulas is far too thick. What you need is a thin spatula, made of what I call "spring steel." This will help you get under the fish without tearing it. Also, I prefer spatulas of normal kitchen length instead of the long-handled type sold for patio cooking.

7. *Use a grilling basket or rig one.* If you grill lots of fish, you might consider getting a hinged grilling basket. I highly recommend the adjustable rectangular models, which can hold small whole fish or thin fillets. Kabob baskets are also available, and there is even a fish-shaped basket for holding whole large fish. Using a basket, of course, facilitates turning the fish without tearing it up.

You can easily rig a sort of grilling basket with two wire racks of equal size. Merely putting the fish on one rack and putting the other rack on top when you are ready to turn the fish will work nicely, if you can make the turn without getting burned. Fireproof gloves will help.

8. *Watch your business.* Unless you are cooking a large fish by the indirect method or are using some sort of combination smoker and cooker, grilling fish is a full-time job. Refuse to answer the telephone or do chores while you man the grill. It's just too easy to burn fish when you are cooking very close to hot coals. In addition to turning and basting the fish properly, you'll need to keep an eye peeled for flare-ups. That's why I often keep a cold beer in hand while grilling.

9. *Serve grilled fish hot.* Large fish cooked by the indirect method may take an hour or longer, but small fish and fillets can be grilled in a matter of minutes. It is therefore sometimes best to have everything else ready to eat before you start grilling.

STEAMING

To steam fish, rig a rack of some sort in a pot of suitable size. Put a little water in the bottom, place the fish above it, bring to a boil, cover tightly, and steam for 10 minutes per inch of thickness. If you are on a mountain or high above sea level, more time will be required.

If you have a Chinese bamboo steamer, use it. When using an ordinary pot, you can build a rack of sorts with carrots and other vegetables. Add a little water and place the fish on top, thereby cooking a whole meal. Also, fish that is put into aluminum foil and grilled over hot coals is really steamed, if the package is properly sealed.

All in all, steaming is an excellent way to cook fish. Properly steamed fish is moist and succulent, and is often served with a sauce.

POACHING

Poaching is an excellent way to cook fish and can be very simple or very complicated. In its simplest form, the fish is merely simmered in water for a few minutes. The general rule—10 minutes per inch of thickness—applies to poaching at sea level, provided that the fish doesn't cool the poaching liquid too much at the outset.

Complicated recipes for poaching usually require either a Court Bouillon (chapter 27) or a sauce of some sort, or both. Many of these recipes are French and require all manner of ingredients, such as sauces needed in order to make sauces in order to make sauces, and are just too complicated, too time-consuming, and too expensive for home use.

For poaching fillets, a large, deep skillet can be used, and I especially like an electric skillet for this purpose. Any pot can be used, such as a Dutch oven, but it doesn't have to be deep.

Large fish that are poached whole require a special pot, such as the French oblong pans designed to fit over two stove burners. The better ones have a lid and a removable rack, which allows the fish to be taken out of the pan easily. The lid and rack also permit the pan to be used for steaming large fish. Some of these fish poachers tend to be expensive, however. While writing this section, I checked the price of an Italian-made poacher marketed by Dean & Deluca of New York City. A 16-inch poacher (their largest) lists for $385. I'll have to look around a little further; sometimes I catch fish longer than 16 inches.

BAKING

Some fatty fish, such as the Atlantic shad, can be baked for long periods of time, but most lean fish tend to dry out when baked. Also, some baking recipes call for putting the fish into a baking bag or encasing it in brown paper. These fish are more steamed than baked, but I'm not going to argue with the results. In any case, here are some tips for cooking better fish in the oven.

1. *Test the accuracy of your thermostat.* Put an oven thermometer in the center of your oven and test it against your thermostat setting. If there is a difference, allow for it when setting your oven temperature.

2. *Bake in the center of the oven.* The temperatures within an oven can vary quite a bit. It's best to adjust the oven racks so that the fish itself is in the middle.

3. *Preheat the oven.* Always heat the oven for about 20 minutes before baking your fish, or until the temperature is at the correct setting for your recipe.

4. *Grease your baking pan.* Although fatty fish don't stick to the bottom of a pan as badly as lean fish, it's always better to grease your pan with at least a light coating of oil or with a cooking spray.

5. *Use a meat thermometer on large fish.* Baking a whole large fish can be tricky, and it's best to insert a meat thermometer into the thickest part of the fish. Start the thermometer in near the head and insert it at an angle, going back toward the tail. Do not touch the rib cage or backbone. The fish is done when the thermometer reads between 140 and 145 degrees. If the fish is stuffed, turn off the oven and leave the fish in it for another 10 minutes or so.

6. *Abide by the general rule.* If you don't use a meat thermometer, which isn't practical on most fillets and small fish, remember the general rule: 10 minutes of cooking time for each inch of thickness in a moderately hot oven (about 350 degrees). If you use a cold baking pan, allow a little more time. This general rule is only a guide, however. When done, most fish will flake easily when tested with a fork.

7. *Baste with pan juices.* Basting the fish from time to time helps it brown and keeps the flesh moist. But opening the oven lets out lots of heat, so don't baste too often, and when you do baste, do so quickly.

8. *Leave the head, skin, fins, and tail on baked whole fish.* These parts will help hold in the juices, especially at the head end. If you must remove the head and tail for the benefit of squeamish guests, leave them on the fish during the baking process and remove them before serving. I also prefer to leave the skin on most baked fish unless there is a good reason for taking it off, such as a strong taste. Also, the head makes very good eating if gnawing and nibbling are permitted at the table.

9. *Bake in a serving pan.* If you have a baking pan suitable for serving, use it. This will minimize handling the fish and will send the fish to the table with all the good pan juices.

10. *Don't overcook.* Cooking a fish in a dry oven for too long is a culinary sin. Use your timer.

Cooking fish in a microwave oven is tricky and, frankly, I don't recommend it. There are other opinions, however, and I would like to refer the reader to Paula J. Del Giudice's *Microwave Game & Fish Cookbook,* published by Stackpole Books.

Also, be warned that some of the new forced-air ovens drastically alter cooking times for some baking recipes. For the recipes in this book, use the oven in its ordinary mode. If you do use the forced-air mode, be sure to read the instructions that came with your unit.

SMOKING

Hot smoking is really slow cooking with the aid of a little smoke for flavor. It can be accomplished in large grills, with the fish on one side and the fire on the other. Hot smoking can also be done in the silo-type smokers fitted with a water pan and fire box. The smoke is usually provided by dry wood chips (usually soaked in water) or sawdust. Also, try freshly cut green hardwood, which doesn't have to be soaked. For best results, hot smoking should be done at temperatures well above 160 degrees to ensure that the fish actually cooks. If you are cooking and smoking at low temperatures, be sure to first treat the fish in a salt cure. You can also grill the fish at high temperatures while at the same time flavoring it with a little smoke, preferably in a covered grill.

Cold smoking should be accomplished at temperatures below 100 degrees, preferably at about 75 degrees. The fish must be treated overnight or longer in a brine or with a salt rub to discourage the growth of bacteria. The smoke itself contributes very little to the curing process. The key is to use plenty of salt for a long enough period of time. Cold-smoked fish may or may not be safe to eat as is. I recommend that it be thoroughly cooked.

APPENDIX B

Ten Steps to Better Saltwater Fish

Few if any recipes can work magic unless the fish is in good shape at the beginning of the cooking process. A great deal depends on what happens to the fish, or doesn't happen to them, between the water and the table. Because saltwater fish are so diverse, however, this section simply cannot be as clear-cut as I would like. Too many ifs, ands, and buts. But here goes.

1. *Know your fish.* Some saltwater fish keep better than others. This book's chapters on the various species should be of help in this regard. If in doubt, assume the worst case: that the fish spoils very quickly and contains urea. If steps 2 and 3 are followed, even the worst-case fish may be of very good flavor. If not, they might well be inedible.

2. *Ice your catch.* Forget about keeping freshly caught saltwater fish on a stringer or in a live well. It's best to ice them down as soon as possible after catching them. Have a bed of ice on the bottom of the cooler. Place the fish on the ice, then add ice on top. The general rule is to have 3 inches of ice under the fish and another 3 inches on top of them.

If you are after sharks, skates, rays, or perhaps large game-fish, consider using slush instead of ice. Slush is made by adding salt water to the ice. The salt causes the ice to melt, and when melting, it draws heat from the fish. This is the same principle that is used in the old-fashioned hand-cranked ice cream freezers. I don't have an exact formula, but equal parts by weight of seawater and ice is about right. You can also apply salt directly to ice, preferably crushed ice, using ½ pound of salt for each 5 pounds of ice.

Large fish should be gutted and ice packed into the body cavity before they are put into the box.

It's best to keep water drained from the bottom of the chest, or to place the fish on a rack so that they will not be in any water that collects on the bottom, or both. In my opinion, however, this step is not as important as having plenty of ice in the chest. Remember to add more ice as needed.

3. *Draw the fish quickly if necessary.* Dress the fish, or at least draw them, as soon as possible after the catch. Some fish should be drawn within 15 to 20 minutes, and I have tried to identify these in the various chapters. Other fish, however, can be kept for several days before drawing if they are promptly and properly iced down. Usually, small fish keep better than large ones, but each species is different.

Almost always, drawing the fish should take precedence over skinning, beheading, scaling, and filleting. These tasks can be performed later. Very large fish, however, should be filleted or cut into chunks so that the ice or slush cools them quickly.

Some people believe in bleeding fish. I feel that gutting the fish quickly is sufficient, but bleed it if you want to. Simply cut the fish on either side just above the tail as soon as it is caught. Usually, bleeding is performed on bloody fish such as tuna and jacks.

4. *Marinate if necessary.* If steps 2 and 3 are not carried out quickly enough, or perhaps in spite of these steps, the fish may smell and taste of ammonia. If so, all may not be lost. A marinade may help alleviate a strong smell or taste. There are, of course, thousands of recipes for marinades, some of which are part of a recipe designed to flavor the fish. The four marinades below are quite basic, designed to make the fish more palatable, and should not be considered a part of the recipe.

Salt Water

The word *marinade* has common roots with *marine* and *mare,* which mean sea. This implies salt water, which is surely the oldest marinade. If using fresh water, mix a brine in the proportions of 1 cup of salt per gallon of water. Put the fish in a nonmetallic container, cover them with water, and refrigerate for 8 hours or longer. Rinse the fish well and pat dry with paper towels before proceeding with the recipe.

Vinegar and Water

Mix ½ cup of white vinegar per gallon of water. Put the fish in a nonmetallic container, cover with the vinegar solution, and marinate in the refrigerator for 4 hours. Rinse well and pat dry before proceeding with the recipe.

Milk or Buttermilk

Ordinary cow's milk (and no doubt other forms of milk) makes a good marinade for fish, venison, and other wild game. I especially like it for fish that is to be fried. Buttermilk also works nicely, and I love shark fingers marinated in buttermilk, dusted with cornmeal, and deep-fried. Place the fish in a nonmetallic container, cover with milk or buttermilk, and marinate several hours or overnight.

Lemon Juice

Lemon juice is often used as a marinade, usually without water, and I like it on fillets that are to be grilled or broiled. Exact measures aren't necessary, but I usually use the juice of 1 lemon to marinate 1 pound of fish. Simply put the fish into a nonmetallic container, squeeze the lemon juice over them, toss about to coat all sides, and refrigerate for an hour or so. Note that using lots of lemon or lime juice will change the texture of the fish, as in seviche.

5. *Cook the fish promptly.* Some fish have soft flesh that deteriorates quickly. Although prompt icing will help, these fish should be cooked as soon as practical. A good deal depends on the species. Sand trout, for example, are very good if they are fried right away—almost out of the water and into the skillet. Knowing your species will help a lot. If, for example, you catch some bluefish and some Spanish mackerel, you should cook the bluefish first.

6. *Don't cook the fish too long.* One of the worst things you can do to most fish is to cook it too long, especially by a dry-heat method such as baking, broiling, or grilling. Even frying too long makes most fish dry and tough. The general rule for cooking is 10 minutes per inch of thickness. Don't ever forget the rule—but break it as needed. Skates or rays, for example, may be ideal with less cooking, whereas eels may require longer cooking in order to be done.

As a rule, fish are done when the flesh flakes easily when tested with a fork. Also, partly done fish will look different near the middle. When done, the flesh of most fish will be opaque; when raw, translucent. A cross section of partly cooked fish will show the difference.

7. *Refrigerate or freeze the catch.* If properly iced and drawn, some fish can be kept in the refrigerator (or on ice) for several days. For longer storage, freeze the fish. (Some fish, however, as indicated in the chapters, really don't freeze well, in which case you should try to eat them right away.)

If possible, I prefer to freeze my fish in a block of water. This can sometimes be a problem, however, because the method requires a container and lots of space. When properly frozen in a block of water, the fish can be kept for long periods of time without freezer burn. Wrapping the fish or fillets in freezer paper helps but is not ideal, and such fish do not keep as well as those frozen in a block of ice.

I prefer to freeze fish with the skin intact, unless I have reason to take it off. Sometimes I even leave the scales on the fish.

Some small-to-medium fish, such as mullet, can be frozen whole—head, fins, guts, and all. I usually wrap these in paper or

256

foil, but this step may not be necessary if the fish is to be cooked within a week or two.

If you are going to freeze a fish, do so as soon as possible after it is caught. Never get into the position of having to freeze fish because they are going bad. On this count, I feel that the commercial fish business could be more successful if the catch (and by-catch) were frozen right away. Far too many supermarket fish are put in a showcase for days, then wrapped, frozen, and sold in the frozen foods section. I know this is done, and I suspect that any food frozen in the store (you can usually tell or guess at the truth by the label) is already getting old.

Ideally, fish should be thawed in the refrigerator, but I confess that I often thaw them in the sink or under running cool water, and I suspect that others do the same. A good microwave oven can also be used to thaw the fish quickly.

8. *Dress and cook by an appropriate method.* Some saltwater fish, usually those that have a high fat content, simply don't fry very well but are great for broiling, grilling, or smoking. The size of the fish and the method of cooking may also influence how the fish should be dressed.

9. *Pay attention to details.* Being a stickler for exact temperatures and cooking times, as well as other fine points of cooking as discussed in appendix A, will help you put better fish on the table. In addition, you should use good ingredients. Fresh herbs and mushrooms, for example, are now widely available in supermarkets and are simply better, for most fish cookery, than dried or canned.

10. *Peace of mind.* If you've got enough fish to feed everybody and want others to enjoy your catch, refrain from discussing the fish at the table. And remember that an orange roughy tastes better than a Pacific slimehead, and that, to many views, mahimahi is better than dolphin.

For your own peace of mind, make sure the fish is safe to eat. In my opinion, eating your own catch, with a little caution and knowledge of species, is much safer than eating supermarket meats and seafood. Still, few things are 100 percent safe these days. If in doubt, throw the fish back and catch another one. Also read the section on safety, below, as well as the information in the chapters on specific fish.

SEAFOOD SAFETY

Although the sportsman's catch from salt water is usually very safe if it is properly handled and cooked, there are several types of food poisoning you need to be aware of.

Ciguatera

Ciguatera is an insidious and highly dangerous poison of concern to people fishing Florida and tropical reef waters. Here's a good summary from a booklet called *Recreational Seafood Safety,* published by the Florida Sea Grant College Program and the Florida Department of Natural Resources: "Ciguatera is a form of seafood poisoning caused by natural toxins that can occasionally be found in certain marine fish from specific tropical reef waters. The natural toxins are formed by microplankton and accumulate in the food chain. Potentially any tropical marine fish participating in a food chain with ciguatoxin could become ciguatoxic, but documented illnesses and some recent analyses indicate some fish are more suspect. In the Caribbean region, the fish with the worst reputations are—amberjacks and other jacks, moray eels, and barracuda. Other fish with concerned reputations are hogfish, scorpion fish, certain triggerfish, and some snappers and groupers.

"Ciguatera is most common in certain true tropical reef areas as in the Caribbean region. Ciguatoxic fish cannot be detected by appearance, taste, or smell. Raw and cooked whole fish, fillets, or parts, have no signs of spoilage, discoloration or deterioration. The toxins present cannot be completely destroyed or removed by cooking or freezing.

"Unfortunately, the documentation, verification and utility of a reliable ciguatoxic fish list is seriously compromised by the diversity of fish species and variable nomenclature. For example, local fishermen may refer to a variety of fish as 'jacks' or 'snappers' when they are actually a mackerel, wrasse, or other species. Certain species of snapper and grouper are never implicated in ciguatera, yet their popular reputation suffers from species misidentification.

"Selecting smaller fish, which are likely to accumulate less toxin, offers limited guidance due to variable sizes per species. Particularly large fish of any tropical species from Caribbean reef zones should be avoided. Likewise, barracuda is a reef fish eater that is not recommended for consumption. [But note that the Pacific barracuda and some other species are perfectly safe in regard to ciguatera.]

"Learning about potential ciguatoxic areas and fish remains the best method for avoiding this unusual form of food poisoning. Consumers purchasing tropical marine fish known to occur about reef waters should patronize reputable dealers and restaurants. Vacationers and experienced recreational fishermen should exercise caution in areas of concern for particular tropical fish."

Amen. The Florida Sea Grant College Program also publishes another booklet called *Ciguatera—An Advisory Note*. If you plan to eat fish from tropical waters, write for a copy to Florida Sea Grant College Program, Building 803, Room 4, University of Florida, Gainesville, FL 32611-0341. Note that the problem is not with a whole species but with individual fish that feed extensively around tropical reefs where the microplankton is present in the food chain. Also note that ciguatera is not caused by the fish spoiling after the catch; that there is no way to determine its presence without the help of a chemical analysis laboratory; and that cooking or freezing will not eliminate ciguatera.

Puffer Poisoning

Some of the puffer fish can contain a deadly poison, tetrodotoxin. In general, puffers from northern waters are safer than those from Florida and other tropical and subtropical waters. Although they contain a very tasty strip of meat down either side of the backbone, most anglers will want to pass on these fish. See chapter 20 for a discussion of these species.

Scombroid and Other Bacterial Poisoning

Fortunately, this poisoning can be prevented by properly handling your catch. It occurs only in fish of the scombroid group, including tuna, mackerel, jacks, and dolphin, and does not occur if the fish are properly handled and iced after the catch. The culprit is a buildup of histamine, caused by bacterial action in the flesh. Be warned that once built up, these toxins are not negated by cooking, freezing, pickling, or canning.

Usually, this poisoning is caused only by gross mishandling of a fish, such as leaving it in the warmth of the sun on a pier or on a boat deck. Thus, scombroid poisoning is a problem that the angler can prevent.

Fish can also become contaminated in the kitchen or even in the refrigerator from chicken and other meats or uncooked foods. This is usually not a problem even if bacteria such as salmonella are present, as cooking will make the fish safe.

Raw fish, as eaten in sushi, can contain harmful bacteria, worms, and parasites. I'll eat raw fish, but I like to catch my own, or at least know where they were caught and how they were handled. Even so, a certain amount of risk is involved. Raw fish can be made safer by freezing it for at least 24 hours at 0 degrees or lower, then thawing it before eating.

Worms and parasites in amberjacks and other fish are killed by cooking and pose no health hazard.

Chemical Contaminants

In some areas, chemical pollutants such as mercury and pesticides can contaminate fish. Usually, eating a few such contaminated fish will not cause serious harm, but eating them frequently over a period of time can be dangerous to your health. At present, this is usually a problem in fresh water and has probably been blown out of proportion. Still, it is a concern, and it has spread to salt water in some areas. The state of Florida, for example, has issued an advisory warning about eating too many sharks, some of which have shown higher-than-normal amounts of methylmercury. The problem is not yet a serious concern, at least not to me, and is related only to specific sites, not to the fish in general.

Having said all of the above, I want to add that saltwater fish is one of the safest kinds of food available to man. I think it is safer than supermarket chicken and hamburger. During a fifteen-year study (from 1973 through 1987), seafood caused only 4 percent of all the food-borne illnesses reported to the Center for Disease Control. Some 85 percent of these were from raw oysters and other shellfish. Thus a little math shows that only 0.06 of 1 percent of all such reported illnesses are caused by fin fish. The odds can be even better, I think, if you catch, care for, and cook your own.

APPENDIX C

Metric Conversion Tables

U.S. Standard measurements for cooking use ounces, pounds, pints, quarts, gallons, teaspoons, tablespoons, cups, and fractions thereof. The following tables enable those who use the metric system to easily convert the U.S. Standard measurements to metric.

Weights

U.S. Standard	Metric	U.S. Standard		Metric
.25 ounce	7.09 grams	11	ounces	312 grams
.50	14.17	12		340
.75	21.26	13		369
1	28.35	14		397
2	57	15		425
3	85	1	pound	454
4	113	2		907
5	142	2.2		1 kilogram
6	170	4.4		2
7	198	6.6		3
8	227	8.8		4
9	255	11.0		5
10	283			

Liquids

U.S. Standard	Metric	U.S. Standard	Metric
¹/₈ teaspoon	.61 milliliter	³/₈ cup	90 milliliters
¹/₄	1.23	¹/₂	120
¹/₂	2.50	²/₃	160
³/₄	3.68	³/₄	180
1	4.90	⁷/₈	210
2	10	1	240
1 tablespoon	15	2	480
2	30	3	720
¹/₄ cup	60	4	960
¹/₃	80	5	1200

To convert	multiply	by
Ounces to milliliters	the ounces	30
Teaspoons to milliliters	the teaspoons	5
Tablespoons to milliliters	the tablespoons	15
Cups to liters	the cups	.24
Pints to liters	the pints	.47
Quarts to liters	the quarts	.95
Gallons to liters	the gallons	3.8
Ounces to grams	the ounces	28.35
Pounds to kilograms	the pounds	.45
Inches to centimeters	the inches	2.54

To convert Fahrenheit to Celsius: Subtract 32, multiply by 5, divide by 9.

INDEX